A
MORE
PERFECT
UNION

BOOKS BY WILLIAM PETERS

A More Perfect Union

A Class Divided

For Us, the Living (with Mrs. Medgar Evers)

The Southern Temper

Passport to Friendship: The Story of the Experiment in International Living

American Memorial Hospital—Reims, France: A History

A MORE PERFECT UNION

WILLIAM PETERS

CROWN PUBLISHERS, INC., NEW YORK

Published by Crown Publishers, Inc., 225 Park Avenue South, New York,
New York 10003 and represented in Canada by the Canadian MANDA
Group
CROWN is a trademark of Crown Publishers, Inc.
Manufactured in the United States of America
Book design by Dana Sloan

Library of Congress Cataloging-in-Publication Data
Peters, William, 1921–
    A more perfect union.

    Includes index.
    1. United States. Constitutional Convention (1787) 2. Constitutional
conventions—United States. 3. United States—Constitutional history.
I. Title.
KF4520.P48   1987   342.73'024   86-16581
ISBN 0-517-56450-5   347.30224
10 9 8 7 6 5 4 3 2 1
First Edition

For Hélène

Contents

A MORE PERFECT UNION

*"Every word of [the Constitution]
decides a question between
power and liberty."*

James Madison, 1792

The Delegates

NEW HAMPSHIRE
Nicholas Gilman
John Langdon

MASSACHUSETTS
Elbridge Gerry
Nathaniel Gorham
Rufus King
Caleb Strong

CONNECTICUT
Oliver Ellsworth
William Samuel Johnson
Roger Sherman

NEW YORK
Alexander Hamilton
John Lansing, Jr.
Robert Yates

NEW JERSEY
David Brearley
Jonathan Dayton
William Churchill Houston
William Livingston
William Paterson

PENNSYLVANIA
George Clymer
Thomas Fitzsimons
Benjamin Franklin
Jared Ingersoll
Thomas Mifflin
Gouverneur Morris
Robert Morris
James Wilson

DELAWARE
Richard Bassett
Gunning Bedford, Jr.
Jacob Broom
John Dickinson
George Read

MARYLAND
Daniel Carroll
Daniel of St. Thomas Jenifer
James McHenry
Luther Martin
John Francis Mercer

VIRGINIA
John Blair
James McClurg
James Madison
George Mason
Edmund Randolph
George Washington
George Wythe

NORTH CAROLINA
William Blount
William Richardson Davie
Alexander Martin
Richard Dobbs Spaight
Hugh Williamson

SOUTH CAROLINA
Pierce Butler
Charles Pinckney
Charles Cotesworth Pinckney
John Rutledge

GEORGIA
Abraham Baldwin
William Few
William Houstoun
William Pierce

1

Fears and Hopes

*"What a triumph for our enemies to verify
their predictions! What a triumph for the advocates of despotism to find that we are incapable of governing ourselves...."*
GEORGE WASHINGTON to JOHN JAY
August 1, 1786

1776–May 24, 1787

A lively city in ordinary times, Philadelphia was touched by a special aura of suspense that May of 1787. Even the rain clouds that darkened the skies for much of the month did nothing to dampen a sense of expectancy that was almost palpable. For once again, as so often in the recent past, this attractive, well-ordered city seemed to its citizens to be at the absolute center of things. Critical decisions were again to be made here, decisions that would surely affect the lives of Americans still unborn. And if there was hope in the general air of anticipation, it was a hope tinged with fear.

That an event of such moment should be taking place in Philadelphia, however, seemed only natural. It had, after all, been here that the First Continental Congress had met in 1774, just thirteen years earlier, in the crisis that followed the British closing of the port of Boston. It was here that the Second Continental Congress, meeting in 1775 after the fighting at Lexington and Concord, had named George Washington commander of a new Continental Army. And it was most emphatically here, as every American and a good many Europeans knew, that the Declaration of Independence had been written, debated, and finally signed. Now Philadelphia was again the focus of attention as host to a federal convention whose goal was nothing less than saving what had become a shaky Union of thirteen states from threatened disintegration.

On May 11, three days before the Convention's scheduled opening, the *Pennsylvania Journal* heralded the importance of the meeting: "A correspondent observes that, as the time approaches for opening the business of the Federal Convention, it is natural that every lover of his country should experience some anxiety for the fate of an expedient so necessary, yet so precarious. Upon the event of this great Council, indeed, depends everything that can be essential to the dignity and stability of the National character. . . . All the fortunes of the future are involved in this momentous undertaking."

Three weeks later, with the Convention under way, Philadelphia newspapers printed a long letter from a local citizen who signed himself "Harrington" and argued strongly for the adoption of a new constitution. "We must," he wrote, "either form an efficient government for ourselves, suited in every respect to our exigencies and interests, or we must submit to have one imposed upon us by accident or usurpation. . . . We are upon the brink of a precipice."

Having described the dangers, the writer went on to express confidence in the ability of the Convention delegates to save the country from the yawning abyss. "Many of them were members of the first Congress that sat in Philadelphia in the year 1774," he reminded his readers. "Many of them were part of that band of patriots who, with halters round their necks, signed the Declaration of Independence on the Fourth of July 1776. Many of them were distinguished in the field and some of them bear marks of the wounds they received in our late contest for liberty.

"Perhaps no age or country ever saw more wisdom, patriotism, and probity united in a single assembly than we now behold in a Convention of the States. . . . Under the present weak, imperfect and distracted government of Congress—anarchy, poverty, infamy and slavery await the United States. Under such a government as will probably be formed by the present Convention, Americans may yet enjoy peace, safety, liberty and glory."

Within weeks, portions of this letter were reprinted in newspapers throughout the country. Reflecting as it did a popular hope that once again, by summoning its ablest citizens to the task, America would somehow prevail against all threats to its existence, it touched a genuinely responsive chord. As for the reality of those threats, there was, by 1787, little argument that government under the Articles of Confederation—the sole tie that bound the states to one another—was almost literally grinding to a halt. Even the wording of the call of the Confederation Congress for the Philadelphia Convention, to "render the federal constitution adequate to the exigencies of government and the preservation of the Union," was admission enough that all was far from well.

The problems went back to the very beginnings of American self-government. Independent initially by their own simple declaration and united mostly by the necessities of their common war with Great Britain, all of the states except the already self-governing colonies of Rhode Island and Connecticut had, between 1776 and 1784, adopted new constitutions. All were frank experiments in republican government.

A major goal of the drafters of these state constitutions was to create governments so structured that the power of those entrusted with governing might never encroach on the liberty of the governed. Tyranny would be made impossible. Using the familiar principle of a separation of powers, they set out to assure that the executive branch, which they naturally identified with the British King and his colonial governors, could neither manipulate nor trespass on the judiciary or, more important, on the legislature, which they envisioned as the true representative of the people. In every way they could think of, they stripped their future governors of powers their colonial governors had abused, transferring them bodily to the legislatures. Then, to make sure that these greatly strengthened legislatures would actually reflect the will of the people, they took steps to make them genuinely representative. The people, through their elected representatives in the legislatures, would be their own rulers.

At the same time that the states were providing for their future government, their representatives in the Continental Congress were drafting plans for a central government that would give them a legal basis for authority they had thus far been exercising without it. Yet even with the sometimes desperate needs of the Revolutionary War to draw the states into some kind of formal union, it took five long years to debate, adopt, and finally ratify the Articles of Confederation. It was the individual states, after all, that had declared themselves independent, and despite much high-sounding rhetoric about union, the loyalties of most Americans were still fiercely attached to their own native spheres. Few had even a theoretical attachment to the idea of a Continental republic.

A major cause of the long delay in ratifying the Articles of Confederation was in fact a spirited contest among the states over the disposition of the Western lands between the Appalachian Mountains and the Mississippi River. States with Western claims—Connecticut, Massachusetts, New York, Virginia, North Carolina, South Carolina, and Georgia—clung tenaciously to their right to dispose of them as they saw fit. States without such claims—New Hampshire, Rhode Island, New Jersey, Pennsylvania, Delaware, and Maryland—pushed for a plan for all Western lands to become a common national domain under the authority of the Confederation Congress. Only the eventual promise of the states with claims to surrender them, which New York and Virginia actually did in 1780 and 1781, finally cleared the way for ratification of the Articles of Confederation. Maryland, the last state to ratify, did so only in 1781.

Even so, the Articles contained a fatal flaw, and in 1785, Connecticut-born Noah Webster, already beginning to demonstrate his facility with language in spelling books and grammars, put it into blunt American words: "So long as any individual state has power to defeat the measures of the other twelve, our pretended union is but a name, and our confederation, a cobweb." Both the flaw of separate and independent states and the fragile cobweb of confederation that resulted from it were heritages of recent American history. For if the new state constitutions reflected a desire to keep power as close as possible to the people, the Articles of Confederation made it clear that the individual states had no intention of granting any but the most limited powers to the Confederation Congress.

It is no exaggeration to say that, after their recent experience with the British, many Americans had an almost pathological fear of powerful government. The "Articles of Confederation and perpetual Union," as the document itself described them, embodied that fear. They created not a nation but "a firm league of friendship" among the thirteen states, each of which retained "its sovereignty, freedom and independence, and every Power, Jurisdiction and right, which is not by this confederation expressly delegated to the United States, in Congress assembled." The words were carefully, even cautiously, chosen, and they meant precisely what they said: the states, united solely by a league of friendship, would give up to a congress assembled of representatives of the states only limited and specified powers. And what the states expressly delegated to the Confederation Congress consisted largely of the power to conduct foreign affairs, make treaties, and declare war, functions that no state could successfully fulfill by itself.

As a formalized continuation of the informal First and Second Continental Congresses, the new Confederation inherited the structure of those bodies: a one-chambered assembly. Powers as limited as those it was granted presumably would not require the separate and independent executive and judicial branches of the states. As constituted, the Confederation

Congress had no power to tax, to regulate commerce, or even to enforce its own laws and treaties. Within it, each state, large or small, had a single vote, and the votes of nine states were required to pass anything of importance.

To raise money, the Confederation Congress would first agree on the needed sum and then apportion it among the states according to the value of their improved land. In actual practice, the states then paid their assessments or not, as they saw fit, for there was no way for the Congress to compel payment. Worse still, the votes of all thirteen states were required to amend the Articles. Every attempt to amend the method of raising money—a crucial and continuing problem—had failed. By 1786, the total income of the firm league of friendship came to less than a third of the interest on its national debt.

During the Revolution, the Confederation Congress had somehow muddled through. But with the coming of peace, sentiment for Union diminished, and the thirteen independent states began to flex their sovereign muscles. When it suited them, states simply ignored the resolutions of Congress, refused to pay their allotted shares of its expenses, sent inferior delegates to represent them, and sometimes sent none at all. Since at least two delegates from at least seven states were required for a quorum, weeks sometimes went by with Congress unable to do business.

The result was predictable. The already loose bonds between the states slackened to the point where the words "perpetual Union" threatened to become one of history's bitter jokes. As early as 1783, just two years after the British surrender at Yorktown, Thomas Jefferson was deeply troubled. "I find . . . the pride of independence taking deep and dangerous hold on the hearts of individual states," he wrote his fellow Virginian, Edmund Randolph. "I know no danger so dreadful and so probable as that of internal contests. And I know no remedy so likely to prevent it as . . . strengthening the band that connects us. We have . . . a Congress of deputies from every state to perform this task: but we have done nothing which will enable them to enforce their decisions. What will be the case? They will not be enforced. The states will go to war with each other in defiance of Congress; one will call in France to her assistance; another Great Britain, and so we shall have all the wars of Europe brought to our own doors."

If anything, things got worse. While the states did not go to war with each other, they wrangled over boundaries and navigation rights. They flouted provisions of the peace treaty with Britain to restore confiscated loyalist property. When the Confederation Congress sought power over commerce to retaliate against European trade restrictions on American goods, the states refused to grant it and instead began passing conflicting restrictions of their own. Connecticut was soon charging higher duties on goods from Massachusetts than on those from Britain. States lacking ports for foreign trade were often taxed by their more fortunate neighbors. As James Madison described it later: "New Jersey, placed between Philadelphia and New York, was likened to a cask tapped at both ends; and North Carolina between Virginia and South Carolina to a patient bleeding at both arms."

Some states treated their own citizens even worse. Seven of them issued paper money, and the subsequent wild fluctuations in value quickly made princes of speculators and paupers of creditors. America's reputation in Europe plunged, along with its credit. At home, men with heavy debts were set against men of wealth and property.

One American who was deeply troubled by this state of affairs was James Madison, and during the spring and summer months of 1786 he deliberately took time off from other affairs to attempt to find a way out. At thirty-five, Madison had served in both the Virginia legislature and the Confederation Congress. He had observed the problems at close hand. He knew from experience the difficulties of attempting to resolve them with the inadequate tools of the Articles of Confederation. A graduate of the College of New Jersey (today Princeton) and a scholar with an unquenchable thirst for knowledge, he plunged into a wide-ranging study of the principles of republican government and the problems of federations.

Isolating himself in his room at Montpelier, his father's plantation house in Orange County, Virginia, Madison daily spent the hours between breakfast and dinner poring over books sent from Paris at his request by his friend Thomas Jefferson, then serving as American Minister to France. Week by week, he worked his way painstakingly through tomes on history, politics, and commerce, analyzing the experiences of both ancient and modern federations and republics. By the time he was forced to turn to other things, Madison knew as much about confederate government as anyone in America. And he was more than ever convinced that if the barely united states did not strengthen the bonds of their union, they faced potential disaster.

The major problem, as he saw it, lay with the state legislatures. It was the legislatures, not the people of the states, that had repeatedly failed to support the Confederation Congress. It was the legislatures, with their paper money, that had destroyed the confidence of many people in popular government. It was the legislatures, deliberately strengthened by the new state constitutions and carefully democratized to provide genuine representation of the people, that in state after state had fallen under the control of small farmers eager to pay off their debts with inflated paper money.

Beneath the struggles over paper money lurked a more basic contest between men of property and wealth and men with little of either. Animosity between the two groups revealed as never before a class struggle whose existence most Americans had either ignored or denied. The rehabilitation of loyalists and the quick restoration of their former social status was deeply resented by many ordinary citizens. The Society of Cincinnati, formed at the end of the war by angry, unpaid Revolutionary officers preparing to return to their homes, raised hackles not only among the lower orders of the army but among genuine republicans everywhere. With a charter calling for hereditary membership, the Cincinnati almost immediately came under suspicion as the potential nucleus of a future aristocracy. Four states actually passed resolutions against the exclusive veterans' organization.

In such a climate, it was inevitable that members of the established class would begin to question their commitment to republican government. From New York, where he served Congress as Secretary of Foreign Affairs, the wealthy and conservative John Jay wrote George Washington in 1786: "What I most fear is that the better kind of people (by which I mean the people who are orderly and industrious, who are content with their situations, and not uneasy in their circumstances) will be led, by the insecurity of property, the loss of confidence in their rulers, and the want of public faith and rectitude, to consider the charms of liberty as imaginary and delusive."

From Mount Vernon and what he fondly hoped was permanent retirement from public life, Washington replied, "What astonishing changes a few years are capable of producing! I am told that even respectable characters speak of a monarchical form of government without horror. From thinking, proceeds speaking, and thence to acting is often but a single step. But how irrevocable and tremendous! What a triumph for our enemies to verify their predictions! What a triumph for the advocates of despotism to find that we are incapable of governing ourselves, and that systems founded on the basis of equal liberty are merely ideal and fallacious!"

In August 1786, James Madison left his books and set out for Annapolis, Maryland, to attend a convention of delegates from the various states to discuss regulating trade. Since states were forbidden by the Articles of Confederation to enter into treaties or alliances with each other without the consent of Congress, the Annapolis Convention, called by the Virginia Assembly at Madison's suggestion, would be of questionable legality. Any action the Convention might attempt to take would be clearly illegal. But Madison, if not yet desperate, was determined to do something.

He was the third to arrive at George Mann's tavern, where the delegates would be staying. A week later, just twelve delegates, representing five states, had turned up. With partial delegations from New York and Pennsylvania and only Delaware, New Jersey, and Virginia with voting quorums, a change of plans was clearly in order. Led by Alexander Hamilton of New York and Madison and Edmund Randolph of Virginia, the twelve in attendance unanimously endorsed a call for yet another convention, this one to meet in Philadelphia the following May, with far broader goals than simply regulating trade.

Delegates to the Philadelphia Convention would meet, in the words of the call, "to take into consideration the situation of the United States, to devise such further provisions as shall appear to them necessary to render the constitution of the federal government adequate to the exigencies of the Union; and to report such an act for that purpose to the United States in Congress assembled as, when agreed to by them and afterwards confirmed by the legislatures of every state, will effectually provide for the same." This, then, was a call to amend the Articles of Confederation.

Because Virginia's approval of the call would be critical to its acceptance by the other states, Madison rode immediately to Richmond to urge the state assembly to elect delegates. Even as he traveled, an unfolding drama in western Massachusetts was providing new and compelling evidence of problems in American self-government.

A post–Revolutionary War depression and the attempt of the Massachusetts legislature to pay off the state's war debt quickly had combined to place an unbearable tax burden on farm property. Petitions by farmers for relief had been ignored by the legislators. Finally, with farm foreclosures increasing and more and more farmers being imprisoned for debt, nearly two thousand farmers had rebelled. Under the reluctant leadership of Daniel Shays, a former Revolutionary officer, they marched on the courthouses of five western Massachusetts counties to prevent further foreclosure proceedings. When the rebels moved against the arsenal at Springfield in January 1787, they were met, defeated, and eventually put to rout by state militia. Still, alarm over the armed rebellion spread quickly through the country. If anything further had been needed to highlight the importance of the Philadelphia Convention, Shays's Rebellion provided it.

General Henry Knox, serving Congress as Secretary of War, was dispatched to western Massachusetts to investigate. "This dreadful situation," he wrote Washington, his former commander, "has alarmed every man of principle and property in New England. They start as from a dream and ask what has been the cause of our delusion? What is to afford us security against the violence of lawless men? Our government must be braced, changed or altered to secure our lives and property. . . ."

Washington, forwarding excerpts of Knox's letter to Madison in Richmond, asked, "What stronger evidence can be given of the want of energy in our governments than these disorders? If there exists not a power to check them, what security has a man for life, liberty, or property? . . . Thirteen sovereignties pulling against each other and all tugging at the federal head will soon bring ruin on the whole, whereas a liberal and energetic constitution, well guarded and closely watched to prevent encroachments, might restore us to that degree of respectability and consequence to which we had a fair claim and the brightest prospect of attaining."

Washington's letter, designed in part to prod the Virginia Assembly to choose delegates to the Philadelphia Convention, had the desired effect. And with Virginia leading the way, New Jersey, New Hampshire, Pennsylvania, North Carolina, Delaware, and Georgia had, by February 10, 1787, committed themselves to the Convention by electing delegates. On February 21, Congress, meeting in New York's City Hall, issued its own call, taking steps at the same time to limit the Convention's purpose. It would meet "for the sole and express purpose of revising the Articles of Confederation."

With a congressional stamp of approval, other states joined the seven that had, in effect, jumped the gun. Only Rhode Island, whose two-house legislature deadlocked over the call, ignored it completely. In the light of Rhode Island's long record of disdain and even defiance of the Confederation Congress, many in the other states were just as happy. Newspapers had recently taken to calling the tiny, divided state "Rogue Island."

The Convention was called for the second Monday in May, which fell on the fourteenth. James Madison, arriving in Philadelphia on the third, was the first out-of-town delegate to show up. Coming down from New York where he had been attending Congress, he went straight to the boardinghouse of Mrs. Mary House, his habitual residence in the city. Mrs. House, an elderly widow, lived with her grown children on the corner of Fifth and Market, just a block from the Pennsylvania State House (today Independence Hall), where the Convention would meet.

Madison had first stayed with Mrs. House seven years earlier, in 1780, when he came to Philadelphia as a new Virginia appointee to the Continental Congress. With a number of other delegates to Congress also lodging there, it proved a congenial place, and Madison had quickly become friendly with the entire House family. It had been at Mrs. House's in 1783 that Madison, then thirty-two, had fallen in love with Catherine Floyd, the sixteen-year-old daughter of New York's congressional delegate, William Floyd. Kitty Floyd returned Madison's affections, and under the delighted eye of Thomas Jefferson, the affair appeared to prosper. Plans were made for a wedding in Mastick, Long Island, that summer. But between April, when Kitty left with her parents for New York, and July, when she wrote Madison to break the news, Kitty changed her mind. It would be eleven years before Madison, still a bachelor at forty-three, married a twenty-six-year-old Quaker widow, Dolley Payne Todd.

Madison brought with him to Philadelphia the results of his studies of federations in the form of a manuscript, "Of Ancient and Modern Confederacies." A second paper, "Vices of the Political System of the United States," contained a distillation of his observations and study of American political experiments since the Declaration of Independence. From his months of study, Madison had also developed ideas for a plan of government that would, he hoped, answer the failures of the Confederation. What he had in mind was a radical departure from the "firm league of friendship," which had proved neither firm nor particularly friendly. It would require a new constitution.

In preparation for the Convention, he had already shared his ideas with George Washington and Edmund Randolph, the latter, at thirty-three, Virginia's governor. Both men would serve with him as Virginia delegates. With Washington, Madison had been blunt and to the point: "Temporizing applications will dishonor the Councils which propose them, and may foment the internal malignity of the disease. . . . Radical attempts, although unsuccessful, will at least justify the authors of them."

Randolph, however, presented a special problem, for in a letter to Madison about the Convention's task, he had expressed his belief that "the alterations should be grafted on the old Confederation." Madison, who most emphatically did not agree, wrote diplomatically: "I think with you that it will be well to retain as much as possible of the old Confederation, though I doubt whether it may not be best to work the valuable articles into the new system, instead of engrafting the latter on the former." Diplomatic or not, Madison left neither man in doubt about his belief in the need for a decidedly different kind of government.

To both, he made clear his conviction that the sovereignty

of the states would have to give way. "I hold it for a fundamental point," he told Randolph, "that an individual independence of the states is utterly irreconcilable with the idea of an
aggregate sovereignty. I think, at the same time, that a consolidation of the states into one simple republic is not less unat-
tainable than it would be inexpedient. Let it be tried, then,
whether any middle ground can be taken, which will at once
support a due supremacy of the national authority, and leave
in force the local authorities so far as they can be subordi-
nately useful."

Now, during the eleven days before the Convention was due
to begin, Madison sought out and talked informally with as
many of the Pennsylvania delegates as he could. All favored a
stronger Union. Madison, preparing for the work that lay
ahead, began drafting a set of principles to submit to his fellow Virginians.

On Sunday afternoon, May 13, George Washington arrived
in Philadelphia. Met in Chester, Pennsylvania, by three generals, two colonels, and two majors of his former command, he
was escorted from Gray's Ferry by Philadelphia's Light Horse
Cavalry. In Philadelphia, where a positive din of cannon,
church bells, and cheering citizens greeted him, the procession
led his carriage to Mrs. House's, where Madison had arranged
quarters for him. There he was met by an old and trusted
friend, Robert Morris, who promptly renewed an invitation to
stay with him that Washington had previously declined. This
time, Washington allowed himself to be persuaded.

It is difficult today to comprehend the awe and veneration in
which the Americans of those times held their former commander in chief. His personal prestige has never been matched
in all our subsequent history. A hero whose very presence
raised hopes and whose reserve and dignity silenced fears, he
was for many a symbol of the American Union.

Accompanying Robert Morris and his wife, Mary, Washington ordered his carriage and baggage taken to their three-

story brick mansion, a short distance up Market Street. It was the finest house in Philadelphia, once the property of William Penn's grandson, Richard, and had been used as a headquarters by both Sir William Howe and Benedict Arnold when the British occupied the city during the Revolution. Enlarged and improved by Morris, it boasted a stable accommodating twelve horses, a French butler, and a large staff of liveried servants.

Morris was America's most successful businessman and, by reputation, its richest citizen. A signer of the Declaration of Independence and the Articles of Confederation, he had served the Continental Congress as Superintendent of Finance. Washington, in particular, had good reason to hold him in high regard, for it was Morris's financial leadership that had somehow kept him and his Continental Army supplied during the darkest days of the Revolutionary War.

Once comfortably settled at the Morrises', Washington set out to call on Benjamin Franklin, President of Pennsylvania's Supreme Executive Council: in effect, the state's governor. Franklin, who lived on Market Street, near Fourth, was world-famous as a diplomat, statesman, scientist, and inventor. An agent in London for Pennsylvania and other colonies before the Revolution, he had returned home in time to help draft the Declaration of Independence. Later, he served as a negotiator of the wartime treaties with France and, still later, the peace treaty with Britain. For sixty years a zealous Englishman, he had become one of the most ardent of Americans. Now, at eighty-one, feeble and often racked with pain from gout and bladder stone, he had nonetheless been elected to serve as one of Pennsylvania's delegates.

On Monday morning, May 14, the day set for the opening of the Convention, about a dozen men showed up at the State House. There were delegates from North Carolina and Delaware, but only Pennsylvania and Virginia had voting quorums. So, after agreeing to stop by each morning until seven of the thirteen states were fully represented, the delegates went their separate ways.

As it happened, the controversial Society of Cincinnati was also convening in Philadelphia, and on Tuesday, May 15, Washington had dinner with its delegates. The Cincinnati had originally chosen him as its president-general, and Washington had accepted the post, but he had had second thoughts when he learned of the Society's charter provision for hereditary membership. When he failed to persuade the members to alter the provision, he had simply stopped attending their conventions. He had, in fact, declined an invitation to this gathering as well.

This had made it awkward for him to accept his later appointment to the federal convention. Chosen as a Virginia delegate at Madison's behest, Washington had at first said that having sent his regrets to the Cincinnati, he could not "with any degree of consistency" appear at another convention in Philadelphia "without giving offense to a very worthy and respectable part of the American community, the late officers of the American army." So convinced were Madison and Edmund Randolph that Washington's presence at the federal convention would be vital to its success, however, that they had persisted in urging him to attend. In the end, he had agreed.

On Wednesday morning, May 16, with a majority of the thirteen states still absent, the delegates agreed henceforth to meet each afternoon at one o'clock to check on new arrivals. That afternoon, Benjamin Franklin had everyone to dinner, tapping a cask of English porter in their honor. Later, writing to the British friend who had sent him the beer, Franklin said, "We have here at present what the French call *une assemblée des notables*, a Convention composed of some of the principal people from the several states of our Confederation. They did me the honor of dining with me last Wednesday, when the cask was broached, and its contents met with the most cordial reception and universal approbation. In short, the company agreed unanimously that it was the best porter they have ever tasted." Many of the delegates would wish for more of such unanimity in the days to come.

The next day, the Virginia delegates held the first of a series of daily meetings. Since Virginia had taken the lead in calling for the Convention, it seemed logical for the Virginians to present it with some kind of working document. This was the moment James Madison had waited for. Knowing what he wanted from the Convention, he now began to lead his fellow Virginians toward it. Besides Madison, Washington, and Randolph, the seven-man delegation included George Mason, sixty-two, the planter-statesman who had written Virginia's famous Declaration of Rights. George Wythe, sixty-one, another delegate, was a judge of Virginia's high court of chancery, a distinguished professor of law at the College of William and Mary, and a signer of the Declaration of Independence. John Blair, at fifty-five the same age as Washington, was, like Wythe, a judge of chancery. The seventh member, Dr. James McClurg, forty-one, was a Richmond physician without political experience. He had been appointed by Governor Randolph when Patrick Henry refused to serve.

On Friday, May 18, Robert Yates, a justice of the New York Supreme Court, and Alexander Hamilton—two of the three-man New York delegation—arrived. Yates and the tardy third New Yorker, John Lansing, Jr., were from Albany. Both were members of the state's dominant political faction led by its antinationalist governor, George Clinton. Angry with Congress for its failure to support New York's claim to Vermont and pleased with their success in taxing their neighbors for goods imported through New York City, the Clintonians saw their state as having the best chance of any to make it on its own. Lansing and Yates, determined to resist any loss of their state's sovereignty, could be counted on to oppose radical changes in the Articles of Confederation. That left the ardent nationalist Alexander Hamilton, who had first urged revising the Articles seven years earlier, an unhappy minority of one in the delegation.

When the Convention still lacked full delegations from seven states on Saturday, the nineteenth, Washington was annoyed. Writing the next day to a friend, he said, "These delays greatly impede public measures, and serve to sour the temper of the punctual members, who do not like to idle away their time." Still, not all of the time was wasted, for among the delegates who had arrived there were serious discussions about the task facing the Convention. George Mason, writing to his son in Virginia, reported that "the most prevalent idea in the principal states seems to be a total alteration of the present federal system, and substituting a great national council or parliament, consisting of two branches of the legislature, founded upon the principles of equal proportionate representation, with full legislative powers upon all the subjects of the Union; and an executive; and to make the several state legislatures subordinate to the national, by giving the latter the power of a negative upon all such laws as they shall judge contrary to the interest of the federal Union."

Mason hoped for "greater unanimity and less opposition, except from the little states, than was at first apprehended." But as always, there were the timid and the bold. It was most likely during this period of waiting before the Convention actually began that Washington made clear to others where he stood: "It is too probable that no plan we propose will be adopted," he said. "Perhaps another dreadful conflict is to be sustained. If to please the people, we offer what we ourselves disapprove, how can we afterwards defend our work? Let us raise a standard to which the wise and honest can repair. The event is in the hand of God."

By Monday, May 21, Mrs. House's boardinghouse was full. George Read, a Delaware delegate who was staying there, wrote that day to his fellow delegate, John Dickinson, who had not yet set out for Philadelphia. Reporting that six states—

New York, Pennsylvania, Delaware, Virginia, and North and South Carolina—were now represented by quorums and that single delegates had turned up from Massachusetts, New Jersey, and Georgia, Read described a system of government he expected to be proposed in which the states would be represented in at least one house of the legislature according to their population.

"By this plan," he wrote, "our state may have a representation in the House of Delegates of one member in eighty. I suspect it is to be of importance to the small states that their deputies should keep a strict watch upon the movements and propositions from the larger states, who will probably combine to swallow up the smaller ones by addition, division, or impoverishment; and if you have any wish to assist in guarding against such attempts, you will be speedy in your attendance."

Read's fears for his state, then the smallest of the thirteen, reflected not only its size but its history. Though Delaware had always had its own legislature, laws, and judicial system, it had, until 1776, when it became a state, shared with Pennsylvania both a proprietor—the Penn family—and a governor. As ready as any man to press for a stronger Union, Read, a fifty-three-year-old lawyer and farmer, a signer of the Declaration of Independence, and a friend of George Washington, had happily signed the call for the Convention at Annapolis eight months earlier. Now he sought some assurance that his state would not be devoured by the larger ones.

For three more days, the delegates reported faithfully to the State House only to learn that they still lacked seven fully represented states. And if there was grumbling over the tardiness of the missing delegates, there was at least the satisfaction that the waiting was being done in Philadelphia.

To most Americans in 1787, Philadelphia would have seemed a teeming metropolis, for most of them lived on the land—some in towns and small villages, others in relative isolation. While only twenty-four clusters of population in the entire country held more than 2,500 people, Philadelphia was already a center of commerce and finance, of science, art, and architecture, of politics, learning, and philanthropy. And conventions.

For even as the delegates waited for the federal convention to begin and some mingled with delegates to the meeting of the Cincinnati, conventions of Presbyterians and Baptists were being held in the city to "clean and distribute the streams of religion throughout the American world," as the *Pennsylvania Packet* put it. The American Philosophical Society, the Pennsylvania Society for Promoting the Abolition of Slavery, and the recently formed Society for Political Enquiry, in all of which Benjamin Franklin had a hand, also met during the month.

An out-of-town delegate to any of these meetings found himself surrounded by sights and sounds, by amusements and distractions unknown in all but a few other places in America. If he wandered to the wharves along the Delaware River, he could see piles of goods from Spain, France, England—even China—waiting to find their way into the city's homes and shops. He had his choice of ten newspapers to read. There was a covered market that two days a week offered fresh fish and meat, dairy products, fruits, and vegetables. There were museums and stores displaying everything from paintings and stuffed animals to French furniture and Chinese silk. Philadelphia offered mansions to gawk at and streetlights to light the way at night, taverns to revel in and churches in which to repent. Even at night, a visitor could hardly forget where he was, for here watchmen called out the time and weather every hour until dawn. Philadelphia was the country's largest city, with a population of 45,000. Today, all of them could be comfortably seated in Veterans Stadium, with room left over for the 13,500 people of Baltimore.

Philadelphia and Baltimore, along with Boston, New York, and Charleston, were in fact the only cities in America with more than 10,000 people. Large as they may have seemed to Americans from the hinterland, they were small towns compared with the great cities of Europe. Paris, for example, had a population of 600,000, and London, nearly a million. In the entire United States, there were actually fewer than four million people, nearly a fifth of them slaves.

But what the country lacked in population it more than made up for in space—from the Atlantic to the Mississippi, from the Great Lakes almost to the Gulf of Mexico. It was a land the size of Italy, France, Germany, Spain, Britain, and Ireland combined. And for Americans dedicated to republican government, that was one of the problems.

As one of the prevailing maxims about government had it, only a small, homogeneous society with similar interests could possibly survive as a republic. That conviction, expressed by Aristotle and made famous by Baron de Montesquieu, the French political philosopher, had taken hold with the force, almost, of law. A political entity the size of one of the American states, therefore, might hope to govern itself on republican principles. And thirteen independent republics, bound by a treaty like the Articles of Confederation, might have some chance of enlarging the sphere of republican government, though the record so far was hardly encouraging. But a continental republic with a single central government, encompassing a widely scattered people with interests as diverse as Gloucester fishermen, Connecticut farmers, New York businessmen, Philadelphia lawyers, and Charleston planters? As Thomas Wait of Maine put it later, "You might as well attempt to rule Hell by prayer."

2

Secrecy

*"I am sorry they began their deliberations by
so abominable a precedent as that of tying up
the tongues of their members."*

THOMAS JEFFERSON to JOHN ADAMS
August 30, 1787

May 25–29, 1787

On Friday, May 25, in a drenching rain, the Convention finally got under way. New York, New Jersey, Pennsylvania, Delaware, Virginia, and North and South Carolina—a majority of the thirteen states—at last had voting quorums. There were still gaping voids. From all of New England, only Rufus King of Massachusetts was present. Georgia's William Few had arrived, but there was as yet no one from Maryland.

Still, twenty-nine men took their seats in the large chamber usually occupied by the Pennsylvania Assembly, the same paneled room with wide, high windows where the Declaration of Independence had been signed. With delegates coming and going throughout the Convention, the average daily attendance would be about thirty. Of the seventy-four delegates chosen by the twelve states that answered the Convention call, only fifty-five would actually make an appearance at one time or another.

From Paris, where he first saw the list of elected delegates, Thomas Jefferson wrote John Adams, then serving as American Minister to Great Britain, "It is really an assembly of demigods." For his part, Adams declared them to be men "of

22

such ability, weight, and experience that the result must be beneficial to the United States." Of the notable Americans who were not delegates, these two—Jefferson and Adams— were by all odds the most conspicuous absentees, though there were others whose presence would have seemed natural: John Hancock, Samuel Adams, John Jay, Benjamin Rush, John Marshall, and Patrick Henry, to name but a few.

Still, not everyone shared Jefferson's and Adams's enthusiasm. John Jay, who felt that only some kind of shocking event would mobilize the people to strengthen the government, wrote Jefferson from New York: "I wish their councils may better our situation, but I am not sanguine in my expectations. There is reason to fear that our errors do not proceed from want of knowledge; and, therefore, that reason and public spirit will require the aid of calamity to render their dictates effectual." And in Boston, Samuel Adams expressed his suspicion "of a general revision of the Confederation."

Patrick Henry, who had rejected his appointment as a Virginia delegate, was equally suspicious, and later, when he emerged as the leader of the opposition to his state's ratification of the Constitution, he was challenged for not having attended. Why, a fellow Virginian asked, had he not lent his aid in making a good Constitution instead of staying at home and later abusing the work of his patriotic compeers? Henry's reply was succinct but hardly enlightening. "I smelt a Rat," he replied.

The fifty-five men who would actually take part in the Convention's deliberations were men of experience. Eight of them had been in that very room eleven years earlier to pledge their lives, fortunes, and sacred honor as they signed the Declaration of Independence. The chamber, the State House—even Philadelphia—were little changed, but the world of those eight men had been altered almost beyond recognition. A revolution had been fought and won. Thirteen colonies had become thirteen states.

Six of the delegates had signed the Articles of Confederation. Now they were here to repair them. The basic question was simple: What kind of a country would the United States be? A true national state, like England or France? Or a league of petty sovereignties, like Germany and Italy?

Forty-two of the fifty-five delegates had served in Congress. Seven had been chief executives of their states. Eight had helped in drafting their states' constitutions. Twenty-one had fought in the Revolutionary War. Yet for all of their collective experience, they were relatively young. Ranging from Jonathan Dayton of New Jersey, at twenty-six, to Benjamin Franklin, at eighty-one, their average age was just over forty-three years.

Most were planters or large-scale farmers, lawyers, merchants, or state officeholders. In terms of wealth, sixteen were born aristocrats, if such a term could be applied to any American. Most of the rest came from families with respectable, if not substantial means. Only a few were of genuinely modest circumstances.

About half had graduated from college, and this in an age when few men even from rich families attended college at all. Princeton alone contributed nine graduates; Yale and William and Mary, four each; Harvard, three; the College of Philadelphia (University of Pennsylvania), two; and King's (Columbia), one, though Alexander Hamilton might well have made it two if he had not dropped out to fight in the Revolution. Two had degrees from abroad: one from Oxford, the other from St. Andrews, in Scotland. Two more had studied law at one of the Inns of Court in London. Several had graduate degrees, and a number had served as professors and tutors. Even the self-educated Franklin boasted an honorary degree, an LL.D. from the University of St. Andrews, conferred in 1759. From that date, he had been known to many as "Doctor" Franklin.

Most of the delegates were at least nominal members of one of the traditional churches of their regions, but most were men who could take their religion or leave it alone. Even with its sprinkling of former preachers, strong Christians, and theologians, the Convention as a whole had a strong rationalist and even secular tone.

Eight of the delegates had been born abroad. Several—Franklin, Randolph, and Gouverneur Morris among them—had seen their families' loyalties split by the Revolution. One—John Dickinson of Delaware—had refused to sign the Declaration of Independence, and another—William Samuel Johnson of Connecticut—had been so widely suspected of loyalism that he was forced in 1779 to take an oath of fealty to the Revolutionary cause. All, without exception, had been born British subjects.

They were also a well-traveled group of men. Besides the eight born outside the United States, sixteen more were not natives of the states they now represented. Eighteen had spent a year or more as adults working or studying abroad.

For many, the Convention had overtones of a reunion. Washington must have known a good thirty of the other delegates, and Robert Morris, at least ten from his service in the Continental Congress and another ten from business activities. James Madison was a Princeton classmate of Gunning Bedford, Jr., of Delaware.

If there was a region of the country that was underrepresented at the Convention, it was what was usually called the backcountry. This was especially true of Massachusetts, Pennsylvania, Virginia, and the Carolinas. Since backcountry Americans could hardly imagine a national government in which they would have much influence, most who even thought about the subject were antinationalist. That left the Convention clearly loaded with men who favored a stronger national government. Because strengthening the national government was the stated purpose of the Convention, however, this would have surprised no one.

If the delegates represented an "elite," it was a political elite that had, after all, been selected by twelve democratically elected legislatures to propose changes in the national government. Opponents of whatever they advocated would have their chance when it came to adopting or rejecting their proposals.

Finally, these men who came together to remake a govern-

ment had rich backgrounds in government-making on which
to draw. Some, like Elbridge Gerry of Massachusetts and John
Rutledge of South Carolina, had served in their respective colonial governments. Others, like Gouverneur Morris of Pennsylvania and George Mason of Virginia, had had a hand in the
making of state constitutions.

We would know very little of what happened in the Convention—on this first day or later—had it not been for James
Madison. In his studies of earlier confederacies and republics,
Madison had often been frustrated by a lack of detail as to
how these governments had come into being. Writing of that
frustration more than forty years later, he said, it "determined
me to preserve as far as I could an exact account of what might
pass in the Convention. . . . I chose a seat in front of the presiding member, with the other members on my right and left
hands. In this favorable position for hearing all that passed, I
noted . . . what was read from the chair or spoken by the members. . . . It happened also that I was not absent a single day,
nor more than a casual fraction of an hour in any day, so that I
could not have lost a single speech, unless a very short one."
It was a staggering task that Madison had set himself, for as
he later described it, "losing not a moment unnecessarily between the adjournment and reassembling of the Convention, I
was enabled to write out my daily notes during the session or
within a few finishing days after its close." The work and con-
finement, as he recalled, almost killed him, but he kept at it
until the Convention adjourned.

Though Madison's notes would be by far the most complete
record of the Convention, more than fifty years would pass
before they were made public. Madison himself felt they
should not be published during his lifetime or, if possible, the
lives of the other delegates. As it turned out, when he died in
1836 in his eighty-sixth year, Madison had outlived them all.

Congress purchased Madison's papers, and Henry D. Gil-
pin, a Philadelphia attorney and writer soon to be appointed

Attorney General by President Martin Van Buren, edited them. They were finally published in 1840, and more than half of the three-volume work turned out to consist of Madison's invaluable notes of the Convention's debates.

When the twenty-nine delegates had settled in their chairs at square tables covered with green baize on that first day of the Convention, Robert Morris, speaking for the Pennsylvania delegation, proposed George Washington as presiding officer. Astonishingly, for a man who had played such a large part in the earlier years of the Union, it was, with the exception of the seconding of a motion a month later, to be Morris's sole speech of the Convention. John Rutledge, a former Governor of South Carolina who had served with Washington in the Continental Congress, seconded the nomination, expressing confidence that the choice would be unanimous. It was.

Escorted by Morris and   to the high-backed presiding officer's chair that stood between marble fireplaces on the chamber's east wall, Washington spoke briefly. Madison, no doubt scribbling furiously, reported that he "thanked the Convention for the honor they had conferred on him, reminded them of the novelty of the scene of business in which he was to act, lamented his want of better qualifications, and claimed the indulgence of the House towards the involuntary errors which his inexperience might occasion."

Then, in an explanatory note, Madison made his own comment on the selection of Washington: "The nomination came with particular grace from Pennsylvania, as Doctor Franklin alone could have been thought of as a competitor. The Doctor was himself to have made the nomination of General Washington, but the state of the weather and of his health confined him to his house."

With Washington in the chair, a secretary was chosen. James Wilson of Pennsylvania nominated Franklin's grandson, Temple, but Major William Jackson of Philadelphia, who had served Congress as Assistant Secretary of War, was nominated by Alexander Hamilton and won election to the position. Next, the credentials of the various delegations were read. Besides naming the delegates selected by each state, the credentials made clear what number of them would constitute a quorum qualified to cast the state's vote.

The credentials from Delaware struck an immediately ominous note, for they categorically forbade the delegation's participation in any attempt to change the one state, one vote provision of the Articles of Confederation. George Read, who five days earlier had urged his colleague John Dickinson to hurry to Philadelphia to prevent just such a change, had arranged to have this restriction inserted in the state's credentials when they were passed three months earlier by Delaware's General Assembly. Foreseeing that the large states would likely press for representation based on population and believing that "the argument or oratory of the smaller State commissioners will avail little," it had been Read's hope to relieve his state's delegates of the necessity of "disagreeable argumentation" by presenting the Convention with a fait acccompli.

Nor did the prohibition fail to attract the desired attention. As Madison noted: "On reading the credentials of the deputies, it was noticed that those from Delaware were prohibited from changing the Article in the Confederation establishing an equality of votes among the states."

Finally, a messenger and doorkeeper were appointed, a committee was chosen to prepare rules, and the Convention adjourned for the weekend.

While the Committee on Rules met to draw up the procedures by which the Convention would be governed, the other delegates relaxed and investigated their surroundings in this largest of American cities. On Sunday, May 27, Washington went, as he wrote in his diary, "to the Romish Church to high mass." The other Virginians had attended Catholic services on the previous Sunday, and George Mason had written his son,

George, Jr., about the experience. They attended, he wrote, "more out of compliment than religion, and more out of curiosity than compliment. There was a numerous congregation; but an indifferent preacher, I believe a foreigner. . . . Altho I have been in a Roman Catholic Chapel before, I was struck with the solemnity of the apparatus and could not help remarking how much everything was calculated to warm the imagination and captivate the senses. No wonder that this should be the popular religion of Europe!"

Mason was staying at the Indian Queen, a tavern on Fourth Street, which had quickly become a kind of informal headquarters for the Convention delegates. He had not been in Philadelphia ten days when he wrote complainingly to his son: "I begin to grow heartily tired of the etiquette and nonsense so fashionable in this city. It would take me some months to make myself master of them."

Reading these lines, his son may well have smiled, for Mason was well known for hating to leave his Virginia home, Gunston Hall. That he had made the trip at all—the longest of his entire life—was eloquent testimony to the importance he ascribed to the Convention.

On Monday morning, May 28, nine new delegates turned up. Rufus King, the handsome thirty-two-year-old lawyer and member of Congress who had been the only New Englander present, was now joined by two of his three fellow Massachusetts delegates, Nathaniel Gorham and Caleb Strong. The fourth, Elbridge Gerry, would appear the next day. Connecticut was represented in the tall, neat, scowling person of Oliver Ellsworth, a widely respected judge of his state's superior court. Ellsworth was known for two eccentricities. Reputed to be the country's largest single consumer of snuff, he also had a disconcerting habit of talking incessantly to himself.

Gunning Bedford, Jr., of Delaware and James McHenry of Maryland also appeared, along with four Pennsylvanians missing on Friday: Benjamin Franklin, George Clymer,

Thomas Mifflin, and Jared Ingersoll. Franklin made the most conspicuous entrance, borne in a sedan chair with glass windows by four strong inmates of the Walnut Street Prison, which stood just across the State House yard. The chair, which Franklin had brought back from Paris, was the only means of transportation that didn't jar him with painful reminders of his gout and bladder stone. In it, he was carried gently into the State House and through the double doors into the Convention chamber itself. There he was helped out and into his armchair at the table set aside for the Pennsylvanians. The sedan chair was placed against the west wall of the room to await his departure.

After the Convention had come to order, the Committee on Rules made its report, and rules were adopted for the conduct of the Convention. Motions for additional rules were referred to the committee. And there was at last word from Rhode Island. Thirteen citizens, representing the state's merchants and tradesmen, wrote to deplore their state's failure to attend and to plead that nothing be done to hurt the state's commercial interests. The letter was read and tabled, and the Convention adjourned.

The next day, with John Dickinson of Delaware and Elbridge Gerry of Massachusetts now in attendance, the Convention completed its action on rules by adopting, among others, a rule of secrecy. Without debate, the delegates agreed "that no copy be taken of any entry on the journal during the sitting of the House without leave of the House; that members only be permitted to inspect the journal; that nothing spoken in the House be printed, or otherwise published or communicated without leave."

It is hard to imagine such a rule being adopted by a Constitutional Convention today. The public outcry would deafen the delegates. Indeed, when Thomas Jefferson heard of it in Paris, he wrote John Adams in London: "I am sorry they began their deliberations by so abominable a precedent as that of tying up the tongues of their members. Nothing can justify

this example but the innocence of their intentions and igno-
rance of the value of public discussions."

Still, it is equally hard not to agree with James Madison,
who insisted years later that "no Constitution would ever have
been adopted by the Convention if the debates had been made
public." Opinions, he told editor and historian Jared Sparks,
"were so various and at first so crude that it was necessary
they should be long debated before any uniform system of
opinion could be formed. Meantime the minds of the members were changing, and much was to be gained by a yielding
and accommodating spirit. Had the members committed
themselves publicly at first, they would have afterwards supposed consistency required them to maintain their ground,
whereas by secret discussion no man felt himself obliged to
retain his opinions any longer than he was satisfied of their
propriety and truth, and was open to the force of argument."

With rules adopted, the Convention proceeded to its main
business. Washington recognized Governor Edmund Randolph, who rose to propose what would quickly come to be
called the "Virginia Plan." It was, in fact, pretty much the plan
that Madison had presented to the Virginians at their daily
meetings before the Convention began.

It would have seemed natural to the delegates for the first
move to come from Virginia. Virginia, in the person of Richard Henry Lee, had moved the resolutions that led, in 1776, to
the Declaration of Independence. Virginia had proposed the
Annapolis Convention, which in turn had proposed this one.
And Virginia had been the first state to respond to the convention call by electing delegates.

Randolph "was made the organ on the occasion," as Madison later explained, "being then the Governor of the State, of
distinguished talents, and in the habit of public speaking.
General Washington, though at the head of the list was, for
obvious reasons, disinclined to take the lead. It was also foreseen that he would be immediately called to the presiding sta-
tion."

If additional reasons had been needed for the choice of Randolph to propose the Virginia Plan, they would not have been hard to find. Six feet tall, portly, and strikingly handsome, Randolph looked every inch a leader. A member of a celebrated Virginia family, he had studied law with his father and opened a practice in Williamsburg. In 1775, when his loyalist father fled to England with the royal governor, Randolph had remained in Virginia with his patriot uncle, Peyton Randolph. A former attorney general of Virginia and a delegate to Congress, he had also served briefly on Washington's staff during the Revolution.

Randolph began with a long prelude, listing the characteristics needed in a revised federal system, enumerating the defects of the Articles of Confederation, and pointing out the dangers of inaction. Turning, then, to the question of a remedy on "the republican principle," he offered fifteen resolutions. The first proposed that the Articles of Confederation "be so corrected and enlarged as to accomplish . . . common defense, security of liberty, and general welfare," but the fourteen that followed proposed a government vastly different from the Confederation. In effect, the Virginia Plan called, as James Madison had intended that it should, for a new constitution of the United States.

It called for a national legislature with two branches in both of which states would be represented in proportion either to their financial contributions or to the number of their free inhabitants. So much for the Confederation's principle of one state, one vote. Members of the lower house would be elected by the people of the various states. Members of the upper house would be elected by the lower house from slates nominated by their state legislatures.

The national legislature would have all the lawmaking powers of the Confederation Congress and could also pass laws in all cases where the individual states were incompetent or where the harmony of the United States might be disturbed by separate state laws. It could also veto state laws it found in conflict with the new constitution and could use force against recalcitrant states.

An executive, chosen by the national legislature and ineligible for reelection, would have general authority to execute the national laws and would enjoy the executive rights currently vested in the Confederation Congress. The executive and a number of national judges would constitute a council of revision with power to veto acts of the national legislature unless the legislature overrode their veto by some proportion of votes to be decided.

A national judiciary, chosen by the national legislature to serve during good behavior, would decide national legal issues. New states would be admitted by something less than a unanimous vote of the legislature. The national government would guarantee the republican institutions and the territory of each state.

Until the new constitution was adopted, the Confederation Congress would continue to govern. Once it was adopted, all state officers would be bound by oath to support it. And finally, the new constitution, after approval by Congress, would be ratified by state conventions chosen by the people of each state.

Governor Randolph ended his presentation with a plea that the Convention not permit this opportunity to establish peace, harmony, happiness, and liberty in the United States to pass without action. The Convention agreed to consider the Virginia Plan in detail beginning the following day.

Then Charles Pinckney, the younger of two Pinckneys on the four-man South Carolina delegation, read to the Convention *his* plan for a new government, admitting that it was based on the same principles as the Virginia Plan. It, too, was postponed until the next day and then simply ignored.

Just before adjournment, Alexander Hamilton rose to speak. The inconsistency between Randolph's call for amending the Articles of Confederation and his proposals for what amounted to a whole new government had not escaped him.

"It strikes me," he said, "as a necessary and preliminary inquiry to the propositions from Virginia, whether the United States are susceptible of one government or require a separate existence connected only by leagues offensive and defensive and treaties of commerce." Since Hamilton's disdain for the states was well known, most of the delegates undoubtedly realized that he was, in effect, suggesting that they be abolished.

Hamilton, as events would soon prove, was the delegate whose ideas about a proper government for the United States diverged most widely from those of the others, though he was certainly not the only man with his own ideas. Time and again in the days to come, individual delegates would find themselves isolated from all or most of their colleagues in their positions on various issues. Yet if there were important and strongly held points of difference among the men of the Convention, there was also an important area of general agreement. The members of the Convention, like all members of the human race before and after them, were, to one degree or another, prisoners of their times, products of their environment, and heirs to the political traditions of their age.

That is not to say, of course, that they were not men of ideas but simply that their ideas were limited to the store available to all men of their time and place. It is not to say that they were incapable of changing their environment; they had done so, through the Revolution, and with crucial results. Nor is it to imply that they were unhappy with the new political traditions they had helped to create for themselves: the ideals of the Revolution so forcefully set forth in the Declaration of Independence. They had, after all, come to Philadelphia to find some way of preserving them. It is, rather, to point out that they held in common important assumptions and beliefs that necessarily shaped their thinking about the government they were there to improve or change.

Basic to their shared assumptions was a belief that just as
there were laws that governed the physical world, there were
natural laws that governed society, laws that could be understood through reason and experience and which men ignored
at their peril. The purpose of civil government, as the seven-
teenth-century English philosopher John Locke had explained,
was to enforce these natural laws, the most important of which
was that no man should take from another his natural rights to
life, liberty, and property. A government that failed to protect
these rights had lost its reason for being and deserved to be
changed or overthrown by the people it governed.

By his very nature, man was a mixture of good and bad
qualities. By encouraging the good in man—his sociability,
reasonableness, generosity, and love of liberty—education,
religion, and government might help to repress the bad—his
selfishness, passion, greed, and corruptibility. And of all potentially corrupting forces, the most dangerous was political
power.

Since man's natural state was one of freedom and equality,
legitimate government represented a mutually agreed compact
among equals who sought protection of their natural rights in
return for their pledge of obedience to its rules. The very basis
of government, therefore, was the consent of the governed.
Those chosen to govern were the servants, not the masters, of
the people. But government, like man, was corruptible, and
the task of those devising a system of government was therefore to prevent corruption and the oppression that would inevitably follow.

Republican government was the best form ever devised, but
it, too, required the constant vigilance of a moral citizenry.
Ideally, republican government should be plain, simple, and
understandable. It should be limited and close to the people.
And it should rest on a written constitution that made it a government of laws and not of men. Such a government, finally,
should limit the right to vote and hold office to those with a
genuine stake in the society, since they alone could make in-

telligent and uncorrupted decisions and alone had the right to agree to laws regulating the use of property.

On these basic principles, there was a general consensus among the delegates, though they differed sharply on precisely how they should be applied and with what emphasis. It was these sharp differences that would have to be resolved in the days ahead.

3

A Leap into the Future

*"We had better take a supreme government
now than a despot twenty years hence, for come
he must."*
GOUVERNEUR MORRIS to the Convention
May 30, 1787

May 30–June 1, 1787

On Wednesday morning, May 30, when the delegates gathered at the State House to consider the Virginia Plan, Connecticut's Oliver Ellsworth was joined by Mayor Roger Sherman of New Haven. A self-taught lawyer who had worked his way up from humble beginnings as a farmer and cobbler, Sherman had been a signer of both the Declaration of Independence and the Articles of Confederation. Bright, honest, pious, and blunt, Sherman at sixty-six was a tall, lean, sharp-nosed, and ungainly man.

When Washington called the delegates to order, the Convention resolved itself into a Committee of the Whole House, a parliamentary device that had come down through the centuries from the British House of Commons. The procedure converted the Convention into a single, inclusive committee whose decisions, like those of other committees appointed by the Convention, would be reported back to the Convention in the form of recommendations. The delegates, then sitting once more as the Convention, could again debate, and finally accept or reject, these recommendations. By making use of the device of the Committee of the Whole, the delegates afforded themselves an opportunity for what amounted to a trial run, a preliminary testing of opinion on various issues, before approaching them more formally.

Nathaniel Gorham of Massachusetts, who had just completed a term as President of the Confederation Congress, was elected Chairman of the Committee of the Whole, and Washington surrendered the chair to him and rejoined the Virginia delegation. Gorham, a forty-nine-year-old Charlestown merchant, was known to favor a stronger national government.

As the members turned to a consideration of Randolph's Virginia Plan, Gouverneur Morris made somewhat the same point Alexander Hamilton had made the day before: the first resolution, calling for amendment of the Articles of Confederation, was simply not compatible with the others. It was, of course, the very point Madison had made in his diplomatically worded letter to Randolph before the Convention.

Challenged once again, Randolph, who had clung to the hope of somehow amending the Articles and thereby avoiding the radical step of starting from scratch to devise a whole new government, now bravely took the plunge. Moving that his first resolution be set aside, he proposed three new ones. The first two, which served as the basis for the third, maintained that neither a confederation of the states nor treaties among them could accomplish "common defense, security of liberty, and general welfare," the stated goals of the Articles of Confederation. It was the third resolution that summed up the true meaning of the Virginia Plan: "That therefore, a national government ought to be established, consisting of a supreme legislature, judiciary, and executive."

The proposal was greeted by silence. Eventually, the stillness was broken by the voice of Virginia's George Wythe. "I presume from the silence of the House that the gentlemen are prepared to pass on the resolution," he said. But the silence was one of shock, not acquiescence.

Charles Pinckney of South Carolina asked Randolph, "Do you mean to abolish the state governments altogether?"

"I mean by these general propositions," Randolph replied, "merely to introduce the particular ones I submitted yesterday."

Pierce Butler of South Carolina said he didn't think the House *was* prepared to vote, and he urged discussion. For himself, he said, "I have opposed the grant of powers to Congress heretofore, because the whole power is vested in one body. The proposed distribution of powers into different bodies changes the case and would induce me to go great lengths."

Charles Pinckney's older cousin, General Charles Cotesworth Pinckney, rose. If the Convention agreed to Randolph's new resolutions, he said, "it appears to me that our business is at an end." The Convention, he pointed out, was empowered to revise the present confederation. To conclude that this was impossible would leave them with nothing further to do.

Elbridge Gerry agreed. But Gouverneur Morris did not. At thirty-five, the youngest of the Pennsylvanians, Morris came from a wealthy New York family that had been split by the Revolution. His mother had applauded the British seizure of New York. His half-brother had served as a major general in the British Army. Morris himself had chosen the patriot side. A bachelor whose "lively intellect" was said to dazzle the ladies, he had lost his left leg when thrown from his carriage in an accident seven years earlier. The substitution of a wooden leg had affected neither his magnificent bearing nor his obvious enjoyment of life.

A federal government, Morris explained, was a mere compact, resting on the good faith of the parties to it. The national, supreme government called for in Randolph's third resolution, on the other hand, would have a complete and compulsive operation. The states, in their appointments to the Convention, and Congress, in its call, he maintained, all pointed directly to the establishment of a supreme government capable of "the common defense, security of liberty, and general welfare."

"I cannot conceive of a government in which there can exist two *supremes*," he said. "A federal government which each party may violate at pleasure cannot answer the purpose. One government is better calculated to prevent wars or render them less expensive or bloody than many. We had better take a supreme government now than a despot twenty years hence, for come he must."

George Mason of Virginia agreed. "The present confederation is not only deficient in not providing for coercion and punishment against delinquent states," he said. "Punishment cannot, in the nature of things, be executed on the states collectively." What was needed was a government that "could directly operate on individuals and would punish those only whose guilt requires it."

But confusion over the terms "federal" and "national" was not easily resolved. For many delegates, the idea of a "national" government carried with it the threat of absorbing and destroying the states. That was not at all what Randolph and the Virginians had in mind.

Under the Confederation, which the delegates generally thought of as a federal government, Congress represented the states, not the people of the states. Acts of Congress therefore operated on the states and not on individuals. And that, of course, was the problem. As Mason had indicated, it was impossible to enforce a law against a state without going to war. The national government Randolph was proposing, on the other hand, would operate directly on individuals. Its laws could be enforced against individual lawbreakers.

Roger Sherman of Connecticut admitted that the Confederation had not given sufficient powers to Congress and that additional powers were necessary. But as Madison noted, "He seemed, however, not disposed to make too great inroads on the existing system."

Finally, on a motion by South Carolina's Pierce Butler, seconded by Edmund Randolph, the Committee of the Whole voted, six states to one, with the New York delegation divided, that a national government consisting of a supreme legislature, executive, and judiciary ought to be established. Connecticut cast the sole negative vote.

It was, as all the delegates were surely aware, a momentous decision. Less than a week after the Convention had formally opened and just a day after Randolph had presented the Virginia Plan, they had voted to abandon the Articles of Confederation and create an entirely new government with vastly increased powers. Nor was that all. For as General Pinckney had noted, the decision was totally at odds with the stipulation by Congress that the Convention had "the sole and express purpose of revising the Articles." And while this, their first major decision, was not a binding one, it was one from which the delegates would never retreat.

Turning, then, to the second of Randolph's original resolutions, they quickly found that the question of the representation of the states in the national legislature would not be decided so easily. The Virginia Plan proposed that representation should be based either on a state's financial contribution to the national government or on its free population. In either case, the small states would lose their cherished equality with the large ones. As he had planned, George Read of Delaware now brought discussion of the question to a dead stop.

"I move that the whole clause relating to the point of representation be postponed," he said. "I would remind the committee that the deputies from Delaware are restrained by their commission from assenting to any change of the rule of suffrage. In case such a change should be fixed on, it might become our duty to retire from the Convention." Delaware's stand for the one state, one vote principle could not have been stated more bluntly.

Gouverneur Morris and James Madison both attempted to push for a vote, at least in the Committee of the Whole, and others decried the idea that the credentials of the Delaware delegates could or should lead them to leave the Convention no matter how the question was decided. But the Committee decided to postpone consideration of the clause, and the Convention adjourned for the day. Madison, though he had failed to prevent a postponement, was not seriously disturbed, for he noted with satisfaction that the proposed change in the representation "would certainly be agreed to," since Delaware alone had objected. His optimism would soon prove to be premature.

Approaching the dignified red-brick State House on Chestnut between Fifth and Sixth streets each morning, the delegates could hear the sounds of Philadelphia growing. Over on Fifth, the American Philosophical Society's building was under construction. Even closer, on Sixth, workmen were completing a large excavation, the cellar of a new county courthouse that would one day become Congress Hall.

A block away on Walnut Street stood the prison, its inmates adding to the general din by crying out for alms and cursing the passerby who dared refuse them. To spare the delegates an additional distraction, the city had spread earth on the cobblestones around the State House to dull the clatter of passing traffic. At the entrances of the State House itself, sentries had been posted to prevent the public from approaching too closely. Passing the sentries on their way in and out doubtless also served as a daily reminder to the delegates of their self-imposed rule of secrecy.

When the Convention came to order on Thursday morning, May 31, William Few was joined by his colleague, William Pierce, giving Georgia a quorum and permitting it to take an active part in the Convention. Pierce, a member of Congress and a hero of the Revolution, would quickly set himself to writing pithy sketches of his fellow delegates.

Resolving themselves again into a Committee of the Whole, the delegates continued their discussion of the Virginia Plan. Without debate, they agreed that the national legislature should have two branches. Next came the proposal that members of the lower house from each state should be elected by the people of those states. Roger Sherman, who had risen straight from the people, had some sharp words on that subject.

"I am opposed to the election by the people," he said. "It ought to be by the state legislatures. The people should have as little to do as may be about the government. They lack information and are constantly liable to be misled."

Elbridge Gerry of Massachusetts was in hearty agreement. A follower of the radical Samuel Adams in the days before the Revolution, Gerry had earnestly supported the break with Britain. As a member of the Continental Congress, he had signed both the Declaration of Independence and the Articles of Confederation. But time and events had changed his perspective. A merchant and trader of inherited wealth, which he had himself significantly increased, Gerry had finally married at the age of forty-one in January 1786. His bride, Ann Thompson, the daughter of a rich New York merchant, was half his age and said by some to be the most beautiful woman in America. Marriage had wrought great changes in Gerry's way of life. Leaving his native Marblehead, he moved to the Cambridge mansion formerly owned by Thomas Oliver, the royal lieutenant governor. In a final irony, the radical who had once railed against Anglican bishops as "Tyrants of Religion," joined Christ Church, the leading Episcopal congregation. Shays's Rebellion, in the winter of 1786–87, had come as a shock to Gerry, badly shaking his already weakened republican principles.

Now, faced with the prospect of having the people of each state elect their representatives in the lower house of the national legislature, Gerry gave vent to his contradictory feelings. "The evils we experience," he began, "flow from the excess of democracy. The people do not lack virtue but are the dupes of pretended patriots. In Massachusetts, it has been fully confirmed by experience that they are daily misled into the most baneful measures and opinions by the false rumors circulated by designing men and which no one on the spot can refute." Complaining of the popular clamor in Massachusetts for reducing the salaries of government administrators, including the governor, he said, "I have been too republican heretofore. I am still republican, but I have been taught by experience the danger of the leveling spirit."

That brought crusty old George Mason to his feet. Slave-owning Virginia planter he might be, but he had lost none of his republican convictions. The larger branch of the legislature, he said, "is to be the grand depository of the democratic principle of the government. It is, so to speak, to be our House of Commons. It ought to know and sympathize with every part of the community and ought, therefore, to be taken not only from different parts of the whole republic, but also from different districts of the larger members of it."

In a concession to Gerry, he added, "I admit that we have been too democratic, but I am afraid we shall incautiously run into the opposite extreme. We ought to attend to the rights of every class of the people. I have often wondered at the indifference of the superior classes of society to this dictate of humanity and policy, considering that however affluent their circumstances or elevated their situations might be, the course of a few years not only may but certainly will distribute their posterity throughout the lowest classes of society. Every selfish motive, therefore, every family attachment, ought to recommend such a system of policy as will provide no less carefully for the rights and happiness of the lowest than of the highest orders of citizens."

As Mason took his seat, James Wilson of Pennsylvania caught the eye of Chairman Gorham and was recognized. A native of Scotland and a graduate of St. Andrews, Wilson had come to America in 1765 at the age of twenty-three. A lawyer now at forty-five, he had signed the Declaration, served in Congress, and built a prosperous Philadelphia practice. Blunt, direct, and logical, he spoke with a soft, Scottish burr. Arguing against Roger Sherman's idea of election of the lower house by the state legislatures, he contended strenuously that it should be drawn immediately from the people.

"I am for raising the federal pyramid to a considerable altitude," he said, "and for that reason, I wish to give it as broad a basis as possible. No government can long subsist without the confidence of the people. In a republican government, this confidence is peculiarly essential. I also think it wrong to increase the weight of the state legislatures by making them the electors of the national legislature. All interference between the general and the local governments should be obviated as much as possible. On examination, it will be found that the opposition of states to federal measures has proceeded much more from the officers of the states than from the people at large."

These were Madison's sentiments precisely and he rose to support them. The contrast between the two men was striking. Small and slightly built, whereas Wilson was tall and thick-muscled, Madison spoke in a voice so soft that people at meetings often called out for him to speak louder. William Pierce, who was perhaps already jotting down his sketches of the delegates, wrote of him, "tho' he cannot be called an orator, he is a most agreeable, eloquent, and convincing speaker."

"I consider the popular election of one branch of the national legislature as essential to every plan of free government," Madison said. "In some of the states, one branch of the legislature is composed of men already removed from the people by an intervening body of electors. If the first branch of the general legislature should be elected by the state legislatures, the second branch elected by the first, the executive by the second together with the first, and other appointments again made for subordinate purposes by the executive, the people will be lost sight of altogether, and the necessary sympathy between them and their rulers and officers, too little felt.

"I am an advocate of the policy of refining popular appointments by successive filtrations," he added, "but I think it may be pushed too far. I wish it to be resorted to only in the appointment of the second branch of the legislature and in the executive and judiciary branches of the government. I think, too, that the great fabric to be raised will be more stable and durable if it rests on the solid foundation of the people themselves than if it stands merely on the pillars of the legislatures."

When the question was put to a vote, election of members

of the lower house by the people of the various states won, six states to two, with two states divided and thus not voting.

Then, unable to agree on a method of electing members of the upper house, which the delegates were already beginning to call the Senate, the Committee of the Whole moved on to consider the powers of the national legislature. With remarkably little discussion, they agreed on sweeping powers: to pass laws wherever the states were not competent and when necessary to preserve harmony among the states, and to veto state laws in conflict with either the new constitution or treaties made under it.

Leaving the chamber that afternoon after adjournment, more than one delegate must have marveled at the radical differences between the old Confederation Congress they were already defying and the new national legislature they were in the process of constructing.

The Convention sat from ten in the morning until three in the afternoon, permitting the delegates to dine about four. In a day when there were only two main meals between sunup and sundown, this was the American custom. On this afternoon, General Washington dined with a Mr. Francis and drank tea with a Mrs. Meredith, according to the entry in his diary. But Philadelphia offered distractions and entertainment even for those not sought out as distinguished visitors by the local worthies.

Charles Willson Peale, the painter of America's great men, had a museum filled not only with his portraits but with all manner of fossil bones and other oddities. There were bookstores where one could buy anything from *The Vision of Columbus*, the new epic poem by America's own Joel Barlow, to Blackstone's *Commentaries* in four volumes. There were shops where Sheffield cutlery, Canton teas, French soap balls, and ivory fans might be had, and shoemakers prepared to make boots to measure in a single day.

In the evening, there were the City Tavern, the Indian

Queen, the George, and the Black Horse, where delegates could meet informally over brandy or Madeira and cautiously avoid talking of the Convention's work in public. A church-inspired ban on stage performances had deprived the city of theater for the past eight years, but Philadelphia had found ways around that. Shakespeare's *Richard III* was advertised as a "series of historical lectures in five parts on the fate of tyranny" and Oliver Goldsmith's *She Stoops to Conquer* was billed as "a lecture on the disadvantages of improper education."

At ten o'clock on Friday morning, June 1, the Convention welcomed the third Georgia delegate, William Houstoun, and resolved itself into a Committee of the Whole to consider Governor Randolph's resolutions on the executive branch of the national government. James Wilson moved that the executive consist of a single person, and Charles Pinckney provided a second. When there was a long silence, Chairman Gorham asked if he should put the question to a vote. Benjamin Franklin struggled to his feet.

"This," he said, "is a point of great importance. I wish the gentlemen would deliver their sentiments on it before the question is put."

John Rutledge of South Carolina was the first to oblige. Trained in the law at London's Middle Temple, Rutledge had built a Charleston practice so lucrative that in just fifteen years he had acquired five plantations. William Pierce, in his sketch, ranked Rutledge "among the American worthies . . . a man of abilities, and a gentleman of distinction and fortune."

Echoing Franklin, Rutledge said, "I must remark on the shyness of the gentlemen on this and other subjects. It appears that you suppose yourselves precluded by having frankly disclosed your opinions from afterwards changing them. I do not take that to be at all the case. I am for vesting the executive power in a single person, though I am not for giving him the power of war and peace. A single man will feel the greatest responsibility and administer the public affairs best."

That loosened some tongues, and one after another, Roger Sherman, James Wilson, Elbridge Gerry, Edmund Randolph, James Madison, and the two Pinckneys spoke out. In the end, though, the delegates could agree only "that a national executive ought to be instituted with power to carry into effect the national laws."

The question of how the executive should be chosen and for how long a term proved equally difficult. After much discussion, they agreed only on a term of seven years.

With the Convention only a week old, George Mason was beginning to fear it might last until August. Writing to his son, George, Jr., in Virginia, he expressed his surprise at the caliber of his fellow delegates. "When I first came here," he wrote, "judging from casual conversations with gentlemen from the different states, I was very apprehensive that, soured and disgusted with the unexpected evils we had experienced from the democratic principles of our governments, we should be apt to run into the opposite extreme . . . of which I still think there is some danger, though I have the pleasure to find in the convention many men of fine republican principles. America has certainly, upon this occasion, drawn forth her first characters. . . .

". . . For my own part, I never before felt myself in such a situation; and declare I would not, upon pecuniary motives, serve in this convention for a thousand pounds per day. The revolt from Great Britain and the formations of our new governments at that time were nothing compared to the great business now before us; there was then a certain degree of enthusiasm which inspired and supported the mind; but to view through the calm, sedate medium of reason the influence which the establishment now proposed may have upon the happiness or misery of millions yet unborn is an object of such magnitude as absorbs, and in a manner suspends, the operations of the human understanding."

Ironically, on the very day that Mason was thus pondering

the immensity of the Convention's task, an event occurred that underscored the need for a government that could, in the words already approved by the delegates, "preserve harmony among the states." Not seventy-five miles north of Philadelphia, on Sandy Hook, New Jersey, stood a lighthouse owned by New York. In April, New York had passed a law imposing entrance and clearance fees—like those imposed on ships from foreign ports—on vessels bound to or from New Jersey or Connecticut. On June 1, New Jersey retaliated by imposing a tax on New York's lighthouse.

4

The People or the States

"The proposed national system is like the solar system, in which the states are the planets and ought to be left to move freely in their proper orbits."

JOHN DICKINSON to the Convention
June 7, 1787

June 2–7, 1787

Most Americans worked a six-day week in 1787, and the Convention delegates were no exception. They met at the State House on Saturday, June 2, as usual.

Three new delegates appeared that morning. The arrival of William Samuel Johnson completed the three-man Connecticut delegation. A modest, scholarly man of fifty-nine with degrees from Yale and Harvard, Johnson had just been offered the presidency of Columbia College in New York. He would accept the position soon after the Convention adjourned.

John Lansing, Jr., of New York, at thirty-three already speaker of his state's assembly and mayor of Albany, brought the three-man New York contingent to full strength. Daniel of St. Thomas Jenifer, sixty-four, a wealthy bachelor who had served in Congress, turned up to help represent Maryland.

The day before, the Committee of the Whole had agreed on an executive term of seven years. Now they accepted the Virginia Plan's proposal that he (or they, since the number had not yet been decided) should be elected by the national legislature and be ineligible for reelection. And they added a provision that the executive should be removable "on impeachment and conviction of malpractice or neglect of duty."

Throughout their discussions of the executive, there would be constant references to monarchs and monarchy, for that was, of course, the form of national executive with which they were most familiar. And while many delegates saw the need for a strong executive, independent of the legislature, most were painfully aware of the potential dangers of giving one man—or even a group of them—too much power. Hence the decision that the executive should be ineligible for reelection. Hence, also, the insistence that there be some means of removing a bad one.

Once again, now, they turned to the question of a single or plural executive. Edmund Randolph, who had opposed a single executive the day before as "the foetus of monarchy," had suggested a three-man executive department. He had not changed his mind. "The permanent temper of the people," he insisted, "is adverse to the very semblance of monarchy." The subject was postponed.

Even in these preliminary stages, with the decisions of the Committee of the Whole committing the Convention to nothing final, it was becoming apparent to those who had not tried it before that framing a constitution was in some ways like creating a mosaic. The selection and placement of each new piece affected those touching it, so that, often, it had to be altered or removed. Each such rearrangement then altered the whole, so that it was necessary, from time to time, to step back to see the emerging pattern. John Dickinson of Delaware now did something very like that.

At fifty-four Dickinson was a man of continental reputation. A veteran of the Stamp Act Congress of 1765 and the First Continental Congress of 1774, his greatest fame had come from his *Letters from a Farmer in Pennsylvania*, published in 1767 and 1768, on the powers of Parliament to tax the colonies. Now, in a speech that ranged over much that had been discussed, he made several key points.

"The legislative, executive, and judiciary departments," he

said, "ought to be made as independent as possible, but such an executive as some seem to have in contemplation is not consistent with a republic. A firm executive can only exist in a limited monarchy." The Convention would have to look elsewhere for stability.

One source, he continued, "is the double branch of the legislature. The division of the country into distinct states forms the other principal source of stability. This division ought therefore to be maintained and considerable powers to be left with the states. This is the ground of my consolation for the future fate of my country. Without this, and in case of a consolidation of the states into one great republic, we may read its fate in the history of smaller ones."

Turning finally to the delicate question of the representation of the states in the national legislature, which his Delaware colleague George Read had successfully postponed, Dickinson said, "It must probably end in mutual concession. I hope that each state will retain an equal voice at least in one branch of the national legislature."

Sometime that Saturday, Dr. Benjamin Rush, the noted Philadelphia physician, wrote to the Welsh philosopher and Unitarian minister, Richard Price, in London. Reporting on the Convention and quoting Price's close friend Benjamin Franklin to the effect that all was going well, he warned that there would be opponents to whatever the Convention might ultimately decide. "You must not be surprised," he wrote, "if you should hear of our new system of government meeting with some opposition. There are in all our states little characters whom a great and respectable government will sink into insignificance. These men will excite factions among us, but they will be of a temporary duration."

Sunday, June 3, dawned fair and warm. Some of the Convention delegates went to the Second Presbyterian Church, where Dr. James Sprout, a student of Jonathan Edwards, preached the sermon. Most, though, were Episcopalians, and many of them attended services at Christ Church, where Bishop White conducted his first ordination of two young ministers.

The Convention had adjourned on Saturday with a motion before the Committee of the Whole that the executive should be a single person, and on Sunday evening James Wilson sat in the library of his house on Market Street preparing his speech in favor of it. When the time came on Monday morning, Wilson rose. "I am in favor of the motion," he said in his Scottish burr. "It was opposed by the gentleman from Virginia," he added, indicating Governor Randolph, "but the arguments used did not convince me. The objections of Mr. Randolph are leveled not so much against the measure itself as against its unpopularity." Wilson could not agree. "On examination," he said, "I can see no evidence of the alleged antipathy of the people. On the contrary, I am persuaded that it does not exist. All know that a single magistrate is not a king.

"One fact has great weight with me," he continued. "All the thirteen states, though agreeing in scarce any other instance, agree in placing a single magistrate at the head of government. The idea of three heads has taken place in none."

When the question was put to a vote, a single executive was agreed to, seven states to three.

Next came the proposal for a council of revision composed of the executive and a number of national judges. The Virginia Plan had assigned to such a council power to veto national legislation. Roger Sherman, who had favored a single executive, favored a council as well, pointing out that in all the states there was a council of advice, without which the executive could not act. Hugh Williamson of North Carolina asked James Wilson if he meant to have a council. Wilson said no. "A council serves oftener to cover, than prevent, malpractices," he added.

Elbridge Gerry of Massachusetts opposed the idea of including judges in any such council. They would, he said, "have a sufficient check against encroachment on their own department by their exposition of the laws, which involves a power of deciding on their constitutionality. In some states," he added, "the judges have actually set aside laws as being against the constitution. This was done, too, with general approbation."

Gerry's assumption that national judges considering ordinary lawsuits would have a similar power to set aside acts of the national legislature that violated the Constitution brought no comment from others. And it is worthy of note that no explicit provision giving the national courts such a power was ever suggested to the Convention, let alone included in the Constitution itself. Yet it was discussed by some delegates as though it existed in the very nature of the judicial process. That, it seems, was Elbridge Gerry's assumption as well. Madison later made the same point even more bluntly, though in connection with another issue. "A law violating a constitution established by the people themselves," he told the Convention on July 23, "would be considered by the judges as null and void."

*　　*　　*

Sixteen years later, in 1803, the Supreme Court arrived at the same conclusion in a case in which, ironically, James Madison was himself the legal target. The decision in *Marbury versus Madison* that the Supreme Court could declare acts of Congress unconstitutional was a landmark in the country's legal history. The background of the case that led to it was, by way of contrast, one of narrow and ugly partisan politics.

It began in 1800 after John Adams's defeat for a second term as President. Embittered at the outcome of the election and deeply troubled by the radical course he expected the victorious Jefferson and his newly elected Republican Congress to take, Adams decided during his last months in office to make the judiciary a bastion of his own Federalist Party. With the enthusiastic backing of the lame-duck Federalist Congress, Adams proceeded to establish sixteen new circuit judgeships, complete with the flock of marshals, attorneys, and clerks that went with them. At the same time, he created forty-two justices of the peace for the thinly populated District of Columbia. Finally, he appointed staunch Federalists to fill all of the new positions. The Federalist Senate obligingly rubber-stamped the appointments.

Next, to postpone the time when Jefferson could name an appointee of his own to the Supreme Court, the Federalist Congress provided that the next vacancy on the Court should not be filled, thereby reducing the Court from six to five justices. And to complete the Federalist seizure of the judiciary, Adams appointed his Secretary of State, John Marshall, to replace the retiring Chief Justice, Oliver Ellsworth.

With all of the pieces in place, Adams spent part of his last night in the still-unfinished White House signing the commissions of his newly appointed justices of the peace. Somehow, in the pressures of the last hours of his administration, the commissions were not delivered to the appointees. When Jefferson learned, after his inauguration, of the appointment of the "midnight justices," he ordered the State Department, now headed by his old friend James Madison, not to deliver the commissions. One of them bore the name of William Marbury, and when Marbury and three of the others asked the Supreme Court to require Madison to hand them over, Chief Justice John Marshall thought he had found a way of striking out at the power and authority of the new President.

In what developed as a classic struggle between two departments of the federal government—the executive and the judiciary—Marshall soon found himself facing an equally classic dilemma. If he ruled in favor of Marbury and his associates and Madison and Jefferson ignored the order of the Court, as they likely would, the Court's then minimal prestige and authority would be further diminished. Yet he could not bring himself to surrender abjectly to Jefferson.

His solution, to which his associates on the bench agreed, was clever, though of shaky legal logic. Marbury and his colleagues, the Court ruled, were entitled to their commissions, and Secretary of State Madison acted in plain violation of the law of the land in denying them. Yet the Court could not issue the requested order for Madison to hand them over, because the provision of the act of Congress which gave the Court that authority was unconstitutional. Joining Marshall in this inspired but highly questionable decision was one of the men who had helped frame not only the section of the law now being struck down but the Constitution which was being cited against it, William Paterson of New Jersey, now an Associate Justice of the Court.

Marbury's commission as a justice of the peace would soon be forgotten, but John Marshall's upholding of the Court's right to nullify an act of Congress that contravened the Constitution would become one of the Supreme Court's most noteworthy decisions. Petty in its origins, mean-spirited in its evolution, and partisan in its motives, *Marbury versus Madison* nonetheless wrote into the Constitution for all time what the members of the Convention had neglected to make explicit. Chief Justice Marshall, writing the opinion of the Court, said: "It is emphatically the province and duty of the judicial department to say what the law is. . . . A law repugnant to the Constitution is void. . . ." And so it has remained.

*   *   *

But all of this was in the future. At the moment, the dispute in the Convention's Committee of the Whole was over the Virginia Plan's proposal for a council of revision, composed of the executive and a number of national judges, with power to veto national legislation. In an attempt to resolve it, Elbridge Gerry moved to give the executive alone the power to veto legislative acts, with the proviso that such a veto could be overridden by a vote of something more than a simple majority of each house of the national legislature. Rufus King seconded the motion of his Massachusetts colleague.

James Wilson and Alexander Hamilton wanted to go even further and give the executive an absolute veto. Gerry and Dr.

Franklin opposed that, as did Roger Sherman. Madison pointed out that if the percentage required of each house to override were large enough, it would have virtually the same effect as an absolute veto. At that point, Pierce Butler of South Carolina rose to speak.

"I was in favor of a single executive magistrate," he said, "but could I have entertained an idea that a complete negative on the laws was to be given him, I certainly should have acted very differently. It has been observed that in all countries the executive power is in a constant course of increase. This is certainly the case in Great Britain. Some gentlemen seem to think that we have nothing to apprehend from an abuse of the executive power. But why might not a Catiline or a Cromwell arise in this country as well as in others?"

Those who favored an absolute veto believed it would rarely be exercised. Wilson, for one, thought its mere existence would prevent the legislature from passing laws it knew would be vetoed. But Gunning Bedford, Jr., of Delaware was opposed to any check whatsoever on the members of the legislature. As the representatives of the people, they would be the best judges, he thought, of what was in the people's interest.

George Mason, who had been out of the chamber when the Committee voted for a single executive, took this opportunity to speak out against too much power in the executive branch. "We are, Mr. Chairman, going very far in this business," he said. "We are not, indeed, constituting a British Government, but a more dangerous monarchy, an elective one. We are introducing a new principle into our system, and one not necessary as in the British Government where the executive has greater rights to defend. Do the gentlemen mean to pave the way to hereditary monarchy? Do they flatter themselves that the people will ever consent to such an innovation? If they do, I venture to tell them they are mistaken. The people will never consent."

Turning back to an earlier theme, Mason continued, "Notwithstanding the oppressions and injustice experienced among us from democracy, the genius of the people is in favor of it, and the genius of the people must be consulted." Then, addressing the question of an absolute veto, he asked, "Will it not be enough to enable the executive to suspend offensive laws till they shall be cooly revised and the objections to them overruled by a greater majority than was required in the first instance? I could never agree to give up all the rights of the people to a single magistrate."

Dr. Franklin rose to express his agreement and, in doing so, made clear his belief that Washington would be the country's first executive. "The first man put at the helm will be a good one," he said. "Nobody knows what sort may come afterwards."

This expectation that Washington would be the first at the helm was, in fact, shared by most, if not all, of the delegates. And it influenced not only the way they envisioned the future presidency but the powers they were willing to assign to that office. As Pierce Butler would write to a relative in England a year later, the powers of the President "are full great, and greater than I was disposed to make them. Nor, Entre Nous, do I believe they would have been so great had not many of the members cast their eyes towards General Washington as President; and shaped their Ideas of the Powers to be given to a President, by their opinions of his Virtue."

When the debate over the executive veto finally ended, Wilson and Hamilton lost their attempt to push through an absolute veto, and the Committee of the Whole voted for an executive veto that could be overridden by two-thirds of each house of the legislature. Then, before adjournment, the Committee voted to establish a national judiciary "to consist of one supreme tribunal and of one or more inferior tribunals."

That afternoon, George Washington and two delegates who had served as generals under him—Thomas Mifflin of Pennsylvania and Charles Cotesworth Pinckney of South Carolina—hurried from the State House to the commons on the outskirts of the city to review Philadelphia's light infantry, cavalry, and a detachment of artillery. A newspaper reported that "the usual maneuvres were performed with alertness and regularity, much to the satisfaction of the Generals, as well as to a vast concourse of respectable inhabitants." But another report left grave doubt that Washington, at least, had seen very much, "so great was the crowd which unceasingly surrounded him and wished to see and talk with him."

On the next day, Tuesday, June 5, Governor William Livingston of New Jersey joined his fellow delegates David Brearley, William Paterson, and William Churchill Houston. The Committee of the Whole turned to the question of how national judges would be chosen. The Virginia Plan had proposed appointment by the national legislature, but James Wilson of Pennsylvania urged appointment by the executive.

Dr. Franklin expressed a wish to hear other suggestions and facetiously offered one of his own which he said he understood was practiced in Scotland. There, he said, "the nomination proceeds from the lawyers, who always select the ablest of the profession in order to get rid of him and share his practice among themselves."

Unable to decide the question, the delegates moved on to other proposals of the Virginia Plan. They agreed to admit new states by something less than a unanimous vote of the legislature and to continue the Confederation Congress until the new constitution had been adopted. Then, after postponing a number of other decisions, they took up the proposal for ratification of the new constitution by state conventions chosen by the people. Roger Sherman, who had earlier expressed his distrust of the people as electors of the lower house of the legislature, objected to this as well. "I think such a popular ratification is unnecessary," he said. "The Articles of Confederation provide for changes and alterations with the assent of Congress and ratification of the state legislatures."

But James Madison, who feared and distrusted the state legislatures, differed strongly. "I think this provision is essential," he said. "The Articles of Confederation themselves are defective in this respect." It was, he thought, "indispensable that the new constitution should be ratified in the most unexceptionable form and by the supreme authority of the people themselves."

Although the question had not yet arisen, Wilson expressed a hope that ratification by a certain number of states might lead to at least a partial union, with the door left open for the rest to join later. Madison took this suggestion as an attempt to frighten the small states of New Jersey and Delaware into accepting proportional representation in the legislature lest they be left out altogether, and he noted that nothing was said in response to it. Indeed, Charles Pinckney went further, expressing a hope that as few as nine states might be authorized to unite if the others held back. But as with other controversial questions, the Committee of the Whole eventually agreed that the entire question of ratification should be postponed.

When the Convention adjourned, the delegates were aware that their earlier decision for election of members of the lower house of the legislature by the people of each state would be challenged in the morning. Charles Pinckney and John Rutledge of South Carolina had sought time to reconsider that decision, and the Committee of the Whole had agreed. Pinckney took it up the first thing Wednesday morning, June 6, with a motion that members of the lower house from each state be elected by their respective state legislatures. This was precisely what Roger Sherman and Elbridge Gerry had unsuc cessfully urged six days earlier. "The people," Pinckney said now, "are less fit judges in such cases, and the legislatures will be less likely to promote the adoption of the new government if they are to be excluded from all share in it." John Rutledge seconded his motion.

This time, Gerry suggested a compromise: that the state legislatures choose members of the lower house from lists of individuals nominated by the people. It was an idea that clearly

reflected Gerry's distrust of both the people *and* the legislature
of his home state of Massachusetts. "I am not," he said with
splendid understatement, "disposed to run into extremes. I am
as much principled as ever against aristocracy and monarchy.
It is necessary, on the one hand, that the people should appoint one branch of the government in order to inspire them
with the necessary confidence. But I wish the election, on the
other hand, to be so modified as to secure more effectually a
just preference of merit."

Roger Sherman was in no mood to compromise, and he endorsed Pinckney's notion of attempting to win the state legislatures to the new plan of government by involving them in it.
"If it is in view to abolish the state governments," he said, "the
elections ought to be by the people. If the state governments
are to be continued, it is necessary, in order to preserve harmony between the national and state governments, that the
elections to the former should be made by the latter. The right
of participating in the national government will be sufficiently
secured to the people by their election of the state legislature."

Then, as John Dickinson had done a few days earlier, Sherman turned from the specific question before them to enlarge
on his ideas about the proper relationship between the states
and the national government. The objects of the Union, he
thought, were few in number: defense against foreign and domestic turmoil, concluding treaties with foreign nations, and
regulating foreign trade. "All other matters, civil and criminal," he said, "would be much better in the hands of the
states."

Expressing his preference for small units of government, the
man from the middle-sized state of Connecticut declared,
"The people are more happy in small than large states. States
may indeed be too small, as Rhode Island, and thereby too
subject to faction. Some others are perhaps too large, the
powers of government not being able to pervade them. I am
for giving the general government power to legislate and execute within a defined province."

It was in many ways a restatement of the classic belief about the impossibility of republican government in a large nation. Combined with Elbridge Gerry's contentions that democratic governments were prone to anarchy and misrule, it was persuasive to many. But Madison, aided by his months of study of republics and confederacies, was convinced that both men were wrong. And now, in his first lengthy speech to the assembled delegates, he took on both aspects of the Gerry-Sherman argument and, in effect, turned them against each other.

"All civilized societies," he said, "will be divided into different sects, factions, and interests as they happen to consist of rich and poor, debtors and creditors, the landed, the manufacturing, the commercial interests, the inhabitants of this district or that district, the followers of this political leader or that political leader, the disciples of this religious sect or that religious sect.

"In all cases where a majority are united by a common interest or passion, the rights of the minority are in danger." What motives, he asked, might restrain such a majority? Neither honesty, respect for character, nor conscience had succeeded in past societies. "Religion itself may become a motive to persecution and oppression." We have, he said, in a reference to slavery, "seen the mere distinction of color made, in the most enlightened period of time, a ground of the most oppressive dominion ever exercised by man over man.

"What has been the source of those unjust laws complained of among ourselves? Has it not been the real or supposed interest of the major number? Debtors have defrauded their creditors. The landed interest has borne hard on the mercantile interest. The holders of one species of property have thrown a disproportion of taxes on the holders of another species. The lesson we are to draw from the whole is that where a majority are united by a common sentiment and have an opportunity, the rights of the minor party become insecure.

"In a republican government," he continued, "the majority, if united, have always an opportunity. The only remedy is to *enlarge* the sphere and thereby divide the community into so great a number of interests and parties that, in the first place, a majority will not be likely at the same moment to have a common interest separate from that of the whole or of the minority and, in the second place, that in case they should have such an interest, they may not be able to unite in the pursuit of it.

"It is incumbent on us then," he concluded, "to try this remedy and, with that view, to frame a republican system on such a scale and in such a form as will control all the evils which have been experienced."

There was more discussion and debate, but Madison had placed before the delegates a masterful argument in favor of large *and* democratic government: that what Gerry had earlier called the evils flowing from an excess of democracy, far from being compounded in an enlarged country, would, by counteracting each other, be reduced and controlled. He had not only challenged the prevailing idea that only a small, homogeneous society could survive as a republic but had also given his fellow delegates reasons for believing that a large, heterogeneous electorate, by taking advantage of shifting coalitions of interests, might actually safeguard the liberty of its citizens.

When the vote finally came, the move by Pinckney and Rutledge to have members of the lower house from each state elected by their state legislatures was defeated, eight states to three. The choice would remain with the people of each state.

That afternoon after adjournment, a number of the delegates adjourned to Dr. Franklin's for dinner. Washington was there, and William Samuel Johnson of Connecticut. And since Franklin's dining room seated twenty-four, we can assume there were others. Gradually, the delegates were concluding that the Convention would drag on, and if Governor Randolph was among the guests, he may have mentioned his plan to bring his wife and infant daughter to Philadelphia to stay with him. Elbridge Gerry had brought his wife and infant daughter with him, and the Gerrys were happily ensconced in a rented house on Spruce Street.

For two days it had rained, and the weather was still show-
ery when the delegates turned up at the State House on
Thursday morning, June 7. With the method of electing members of the lower house decided for the second time, the Committee of the Whole turned back to the question of electing
Senators, which had been postponed. John Dickinson of Delaware moved for their election by the state legislatures, and
Roger Sherman seconded the motion.

The debate lasted throughout the day, with Wilson and
Madison arguing strenuously for the direct election of Senators by the people of the states and Dickinson, Sherman, and
Gerry just as vigorously for their election by the state legislatures. And while the specific question was how the members
of the Senate would be chosen in each state, it was soon clear
that other considerations were being taken into account by
various delegates.

Charles Pinckney, who obviously assumed that the number
of Senators from each state would be in proportion to a state's
population, said, "If the small states should be allowed one
Senator only, the number will be too great. There will be
eighty, at least."

John Dickinson, on the other hand, clearly assumed that
while in the lower house the states might be represented in
proportion to their population, that would not be the case in
the Senate. It had been Dickinson, after all, who just five days
earlier had expressed the hope that each state would retain an
equal vote in at least one branch of the national legislature.
Now, addressing himself to the question of how members of
the Senate should be chosen, he said, "The proposed national
system is like the solar system, in which the states are the
planets and ought to be left to move freely in their proper
orbits. The gentleman from Pennsylvania, Mr. Wilson, wishes
to extinguish these planets. If the state governments are excluded from all agency in the national one, and all power is
drawn from the people at large, the consequence will be that
the national government will move in the same direction as the

state governments now do and will run into all the same mischiefs."

Wilson, who had studied law under Dickinson, had an answer for his mentor. "I do not see the danger of the states being devoured by the national government. On the contrary, I wish to keep them from devouring the national government. I am not, however, for extinguishing these planets as is supposed by Mr. Dickinson. But neither do I, on the other hand, believe that they will warm or enlighten the sun. Within their proper orbits they must still be suffered to act for subordinate purposes, for which their existence is made essential by the great extent of our country."

The two men differed as well in their views of the proper membership of the new Senate. Dickinson said, "I wish the Senate to consist of the most distinguished characters, distinguished for their rank in life and the weight of their property, and bearing as strong a likeness to the British House of Lords as possible."

Wilson replied, "The British Government cannot be our model. We have no materials for a similar one. Our manners, our laws, the abolition of entails and of primogeniture, the whole genius of the people are opposed to it."

Finally, shortly before adjournment, George Mason spoke up. "Whatever power may be necessary for the national government, a certain portion must necessarily be left in the states. It is impossible for one power to pervade the extreme parts of the United States so as to carry equal justice to them. The state legislatures also ought to have some means of defending themselves against encroachments of the national government. In every other department, we have studiously endeavored to provide for its self-defense. Shall we leave the states alone unprovided with the means for this purpose? And what better means can we provide than to make them a constituent part of the national establishment?"

When a vote was taken, it was unanimously in favor of the election of Senators by the state legislatures, ten states to none. Wilson and Madison were outvoted even in their own state delegations.

*   *   *

It took 126 years for the views of Wilson and Madison to finally prevail. Then, on May 31, 1913, William Jennings Bryan, Secretary of State under President Woodrow Wilson, signed the document promulgating the Seventeenth Amendment to the Constitution, which mandated the direct election of United States Senators by the people of the states. Proposed by Congress in 1912, the amendment was ratified by the legislatures of the required thirty-six states in just under a year.

The idea that there should *be* a Senate was never questioned in the Convention, though Thomas Jefferson is said to have raised the point sometime after his return from France in 1789 to become Washington's Secretary of State. It came up when the two men were breakfasting and Jefferson called Washington to account for having agreed to a second chamber of Congress.

"Why," asked Washington in response, "did you pour that coffee into your saucer?"

"To cool it," answered Jefferson.

"Even so," said Washington, "we pour legislation into the senatorial saucer to cool it."

*   *   *

After the Convention's adjournment that day, Washington had dinner with a group of delegates at the Indian Queen. Others may well have taken the leisurely ride out to Gray's Ferry where, on Thursdays during the summer, there was an outdoor concert from four in the afternoon until nine at night.

5

The Small States
and the Large

"There is no more reason that a great individual state, contributing much, should have more votes than a small one, contributing little, than that a rich individual citizen should have more votes than an indigent one."
WILLIAM PATERSON to the Convention
June 9, 1787

June 8–14, 1787

On Friday, June 8, the delegates began their third week of deliberations. At the request of Charles Pinckney of South Carolina the day before, the Commitee of the Whole had agreed to reconsider the clause giving the national legislature power to veto state laws in conflict with the new constitution or treaties made under it. It had been accepted more than a week earlier without debate or dissent. Pinckney now moved to broaden the veto power to include any state law the national legislature judged to be improper. Madison, still seeking to strengthen the national government at the expense of the states, seconded the motion.

The delegates argued for the entire day about this idea. Pinckney, defending it, said, "The states must be kept in due subordination to the nation; if they are left to act of themselves in any case, it will be impossible to defend the national prerogatives, however extensive they may be on paper. The acts of Congress have been defeated by this means, nor have foreign treaties escaped repeated violations."

Madison backed him up. "I cannot but regard an indefinite power to veto legislative acts of the states as absolutely necessary to a perfect system," he said. "Experience has evinced a constant tendency in the states to encroach on the federal authority, to violate national treaties, to infringe the rights and interests of each other, to oppress the weaker party within their respective jurisdictions.

"A veto is the mildest expedient that could be devised for preventing these mischiefs," he continued. "The existence of such a check will prevent attempts to commit them. If no such precaution is adopted, the only remedy will lie in an appeal to coercion. Is such a remedy desirable? Is it practicable? Could the national resources, if exerted to the utmost, enforce a national decree against Massachusetts, abetted perhaps by several of her neighbors?" It would not, he declared, be possible.

"In a word," he said, finally, "to recur to the illustrations borrowed from the planetary system, this prerogative of the general government is the great pervading principle that must control the centrifugal tendency of the states which, without it, will continually fly out of their proper orbits and destroy the order and harmony of the political system."

But Hugh Williamson of North Carolina was against giving the national legislature a power that might, as he saw it, prevent the states from regulating their internal police. And Elbridge Gerry said, "The national legislature with such a power might enslave the states. Such an idea as this will never be acceded to. It has never been suggested or conceived among the people." It was, he insisted, "a leap in the dark."

Roger Sherman suggested that the cases in which a veto might apply could be listed, but James Wilson dismissed that as impractical. In rebuttal, he resorted to a brief review of recent history. "Among the first sentiments expressed in the First Continental Congress," he reminded the delegates, "one was that Virginia is no more, that Massachusetts is no more, that Pennsylvania is no more, and so on. We are now one nation of brethren. We must bury all local interests and distinctions." This rhetoric in favor of the broader interests of the Union, he pointed out, "continued for some time.

"The tables at length began to turn. No sooner were the state governments formed than their jealousy and ambition began to display themselves. Each endeavored to cut a slice from the common loaf to add to its own morsel, till at length the confederation became frittered down to the impotent condition in which it now stands.

"Review the progress of the Articles of Confederation through Congress and compare the first and last drafts of it. To correct its vices is the business of this convention. One of its vices is the want of an effectual control in the whole over its parts. What danger is there that the whole will unnecessarily sacrifice a part? But reverse the case and leave the whole at the mercy of each part, and will not the general interest be continually sacrificed to local interests?"

This time John Dickinson agreed with his former law student and favored giving the national legislature the increased veto power over state legislation that Pinckney's motion would provide. "We must," he said, "take our choice of two things. We must either subject the states to the danger of being injured by the power of the national government or the latter to the danger of being injured by that of the states. I think the danger is greater from the states."

Gunning Bedford, Jr., as Attorney General of Dickinson's state of Delaware, must have found this conclusion appalling, for he addressed his reply directly to Dickinson. "In answer to my colleague's question—where would be the danger to the states from this power—I would refer him to the smallness of his own state, which can be injured at pleasure without redress. It is meant, I find, to strip the small states of their equal right of suffrage. In this case, Delaware will have about one-ninetieth for its share in the general councils, whilst Pennsylvania and Virginia will possess one-third of the whole. Is there no difference of interests, no rivalry of commerce, of manufactures? Will not these large states crush the small ones whenever they stand in the way of their ambitions or interested views?" But Bedford was not through.

"It seems," he said, "as if Pennsylvania and Virginia, by the conduct of their deputies, wish to provide a system in which they will have an enormous and monstrous influence."

That thrust, directed at Wilson and Madison, apparently had its effect, for the attempt to broaden the legislature's veto power was defeated, seven states to three. Thus far, at least, the Committee of the Whole had rejected every attempt to change its earlier decisions.

Leaving the State House that afternoon, delegates who bought copies of the *Pennsylvania Herald* might well have wondered if their secrecy rule had been such a good idea. For the *Herald* reported that the Convention had decided to throw Rhode Island out of the Union. It wasn't true, of course, but ten days passed before a letter from Philadelphia went out to newspapers around the country reminding readers that none of the Convention's actions had been officially divulged. "The mere idle reports of busy bodies and the absurd foolish suggestions of idle pretenders are not to be viewed and considered as the real and regular proceedings of the Convention," the letter warned.

On Saturday, June 9, Maryland's Attorney General, Luther Martin, joined his colleague Daniel of St. Thomas Jenifer, at the Convention. Born on a small New Jersey farm, Martin had graduated with honors from Princeton. After teaching school in Maryland, he had gone into the law. Delegates who had served with him in Congress were inclined to associate his permanently red face with his frequently high alcoholic content. At thirty-nine, the broad-shouldered, carelessly dressed Martin was ornery, impulsive, brilliant, and a committed anti-nationalist.

The question of how the states would be represented in the two houses of the legislature had come up first on May 30, the day the Virginia Plan came under discussion. It had been postponed when George Read of Delaware warned that any change in the one state, one vote formula of the Articles of Confederation might force his delegation to leave. But Gunning Bedford, Jr., also from Delaware, had raised the question forcefully in his attack on Wilson and Madison the day before, and now William Paterson of New Jersey, another small state, moved to take it up. His colleague David Brearley seconded him.

The *means of electing* members of the legislature had by now been decided. Representatives in the lower house would be chosen by the people of their states; Senators, by their state legislatures. The question now was whether a state's representation in each of the two houses would be proportional to its free population or contributions to the national government, as the Virginia Plan proposed, or whether each state would have an equal representation, as in the Confederation Congress. It was a question that everyone knew would divide the small and large states.

David Brearley, just short of his forty-second birthday, was New Jersey's chief justice. He spoke first, remarking that he was sorry the question of representation had even come up. "It was much agitated in Congress at the time of forming the Confederation," he reminded the delegates, "and was then rightly settled by allowing to each sovereign state an equal vote. Otherwise, the smaller states would have been destroyed instead of being saved.

"The substitution of a ratio, I admit, carries fairness on the face of it. But on a deeper examination, it is unfair and unjust." Massachusetts, Pennsylvania, and Virginia would carry everything before them. What then was the remedy? There was only one—"that a map of the United States be spread out, that all existing boundaries be erased, and that a new partition of the whole be made into thirteen equal parts."

William Paterson, a forty-two-year-old lawyer, was a graduate of Princeton and a former attorney general of New Jersey.

Speaking in deadly earnest, he went back to question the very first decision made by the Committee of the Whole: that a national government ought to be established. The call of the Confederation Congress for the Convention, he pointed out, had specifically limited its purpose to amendment of the Articles of Confederation. Referring to that call, he said, "We ought to keep within its limits, or we shall be charged by our constituents with usurpation. The people of America are sharp-sighted and not to be deceived." The idea of a national government as distinguished from a federal one, he said, "never entered into the mind of any of them, and to the public mind we must accommodate ourselves. We have no power to go beyond the federal scheme, and if we had, the people are not ripe for any other. We must follow the people; the people will not follow us."

Then, turning to the specific proposal for a proportional representation of the states, he said, "There is no more reason that a great individual state, contributing much, should have more votes than a small one, contributing little, than that a rich individual citizen should have more votes than an indigent one."

Finally, turning to James Wilson's earlier remark that he hoped ratification by a certain number of states might lead to at least a partial union, he labeled it a hint that the large states might unite despite the refusal of the small states to agree with them on a form of government. "Let them unite if they please," he said, "but let them remember that they have no authority to compel the others to unite. New Jersey will never confederate on the plan before the Committee. She would be swallowed up. I would rather submit to a monarch, to a despot, than to such a fate. I will not only oppose the plan here, but on my return home, do everything in my power to defeat it there."

Paterson was a small man, at five feet two, a full four inches shorter than Madison, but he clearly impressed William Pierce of Georgia. In his sketch, Pierce wrote, "Mr. Paterson is one of those kind of men whose powers break in upon you and create wonder and astonishment. He is a man of great modesty, with looks that bespeak talents of no great extent, but he is a classic, a lawyer, and an orator."

James Wilson was not intimidated. "I hope," he said, "if the Confederacy should be dissolved, that a majority, nay even a minority, of the states will unite for their safety, and the rest may do as they please." Since all authority was derived from the people, he continued, "equal numbers of people ought to have an equal number of representatives." This principle had been improperly violated in the Confederation because of the urgent circumstances of the time. "Are not the citizens of Pennsylvania equal to those of New Jersey?" he asked. "Does it require a hundred and fifty of the former to balance fifty of the latter?"

Then, paraphrasing Paterson's defiant statement, Wilson said, "If the small states will not confederate on this plan, Pennsylvania, and I presume some other states, will not confederate on any other." Turning to Paterson, he said, "The gentleman from New Jersey is candid in declaring his opinion. I commend him for it. I am equally so. I say again, I will never confederate on his principles. If no state will part with any of its sovereignty, it is in vain to talk of a national government."

Perhaps wisely, Paterson moved to postpone a decision, and the Convention adjourned to take up the subject again on Monday.

Just three days earlier, Madison had written optimistically to William Short, the secretary of the American legation in Paris: "The personal characters of the members promise much. The spirit which they bring with them seems in general equally promising." But that was three days ago, the day of Madison's masterful speech on democracy in a large country. Until then, he and his major ally, James Wilson, had had things pretty much their way.

Now the climate had begun to change, both inside the Con-

vention chamber and in Philadelphia itself. The exchange between Paterson and Wilson had been rancorous, and Madison
must have felt things beginning to slip out of control. To make
matters worse, the temperature had begun to rise, and those
who knew Philadelphia summers sensed a heat wave coming
on.

The next day was a Sunday, and for those who went to
church, there was more than usual reason to pray for their
country.

On Monday morning, June 11, the delegates arrived at the
State House in a withering heat that could only grow worse as
the sun rose higher. Abraham Baldwin, a member of Congress
like his three colleagues from Georgia, arrived from New York
to join them. Born and raised in Connecticut, a graduate of
Yale, a licensed preacher and a lawyer, Baldwin had moved to
Augusta only three years earlier.

Moving into the chamber, the delegates took their seats, and
when the formality of resolving the Convention into a Committee of the Whole was completed, Roger Sherman of Connecticut took the floor. Of Sherman, William Pierce wrote in
his sketch: "Mr. Sherman exhibits the oddest-shaped character I ever remember to have met with. He is awkward, un-
meaning, and unaccountably strange in his manner. But in his
train of thinking there is something regular, deep and comprehensive; yet the oddity of his address, the vulgarisms that
accompany his public speaking, and that strange New England
cant which runs through his public as well as his private
speaking make everything that is connected with him gro-
tesque and laughable; and yet he deserves infinite praise—no
man has a better heart or a clearer head."

Sherman was brief and to the point. He suggested a compromise. "I propose that the proportion of suffrage in the first
branch should be according to the respective numbers of free
inhabitants; and that in the second branch, or Senate, each
state should have one vote and no more. As the states will re-

main possessed of certain individual rights, each state ought to be able to protect itself. Otherwise a few large states will rule the rest."

After some discussion of whether financial contributions were a better way of allocating representation than simple population, Rufus King of Massachusetts moved to establish at least the principle that voting in the lower house should be "according to some equitable ratio of representation." James Wilson seconded the motion, but before a vote was taken, Benjamin Franklin was recognized. He had written out his speech, and Wilson read it for him.

"It has given me a great pleasure," he read, "to observe that till this point—the proportion of representation—came before us, our debates were carried on with great coolness and temper. If anything of a contrary kind has on this occasion appeared, I hope it will not be repeated; for we are sent here to *consult*, not to *contend*, with each other; and declarations of a fixed opinion, and of determined resolution never to change it, neither enlighten nor convince us."

When the vote was taken on King's motion for state representation in the lower house according to some equitable ratio, it passed, seven states to three. Connecticut voted with the large states in accordance with Roger Sherman's suggested compromise.

That much accomplished, James Wilson moved to establish population as the equitable ratio to be used. To keep the Southern states with him, he tactfully worded his motion to provide that the representation of each state in the lower house be in proportion to the number of free inhabitants and three-fifths of all other persons except nontaxpaying Indians. Charles Pinckney of South Carolina seconded the motion.

The three-fifths formula, which referred, of course, to slaves, was no sudden inspiration of Wilson's. Congress itself had proposed that proportion in 1783 when the issue was levying direct taxes. Southern states would be undertaxed, Northerners had then insisted, unless *all* slaves were counted in the total population. Southerners naturally held the opposite view. The proposed compromise had been to count three-fifths of the slaves. By the time of the Convention, eleven of the thirteen states—all but New Hampshire and Rhode Island—had voted their approval of that proportion.

Elbridge Gerry immediately objected to Wilson's proposal. "Property is not the rule of representation," he said. "Why then should the blacks, who are property in the South, be in the rule of representation more than the cattle and horses of the North?"

No one bothered to answer, and when the vote was taken, Wilson's motion passed, nine states to two.

Roger Sherman, who had seen the first part of his compromise adopted, now moved for the rest: that each state should have a single vote in the Senate. "Everything," he said, "depends on this. The smaller states will never agree to the plan on any other principle than an equality of suffrage in this branch." Oliver Ellsworth of Connecticut seconded the motion. It was close, but Sherman lost, six states to five.

James Wilson, seconded by Alexander Hamilton, seized the moment to move that representation in the Senate should be by the same rule as in the lower house, and his motion carried, six states to five. The five losers in both votes were Connecticut, New Jersey, Delaware, Maryland—four small states—and New York, with Hamilton outvoted by his two antinationalist New York colleagues. Wilson and Madison had won their fight to keep the Confederation's one state, one vote principle of state sovereignty out of the new government. The states would be represented in both houses of the national legislature according to their population. The defeat of the small states, though narrow, appeared to be decisive. As later events would prove, however, it was anything but final.

Moving on, the Committee of the Whole approved a slightly altered Virginia Plan resolution that "a republican constitution and its existing laws ought to be guaranteed to each state by the United States." Then, after a brief debate, the resolution requiring oaths by state officials to support the new constitution and national laws was also approved, and the Convention adjourned.

The heat wave continued, though tempers inside the Convention chamber appeared to have been cooled by Benjamin Franklin's admonition. On Tuesday, June 12, the delegates reached Edmund Randolph's final resolution calling for ratification of the new constitution by state conventions chosen by the people. Postponed a week earlier after Roger Sherman objected to it, the resolution was now agreed to without debate. The delegates then turned back to fill in some of the gaps they had left.

With little argument, they agreed on three-year terms for Representatives and seven-year terms for Senators, with both eligible for reelection. And while they rejected a minimum age for members of the lower house, they decided that Senators should be at least thirty. Both would be paid a fixed compensation out of the national treasury, and both would be ineligible to hold any state or national office while serving in the national legislature and for one year thereafter.

There were two main reasons for this prohibition. First, the delegates knew that resentment and jealousies had arisen in some of the states over the policy of the Confederation Congress of appointing its own members to various diplomatic and executive positions. And second, as Pierce Butler would put it some days later, it was a precaution against intrigue. "Look at the example of Great Britain," he said, "where men get into Parliament that they may get offices for themselves or their friends. This is the source of the corruption that ruined their government."

On most of these provisions, as with many others, the delegates would later change their minds.

On Wednesday, in stifling heat, they turned to the judiciary. In short order, they agreed that the national judiciary should decide cases involving the collection of national revenue, impeachment of national officers, and the national peace and harmony. Judges, they agreed, should be appointed by the Senate.

And with that, the Committee of the Whole resolved itself back into the Convention, George Washington replaced Nathaniel Gorham in the chair, and Gorham read out the nineteen resolutions the Committee had adopted. The Convention, which would consider them all again, put off beginning that task until the next day. And for some time after adjournment, members busied themselves copying the resolutions to study overnight.

In one day short of three weeks, the delegates had organized the Convention and heard, debated, and revised the Virginia Plan. And while their decisions were tentative and stated mostly in general terms, they had agreed on the outline of a federal republic radically different from the existing Confederation. They had found a consensus for a national government operating directly on individual citizens and based to a significant degree on the will of those citizens. Their distrust of the state legislatures stood in marked contrast to their faith in the intelligence of their fellow Americans, for in the hands of the people themselves they had placed not only the election of members of the lower house of the national legislature but the ratification of the plan itself.

While members of the Senate would be elected by the state legislatures, giving the state governments a voice in the national government, the national legislature would have broad powers, including a veto over state laws in conflict with the new constitution and treaties made under it. And membership in both houses of the legislature would adhere to democratic principle by being proportional to state populations.

The executive, chosen by the national legislature, would be a single person with a limited power to veto legislation. The national judiciary would have jurisdiction over questions involving the national peace and harmony. James Madison had lost his plan for a council of revision with power to veto national legislation, but he had won virtually everything else he had worked for.

As the delegates left the State House that afternoon, they took with them their scribbled copies of the nineteen resolutions they had agreed on. Examining the broad outline of government that afternoon and evening, they could see the mosaic beginning to take shape. It was crude; it lacked details; but it was clearly so different from what many of the delegates from small states had envisioned that more than a few of them were aghast. The tidy work of three weeks threatened to unravel the next day.

The sweltering heat persisted. On Thursday morning, June 14, William Paterson, the diminutive attorney from New Jersey who had told James Wilson that his state would never confederate on the Virginia Plan, took the floor.

"It is the wish of several deputations," he said, "particularly that of New Jersey, that further time might be allowed them to contemplate the plan reported from the Committee of the Whole and to prepare another purely federal system of government materially different from the system now under consideration." He asked for a day's postponement.

Governor Randolph graciously moved for an adjournment, Paterson seconded, and the Convention adjourned until eleven o'clock the next day.

It was most likely on this morning, after all the copying of resolutions the day before, that General Washington rose from the chair to speak.

"I am sorry," he said, "to find that some one member of this body has been so neglectful of the secrets of the Convention as to drop in the State House a copy of their proceedings, which by accident was picked up and delivered to me this morning. I must entreat gentlemen to be more careful lest our transactions get into the newspapers and disturb the public repose by premature speculations. I know not whose paper it is, but there it is."

He threw the paper onto the table. "Let him who owns it take it." With that, he bowed, picked up his hat, and left the chamber.

William Pierce, feeling in his pocket for his papers, was alarmed to find them missing. A quick glance at the paper on the table, however, showed it to be in someone else's handwriting. He found his own papers in his room at the Indian Queen. Writing about it later, he said, "It is something remarkable that no person ever owned the paper."

6

A Backward Step

"Is it probable that the states will adopt and ratify a scheme which they have never authorized us to propose?"

JOHN LANSING to the Convention
June 16, 1787

June 15–26, 1787

The heat in the Convention chamber was still oppressive when the delegates assembled at eleven o'clock on Friday morning, June 15, to hear William Paterson's "purely federal" plan of government. It is not hard to imagine some unhappy fidgeting on the part of Madison, Wilson, King, and other strong nationalists as the New Jersey lawyer read out nine resolutions designed to amend the Articles of Confederation.

The New Jersey Plan, as it would be called, was actually a product of that state's delegates along with others from Connecticut, New York, Delaware, and Maryland. It called for some additional powers for the Confederation Congress, an executive of several persons elected by the Congress, and a judiciary appointed by the executive. Madison, for one, saw it as totally inadequate, for while it took a few steps in what he considered the right direction, it retained all of the Confederation's fatal flaws. The states would remain sovereign, for example, and each would have a single vote.

Madison moved successfully to refer the New Jersey Plan to the Committee of the Whole, but he was distressed when John

Rutledge of South Carolina succeeded in referring the Virginia Plan back to the Committee as well. That meant that all of the important decisions already taken would immediately be open to reconsideration. Once again, there was an early adjournment and much copying of the new resolutions before the delegates went their several ways.

Meanwhile, John Dickinson of Delaware approached Madison. "You see the consequence of pushing things too far," he said. "Some of the members from the small states wish for two branches in the general legislature and are friends to a good national government; but we would sooner submit to a foreign power than submit to be deprived of an equality of suffrage in both branches of the legislature and thereby be thrown under the domination of the large states." It is a mark of Madison's fairness as a reporter that he included this private scolding in his notes on the Convention.

The heat wave had mercifully broken when the delegates showed up at the State House on Saturday morning, but the cooler temperatures had done little to bank the fires of contention between the small and large states. There were two anomalies in that lineup. One was New York, a large state, which, through its two-man majority of Lansing and Yates, had allied itself with the small states. The other was Georgia. Smaller in white population than Rhode Island yet larger in area than Virginia and North Carolina combined, Georgia's delegates had cast their lot with the larger states.

Both Georgians and New Yorkers generally believed that their states would soon be among the most populous in the country; yet that common belief led each of the two delegations to opposite conclusions. For Lansing and Yates, as followers of the political leadership of New York's Governor George Clinton, it called for opposition to a strong national government which could be expected to oppose New York's profitable use of its harbor to the disadvantage of neighboring states. For the delegates of Georgia, whose state was weak and vulnerable to both Indians and the Spanish on her frontiers, the protection of a strong national government seemed essential until the state was populous enough to defend itself.

And even this did not tell the whole story, for there was often division within the delegations of both small and large states as well. Alexander Hamilton was a good example. A New Yorker, he was also a strong nationalist. And as the future would prove, there were among the delegates from small states many who needed only some assurance that their states would not, in fact, be dominated by the large states to reveal themselves as the nationalists they really were.

When the Convention had resolved itself once more into a Committee of the Whole, John Lansing, Jr., called for a reading of the first resolution of each of the two plans. When it was completed, he rose to compare them. "That of Mr. Paterson," he said, "sustains the sovereignty of the respective states. That of Mr. Randolph destroys it." He was, he said, decidedly of the opinion that the power of the Convention was limited to proposing amendments to the Articles of Confederation. "New York would never have concurred in sending deputies to the Convention if she had supposed the deliberations were to turn on a consolidation of the states and a national government.

"Is it probable that the states will adopt and ratify a scheme which they have never authorized us to propose?" he asked. The states, he concluded, "will never feel a sufficient confidence in a general government to give it a negative on their laws. The scheme is itself totally novel. There is no parallel to it to be found."

Paterson then rose to defend the New Jersey Plan. He preferred it, he said, because it accorded with both the powers of the Convention and the sentiments of the people. "If the confederacy is radically wrong, let us return to our states and obtain larger powers, not assume them ourselves."

James Wilson of Pennsylvania was then recognized. After

comparing the two plans point by point, he said, "With regard to the power of the Convention, I conceive myself authorized to *conclude nothing* but to be at liberty to *propose anything.*" As for the sentiments of the people, he added, "I conceive it difficult to know precisely what they are. Those of the particular circle in which one moves are commonly mistaken for the general voice. I cannot persuade myself that the state governments and sovereignties are so much the idols of the people nor a national government so obnoxious to them as some suppose. Why should a national government be unpopular? Has it less dignity? Will each citizen enjoy under it less liberty or protection? Will a citizen of Delaware be degraded by becoming a citizen of the United States?"

Governor Randolph addressed himself to the Convention's power to go beyond amending the Articles of Confederation. "When the salvation of the Republic is at stake," he said, "it would be treason to our trust not to propose what we find necessary." He would not "leave anything that seems necessary undone. The present moment is favorable and is probably the last that will offer."

The Convention adjourned for the weekend with nothing settled. Those delegates who read the *Independent Gazetteer* that evening were told that "the greatest unanimity subsists in the councils of the Federal Convention." They must have wondered if they had spent the day dreaming.

By Monday, June 18, the stifling heat had returned. Alexander Hamilton, who had been consistently outvoted by Lansing and Yates in the New York delegation, took the floor. Handsome, impeccably dressed, the former aide to Washington had risen in his mere thirty years from obscurity to a continental reputation as a New York lawyer and politician. A man of style, skill, vision, ambition, and energy, Hamilton was utterly nationalistic. He had first suggested a constitutional convention in 1780.

He was obliged, he said, "to declare myself unfriendly to

both plans. I am particularly opposed to that from New Jersey, being fully convinced that no amendment of the confederation leaving the states in possession of their sovereignty could possibly answer the purpose."

Then, after criticizing both plans and declaring that he almost despaired that a republican government could be established over such a large country, he said, "I am sensible at the same time that it would be unwise to propose one of any other form. In my private opinion, I have no scruple in declaring, supported as I am by the opinions of so many of the wise and good, that the British Government is the best in the world, and that I doubt much whether anything short of it will do in America."

Their House of Lords, he declared, "is a most noble institution." As to the executive, "the English model is the only good one on this subject. The hereditary interest of the King is so interwoven with that of the nation, and his personal emoluments so great, that he is placed above the danger of being corrupted from abroad, and at the same time is both sufficiently independent and sufficiently controlled to answer the purpose of the institution at home."

Hamilton then sketched a plan of government which he offered, he said, not as a proposal to the delegates, but simply to give a more correct view of his ideas. It called for a national legislature of two houses "with power to pass all laws whatsoever." Members of the lower house would be elected by the people for three-year terms. Senators would be elected for life by electors chosen by the people.

A national executive, also elected for life by electors chosen by the people, would have a veto over "all laws about to be passed." Judges of the national court would also serve for life. All state laws contrary to the constitution or national laws would be void, and to prevent such laws from being passed, a governor of each state, appointed by the national government, would have power to veto state "laws about to be passed."

Hamilton spoke for four or five hours, taking up the entire

day's session. Before he sat down, he said, "I confess that this plan and that from Virginia are very remote from the idea of the people. Perhaps the New Jersey Plan is nearest their expectation. But the people are gradually ripening in their opinions of government. They begin to tire of an excess of democracy. And what is even the Virginia Plan but pork still, with a little change of the sauce."

Hamilton's speech must have come as a jolt to Roger Sherman and William Paterson, who had emerged as the spokesmen for the small states. Wilson and Madison, on the other hand, can be imagined squirming in discomfort at the suggestion of a national government as blatantly powerful as the one Hamilton outlined. In any case, there was no response from anyone, either that day or the next, and the plan was never acted upon. If it served any purpose, it was most likely to make the Virginia Plan seem moderate by comparison.

The next day, Tuesday, June 19, James Madison spoke at some length. Ranging over the histories of the Confederation and confederacies of the past, he endeavored to show that the New Jersey Plan was inadequate either to preserve the Union or to provide a government that would remedy the evils that had brought them all to Philadelphia. Then, speaking directly to the small-state delegates, he urged them to consider their situation if their opposition to the Virginia Plan prevented the adoption of any plan at all.

"Let the union of the states be dissolved," he said, "and one of two consequences must happen. Either the states must remain individually independent and sovereign, or two or more confederacies must be formed among them." If all the states remained independent, he asked, "would the small states be more secure against the ambition and power of their larger neighbors than they would be under a general government pervading with equal energy every part of the empire and having an equal interest in protecting every part against every other part?" If, on the other hand, two or more confederacies were formed among the states, "can the smaller states expect that their larger neighbors will confederate with them on the principle of the present confederacy, which gives to each member an equal suffrage, or that they would exact less severe concessions from the smaller states than are proposed in the scheme of Mr. Randolph?"

The prospect of many new states in the West, he added, "is another consideration of importance. If they should come into the Union at all, they will come when they contain but few inhabitants. If they should be entitled to vote according to their proportions of inhabitants, all will be right and safe. Let them have an equal vote, and a more objectionable minority than ever might give the law to the whole."

There the debate ended. On a motion by Rufus King of Massachusetts, the Committee of the Whole rejected the New Jersey Plan, seven states to three, and voted to place the Virginia Plan again before the Convention. Only New York, New Jersey, and Delaware voted against the motion. Maryland, with only two delegates in attendance, divided, and thereby lost its vote. Connecticut, clearly hoping for a compromise within the Virginia Plan, voted with the large-state bloc.

William R. Davie, a thirty-one-year-old Revolutionary War veteran and a delegate from North Carolina, wrote that day to his governor, Richard Caswell. "We move slowly in our business," he admitted. "It is indeed a work of great delicacy and difficulty, impeded every step by jealousies and interest." As a summary of nearly four weeks of deliberations, Davie's description was succinct and accurate.

Wednesday, June 20, was an anticlimax. As the Convention turned to a clause-by-clause reconsideration of everything the Committee of the Whole had decided in its examination of the Virginia Plan, Oliver Ellsworth of Connecticut moved to replace the words "national government" in the first resolution with "Government of the United States." Randolph graciously agreed, and the Convention adopted the change unanimously. The offensive word "national" disappeared.

But then John Lansing, Jr., of New York, supported by Luther Martin of Maryland and Roger Sherman of Connecticut, made a last-ditch effort to preserve the Confederation Congress as the heart of the new government. They failed, as they must have known they would. But once again, Sherman suggested a compromise.

"If the difficulty on the subject of representation can not be otherwise got over," he said, "I would agree to have two branches of the legislature and a proportional representation in one of them provided each state has an equal voice in the other." It was of course the same compromise he had suggested nine days earlier, when it had been defeated, six states to five.

This was the beginning of a solid month of debate in which the issue of representation—apparently already decided— would dominate the Convention. Madison, Wilson, and their nationalist allies had established that they had a majority of the states in favor of proportional representation in both houses, but as the debate wore on, it became increasingly clear that a simple majority would probably not be enough. A constitution adamantly opposed by even as few as three or four of the states represented in the Convention would have little chance of success in the country at large. What was needed was consensus.

Over the next few days, the Convention worked away at confirming or altering the previous decisions of the Committee of the Whole. The legislature, the Convention agreed, *would* have two branches. Members of the lower house *would* be elected by the people but for terms of two, not three, years. George Mason objected to the idea of not including a minimum age for members of the lower house. "I think it absurd that a man today should not be permitted by the law to make a bargain for himself and tomorrow should be authorized to manage the affairs of a great nation," he said.

"It is the more extraordinary as every man carries with him in his own experience a scale for measuring the deficiency of young politicians, since he would, if interrogated, be obliged to declare that his political opinions at the age of twenty-one were too crude and erroneous to merit an influence on public measures. It has been said," he added wryly, "that Congress has proved a good school for our young men. It may be so, for anything I know, but if it is, I choose that they should bear the expense of their own education."

Mason moved to insert the age of twenty-five as a qualification for members of the lower house, and the Convention agreed, seven states to three.

As for Senators, they would, as the Committee of the Whole had decided, be elected by the state legislatures but for terms of six, not seven, years. To provide for a rotation in office, a third of them would be elected every two years.

In the midst of this process of refinement of their previous decisions, young Charles Pinckney rose to speak. A lawyer who had served as an officer in the defense of Charleston during the Revolution, Pinckney had put in three active years as the youngest member of the Confederation Congress. A confirmed nationalist, handsome, eager to make a name for himself, his vanity and ambition to be known as a young man wise beyond his years had led him to leave the impression with others at the Convention that he was just twenty-four years old, and hence, the youngest delegate. Though he managed to keep the exact date of his birth a permanent secret, he was between twenty-eight and thirty when he set out for Philadelphia and, hence, older than the twenty-six-year-old Jonathan Dayton of New Jersey.

From the beginning of their discussions, delegates had invoked the experience of Great Britain, of Greece and Rome, and of other governments in history to back up their arguments. Pinckney brought them sharply back to America. "The people of the United States," he said, "are perhaps the most singular of any we are acquainted with. Among them, there are fewer distinctions of fortune and less of rank than among the inhabitants of any other nation. Every freeman has a right to the same protection and security, and a very moderate share of property entitles them to the possession of all the honors and privileges the public can bestow.

"Hence arises a greater equality than is to be found among the people of any other country, and an equality which is more likely to continue. I say this equality is likely to continue because in a new country, possessing immense tracts of un-cultivated lands, where every temptation is offered to emigration and where industry must be rewarded with competency, there will be few poor and few dependent. Every member of society almost will enjoy an equal power of arriving at the supreme offices and consequently of directing the strength and sentiments of the whole community. None will be excluded by birth and few by fortune from voting for proper persons to fill the offices of government."

Then after pointing out significant differences between the American and British people and societies, Pinckney said, "The people of this country are not only very different from the inhabitants of any state we are acquainted with in the modern world, but I assert that their situation is distinct from either the people of Greece or Rome or of any state we are acquainted with among the ancients."

Turning from the past to the present, Pinckney continued, "Our true situation appears to me to be this: a new extensive country containing within itself the materials for forming a government capable of extending to its citizens all the blessings of civil and religious liberty—capable of making them happy at home. This is the great end of republican establishments. We mistake the object of our government if we hope or wish that it is to make us respectable abroad. Conquest or superiority among other powers is not or ought not ever to be the object of republican systems. If they are sufficiently active and energetic to rescue us from contempt and preserve our domestic happiness and security, it is all we can expect from them. It is more than almost any other government ensures to its citizens.

"I believe this observation will be found generally true: that no two people are so exactly alike in their situation or circumstances as to admit the exercise of the same government with equal benefit; that a system must be suited to the habits and genius of the people it is to govern and must grow out of them."

The Convention must, Pinckney concluded, "suit our government to the people it is to direct. These are, I believe, as active, intelligent, and susceptible of good government as any people in the world. The confusion which has produced the present relaxed state is not owing to them. It is owing to the weakness and defects of a government incapable of combining the various interests it is intended to unite, and destitute of energy. All that we have to do then is to distribute the powers of government in such a manner and for such limited periods as, while it gives a proper degree of permanency to the magistrate, will reserve to the people the right of election they will not or ought not frequently to part with. I am of the opinion that this may be easily done and that, with some amendments, the propositions before the Committee will fully answer this end."

In a way, Charles Pinckney's speech was an answer to Alexander Hamilton's, with its praise of the excellence of the British government. For his fellow nationalists, Pinckney's genuinely American approach to the problems they faced in devising a new government would surely have been refreshing. His optimism that it could all be accomplished with ease, however, must have raised more than a few eyebrows.

For today's Americans, living in a world in which powerful nations routinely attempt to impose their political and economic systems on less powerful ones, there is something decidedly enlightened in Pinckney's notion that no two peoples are so alike as to benefit equally from the same system of government. Yet it was, after all, from a deep-seated belief in this very principle that the delegates to the Convention were at that very moment laboring to create a government uniquely suited to the habits and genius of their own people.

7

Deadlock

"The large states dare not dissolve the Confederation. If they do, the small ones will find some foreign ally of more honor and good faith who will take them by the hand and do them justice."
GUNNING BEDFORD, JR., to the Convention
June 30, 1787

June 27–July 10, 1787

Despite Charles Pinckney's optimism, the members of the Convention knew, as they confirmed or altered decisions they had made in the Committee of the Whole, that they would eventually have to face once more the most divisive issue they had yet encountered. They had approved proportional representation based on population for both houses of the legislature in the Committee of the Whole. But would that vote stand up when the subject came before the Convention itself?

There had been a welcome spell of cool weather for four days, but now, on Wednesday morning, June 27, the heat wave returned. The New England delegates, dressed mostly in woolen suits, must have suffered distressingly. Almost as though the rising temperature were a kind of signal, John Rutledge of South Carolina moved to take up the explosive subject. The Convention agreed.

Attorney General Luther Martin of Maryland took the floor—and held it for more than three hours. Then, too exhausted to finish, he announced he would continue the next day. The thrust of his all but interminable speech was simple. The Convention had no power to diminish the sovereignty of the states. Virginia, Massachusetts, and Pennsylvania—the large states—were plotting, through proportional representation, to oppress the others.

His delivery was rambling and obtuse. Robert Yates of New York, who supported Martin's position, found his arguments "too diffuse . . . to trace." Much later, Connecticut's Oliver Ellsworth charged Martin with having made a speech "which might have continued two months, but for those marks of fatigue and disgust you saw strongly expressed on whichever side of the house you turned your mortified eyes."

When Martin had finally finished, the argument over representation went on. And on. Eventually, Dr. Franklin struggled to his feet. "The small progress we have made after four or five weeks close attendance and continual reasonings with each other," was, he thought, "a melancholy proof of the imperfection of human understanding. We indeed seem to feel our own want of political wisdom, since we have been running around in search of it. We have gone back to ancient history for models of government and examined the different forms of those republics which, having been formed with the seeds of their own dissolution, now no longer exist. And we have viewed modern states all round Europe but find none of their constitutions suitable to our circumstances.

"In this situation of this assembly, groping as it were in the dark to find political truth, and scarce able to distinguish it when presented to us, how has it happened," he wondered aloud, "that we have not hitherto once thought of humbly applying to the Father of lights to illuminate our understandings?"

Recalling the daily prayers of the Continental Congress in that very room at the beginning of the Revolution, Franklin, addressing himself to Washington as presiding officer, declared, "Our prayers, Sir, were heard, and they were graciously answered. All of us who were engaged in the struggle must have observed frequent instances of a superintending providence in our favor. To that kind providence we owe this happy opportunity of consulting in peace on the means of establishing our future national felicity. And have we now forgotten that powerful friend? Or do we imagine that we no longer need his assistance?

"I have lived, Sir," he continued, "a long time, and the longer I live, the more convincing proofs I see of this truth—that God governs in the affairs of men. And if a sparrow cannot fall to the ground without his notice, is it probable that an empire can be raised without his aid?"

Franklin offered a motion "that henceforth prayers imploring the assistance of Heaven and its blessings on our deliberations be held in this assembly every morning before we proceed to business, and that one or more of the clergy of this city be requested to officiate in that service." Roger Sherman seconded the motion.

Hamilton and others worried that instituting prayers at this late date might lead the public to suspect "embarrassments and dissention within the Convention." Hugh Williamson of North Carolina pointed out that the Convention had no funds to pay a clergyman. Then, as Madison noted, "After several unsuccessful attempts for silently postponing the matter by adjourning, the adjournment was at length carried without any vote on the motion."

Much later, a story made the rounds that Hamilton had opposed the motion on the grounds that the Convention was not in need of "foreign aid." There is nothing in the record to support this. Franklin himself noted: "The Convention, except for three or four persons, thought prayers unnecessary." So, without benefit of clergy, the battle over representation in the legislature continued.

The next day, Friday, June 29, William Samuel Johnson of Connecticut argued once more for his colleague Roger Sherman's compromise: "that in *one* branch the *people* ought to be represented; in the *other*, the *states.*" Nationalists, led by Madison, Wilson, and King, remained opposed, fearing that even such a vestige of state sovereignty as equal state representation in the Senate would continue the evils of the Confederation.

When the Convention finally voted, six states to four, with Maryland divided, that representation in the lower house *not* be on a one state, one vote basis, the argument turned again to representation in the Senate, and the battle erupted with renewed vigor.

Later that day, Hamilton, frustrated at being consistently outvoted by his two New York colleagues, left Philadelphia. From New York, he wrote Washington that he would return if he felt it would not be a "mere waste of time."

In the course of the long debate over representation of the states in the Senate, Madison declared once more that the small states had nothing to fear from the large ones. And then, perhaps to divert the small-state bloc, he challenged the whole idea of an inherent conflict between small and large states. "If there were real danger," he insisted, "I would give the smaller states the defensive weapons. But there is none from that quarter. The great danger to our general government is the great southern and northern interests of the continent being opposed to each other. Look at the votes in Congress, and most of them stand divided by the geography of the country, not according to the size of the states."

The next day, Saturday, he made the same point more explicitly. "The states," he said, "are divided into different interests, not by their difference of size, but by other circumstances, the most material of which result partly from climate but principally from the effects of their having, or not having, slaves. These two causes concur in forming the great division of interests in the United States."

*   *   *

Whatever Madison's immediate motives in raising the issue, his words were prophetic. The division between Northern and

Southern states over the issue of slavery would widen steadily over the years until, in 1861, just seventy-four years after Madison spoke, it had become the gaping chasm that split the Union in a bloody civil war. That horror, however, lay in the future, and for the delegates at the Convention, the immediate division of interests remained that of the small and the large states.

*   *   *

The debate grew more and more heated. Rufus King of Massachusetts declared himself "filled with astonishment that, if we are convinced that every *man* in America is secure in all his rights, we should be ready to sacrifice this substantial good to the phantom of *state* sovereignty. My feelings," he said, "are more harrowed and my fears more agitated for my country than I can express. I conceive this to be the last opportunity of providing for its liberty and happiness. I cannot, therefore, but repeat my amazement that when a just government, founded on a fair representation of the *people* of America is within our reach, we should renounce the blessing from an attachment to the ideal freedom and importance of the *states*. Should this wonderful illusion continue to prevail, my mind is prepared for every event rather than sit down under a government founded in a vicious principle of representation which must be as shortlived as it would be unjust."

Jonathan Dayton of New Jersey rose to reply. "When assertion is given for proof," he said acidly, "and terror substituted for argument, I presume they will have no effect, however eloquently spoken." And referring to the plan for proportional representation in both houses of the legislature, he said, "I consider the system on the table as a novelty, an amphibious monster, and am persuaded that it never will be received by the people."

Gunning Bedford, Jr., of Delaware, who had earlier charged Wilson and Madison with attempting to create a government in which Pennsylvania and Virginia would have "an enormous and monstrous influence," now rose to take on Massachusetts and Rufus King. "The larger states proceed as if our eyes were already perfectly blinded," he charged. "Impartiality, with them, is already out of the question: the reported plan is their political creed, and they support it, right or wrong." Their cry, he said, is "where is the danger? And they insist that although the powers of the general government will be increased, yet it will be for the good of the whole; and although the three great states form nearly a majority of the people of America, they never will hurt or injure the lesser states. *I do not, gentlemen, trust you.*"

Turning his attack then on King himself, Bedford said, "We have been told with a dictatorial air that this is the last moment for a fair trial in favor of a good government. It will be the last indeed if the propositions reported by the Committee go forth to the people. I am under no apprehensions. The large states dare not dissolve the Confederation. If they do, the small ones will find some foreign ally of more honor and good faith who will take them by the hand and do them justice."

Rufus King could not let that pass. "It is not I," he said, "that has uttered a dictatorial language. That intemperance marks the honorable gentleman himself. It is not I who, with a vehemence unprecedented in this house, declare myself ready to turn my hopes from our common country and court the protection of some foreign hand. This, too, is the language of the honorable member himself. I am grieved that such a thought has entered into his heart. I am more grieved that such an expression has dropped from his lips. The gentleman can only excuse it to himself on the score of passion. For myself, whatever may be my distress, I will never court relief from a foreign power."

Perhaps to forestall further heated argument, the Convention adjourned for the weekend.

Sometime that day, George Mason tried to pinpoint the Convention's progress in a letter to the lieutenant governor of Virginia. Things, he wrote, "are now drawing to that point on which some of the fundamental principles must be decided, and two or three days will probably enable us to judge—which is at present very doubtful—whether any sound and effectual system can be established or not. If it cannot, I presume we shall not continue here much longer; if it can, we shall probably be detained 'til September."

Over the weekend, two of the Georgians, William Few and William Pierce, left for New York to attend Congress. Pierce had an additional engagement: to fight a duel. Alexander Hamilton, already in New York, had been chosen to act as second to Pierce's adversary. This duel was eventually called off, but seventeen years later, in 1804, Hamilton himself would be mortally wounded in a duel with Aaron Burr.

The vote on representation in the Senate came first thing Monday morning, July 2, on a motion by Oliver Ellsworth that each state should have a single vote. To the surprise of all and the dismay of many, it was a tie, five states to five, with Georgia divided and hence not voting. Massachusetts, Pennsylvania, Virginia, and North and South Carolina—the large-state bloc, minus its usual adherent, Georgia—voted against Ellsworth's motion. Connecticut, New York, New Jersey, Delaware, and Maryland—the small states, plus New York—voted in favor. But a simple tally of the vote by states conceals more than it reveals.

Maryland's vote in favor of a single vote for each state in the Senate was cast by Luther Martin, the sole Maryland delegate then on the floor. Moments later, Daniel of St. Thomas Jenifer, the only other Maryland delegate then in Philadelphia, entered the chamber. Had he not overslept, he would have opposed equal representation, dividing Maryland and leaving it without a vote. The five large states would then have won, five to four.

With Jenifer now in the chamber, Rufus King of Massachusetts asked Washington, as presiding officer, to allow an immediate second vote. The Convention's rules were cited against the request, and it was denied.

Yet even with Maryland's vote in favor of the motion, the large states would still have won if Georgia had joined them as anticipated. As it happened, with Few and Pierce having left for New York, Georgia had only two delegates on the floor. One of the two, William Houstoun, voted with the large states as expected. The other, Abraham Baldwin, born and bred in Connecticut and a resident of Georgia for only three years, chose at the last moment to change his vote to favor equal state representation in the Senate, thereby dividing his state and leaving it without a vote. Since Georgia voted last and the final tally depended on Baldwin's vote, there was no question that he had deliberately caused the tie. But why?

Luther Martin believed it was out of fear that if the small states lost, they would walk out, dissolving the Convention. Others have speculated that Baldwin fell under the influence of the three leading men of his native state, Connecticut's Ellsworth, Sherman, and Johnson. Whatever the explanation, the deed was done, and the Convention was deadlocked. It seemed clear that on this point, at least, the small states would not surrender. If there were to be compromise, this was the moment for it. As Luther Martin put it later, "We were on the verge of dissolution, scarce held together by the strength of a hair."

General Charles Cotesworth Pinckney of South Carolina proposed that a committee with one member from each state be appointed to devise a compromise. Only Wilson and Madison objected, with Wilson pointing out that such a committee would vote by the very means—one state, one vote—opposed by one side of the controversy. Madison had an additional reason. "I have rarely seen any other effect than delay from such committees in Congress," he said. "Any scheme of compromise that could be proposed in the committee might as easily be proposed in the house."

The Convention decided otherwise. The committee, elected by ballot, was clearly loaded by a Convention determined to find a compromise. Madison and Wilson were passed over;

Mason and Franklin would represent Virginia and Pennsylvania. William R. Davie of North Carolina, who had shown some inclination to compromise, was selected, as was Abraham Baldwin, whose vote had produced the tie. Luther Martin, who had cast Maryland's vote in the absence of Jenifer, was also chosen. The rest were either large-state men ready to compromise or small-state men who would not yield. Whatever compromise such a committee might devise could hardly please Wilson and Madison. To give it time to do its work and to permit everyone to celebrate the eleventh anniversary of the Declaration of Independence, the Convention adjourned until Thursday, July 5.

Early the next morning, Tuesday, July 3, General Washington left Robert Morris's house on Market Street for an appointment at the home and gallery of artist Charles Willson Peale at Third and Lombard. Peale had painted Washington before and would do so again. On this occasion, Washington sat for a head and shoulders portrait in his famous blue and buff uniform with three gold stars on the epaulets.

Later, still in uniform, he went to the State House to observe the meeting of the grand committee of the states, as the compromise committee was called. With Elbridge Gerry as its elected chairman, the committee fell immediately into the very arguments it had been chosen to resolve. Driven by the urgent need for compromise, however, the committee kept at it, for without accommodation from some quarter, the Convention seemed clearly at an end.

No one expected a perfect solution; there seemed to some no solution at all. But if the committee members were divided among themselves, each was, to one degree or another, also divided within himself. Each, by his very presence at the Convention, was being forced to play two simultaneous roles: that of the politician, representing the interests of his state, and that of statesman, seeking the permanent good of the union of states. Whatever the demands of the politician within each member of the committee, statesmanship now required an earnest effort at compromise.

Eventually, Dr. Franklin made a suggestion, and after amendment, it became the committee's recommendation. In the lower house, each state would have a representative for every 40,000 of its free inhabitants, with three-fifths of its slaves added to the total. States with fewer than 40,000 people would be allowed a single representative. All bills dealing with money would originate in the lower house and could not be amended in the Senate. In the Senate, each state would have an equal vote. Finally, to preclude endless attempts to amend it and because some members of the committee refused to support it otherwise, the committee provided that the compromise must be adopted or rejected by the Convention as a package.

The provision that money bills must originate in the lower house probably came from Gerry. Three weeks earlier, he had moved unsuccessfully to accomplish this end. The lower house, he had said then, "is more immediately the representatives of the people, and it is a maxim that the people ought to hold the purse strings." At that time, however, the Committee of the Whole had approved proportional representation in both houses of the legislature, and Pierce Butler and General Pinckney of South Carolina, James Madison of Virginia, and Rufus King of Massachusetts, all large-state nationalists, had opposed any limitation on the Senate's ability to originate bills. Now, with a compromise that would give each state an equal vote in the Senate, Gerry clearly hoped to find additional support for the restriction.

The Fourth of July dawned hot and humid. Early in the morning, the city cavalry, the light infantry, a train of artillery, and a battalion of militia assembled on the Philadelphia commons. After performing various military maneuvers, they fired a *feu de joie*, each man firing a blank cartridge in rapid order from right to left. The artillery then fired the salute of the United States—three times thirteen rounds—after which the militia, joining the Pennsylvania Society of Cincinnati at the State House, paraded to the German Lutheran Church on Race Street to hear a patriotic oration by a law student, James Campbell. Later, there were parties and entertainments at inns and taverns throughout the city.

On Thursday morning, July 5, refreshed by their celebration of Independence Day, the delegates filed into the State House to hear the report of the grand committee of the states. Elbridge Gerry delivered it. And no one had a kind word for it. The wrangling began all over again. Madison immediately attacked the money bill provision, which the compromise committee had hoped would somehow pacify the large states. "I cannot regard the exclusive privilege of originating money bills as any concession on the side of the small states," he said bluntly. "Experience has proved that it has no effect." Since it was not a concession, he continued, it "leaves in force all the objections which prevailed against allowing each state an equal voice.

"I conceive," he concluded, "that the Convention is reduced to the alternative of either departing from justice in order to conciliate the smaller states and the minority of the people of the United States or of displeasing them by justly gratifying the larger states and the majority of the people. I cannot myself hesitate as to the option I ought to make. The Convention, with justice and the majority of the people on our side, has nothing to fear."

Gouverneur Morris of Pennsylvania, who had returned to the Convention after attending the funeral of his mother in New York, rose to object both to the idea that the compromise had to be voted on as a package and to its contents as well. "I came here," he said, "as a representative of America. I flatter myself that I came here in some degree as a representative of the whole human race, for the whole human race will be affected by the proceedings of this Convention. I wish the gentlemen would extend their views beyond the present moment of time, beyond the narrow limits of place from which they derive their political origin. If I were to believe some things which I have heard, I would suppose that we are assembled to truck and bargain for our particular states."

Turning to the effects of a possible union of the larger states from which the smaller states abstained, he predicted that the smaller states would soon join in. "This country," he declared, "must be united. If persuasion does not unite it, the sword will. I beg that this consideration have its due weight. The scenes of horror attending civil commotion can not be described, and the conclusion of them will be worse than the term of their continuance. The stronger party will then make traitors of the weaker, and the gallows and halter will finish the work of the sword. How far foreign powers will be ready to take part in the confusions, I will not say. Threats that they will be invited have, it seems, been thrown out." That barb was obviously intended for Gunning Bedford, Jr., of Delaware.

State attachments and state importance, Morris continued, "have been the bane of this country. We cannot annihilate, but we may perhaps take out the teeth of the serpents. I wish our ideas to be enlarged to the true interest of man, instead of being circumscribed within the narrow compass of a particular spot. And after all, how little can be the motive yielded by selfishness for such a policy? Who can say whether he himself, much less whether his children, will the next year be an inhabitant of this or that state?"

Bedford rose immediately to attempt to explain his earlier harsh words. They had, he said, been misunderstood. "I did not mean that the small states would court the aid and interposition of foreign powers," he said. "I meant that foreign powers would not consider the federal compact as dissolved until it should be so by the acts of the large states. In this case, the consequence of the breach of faith on their part and the readiness of the small states to fulfill their engagements to foreign powers would be that foreign nations having demands on this country would find it in their interest to take the small states by the hand in order to do themselves justice. This is what I meant."

If this was, indeed, what Bedford had meant, he all but denied it with his next words. For he immediately added, "But no man can foresee to what extremities the small states may be driven by oppression."

In apology for his earlier statement, Bedford noted that, as a lawyer, "some allowance ought to be made for the habits of my profession, in which warmth is natural and sometimes necessary." Pointing then to the concessions already made by the small states in proportional representation of the lower branch of the legislature and on the question of money bills, he asked, "If the smaller states be not gratified by correspondent concessions as to the second branch, is it to be supposed they will ever accede to the plan? And what will be the consequence if nothing should be done? The condition of the United States requires that something should be immediately done."

Hugh Williamson of North Carolina thought the propositions of the compromise report "the most objectionable of any I have yet heard." Gerry, who had headed the committee that prepared them, admitted to having objections to some of them. But he echoed Bedford's sense of urgency. "If no compromise should take place," he asked, "what will be the consequence? A secession, I foresee, will take place, for some gentlemen seem decided on it. Two different plans will be proposed, and the result no man can foresee. If we do not come to some agreement among ourselves, some foreign sword will probably do the work for us."

George Mason also pleaded for compromise. "Accommodation," he said, "was the object of the house in the appointment of the committee and of the committee in the report they have made. And however liable the report might be to objections, I think it preferable to an appeal to the world by the different sides as has been talked of by some gentlemen. It cannot be more inconvenient to any gentleman to remain absent from his private affairs than it is for me, but I will bury my bones in this city rather than expose my country to the consequences of a dissolution of the Convention without anything being done."

Debate over the recommended compromise would continue for a week and a half. The first proposal to come under attack was the recommendation for each state to have one representative in the lower house for each 40,000 inhabitants. Gouverneur Morris objected. "I think property ought to be taken into the estimate as well as the number of inhabitants," he said. "Life and liberty are generally said to be of more value than property. An accurate view of the matter will nevertheless prove that property is the main object of society."

He was concerned also with "that range of new states which will soon be formed in the west. I think the rule of representation ought to be so fixed as to secure to the Atlantic states a prevalence in the national councils. The new states," he added, "will know less of the public interest than these; will have an interest in many respects different; in particular, will be little scrupulous of involving the community in wars, the burdens and operations of which will fall chiefly on the maritime states. Provision ought therefore to be made to prevent the maritime states from being hereafter outvoted by them."

John Rutledge of South Carolina agreed with both of Morris's positions, but George Mason of Virginia replied that he was decidedly of the opinion that if Western states became part of the Union, "they ought to be subject to no unfavorable discriminations."

When the discussion continued the next day, Gouverneur Morris moved to refer the question of representation in the lower house to a new committee. "My view," he said, "is that they might absolutely fix the number for each state in the first instance, leaving the legislature at liberty to provide for changes in the relative importance of the states and for the case of new states."

Nathaniel Gorham thought that population was the true guide to representation, but his Massachusetts colleague Elbridge Gerry favored a combination of population and wealth. Rufus King agreed with Gerry. Pierce Butler of South Carolina thought wealth should be the only consideration.

When it came to a vote, Gouverneur Morris's motion to refer the question to a new committee passed, seven states to three, and the very thing the compromise committee had tried to prevent had happened. Far from being considered as a package, the compromise report would be debated and voted on piecemeal. A five-man committee to consider this first piece was chosen by ballot. Of the five—Gouverneur Morris, John Rutledge, Rufus King, Edmund Randolph, and Nathaniel Gorham—the first three had spoken in favor of wealth or property as a consideration in representation. Only Gorham had spoken against it.

When the committee reported three days later, it recommended specific numbers of representatives for each of the thirteen states for the first meeting of the lower house. The legislature itself would then be permitted to make whatever adjustments were indicated by changes in wealth and population among the original states and to decide, on the same basis, the representation of new states. No mention was made of the much earlier agreement that three-fifths of the slaves would be counted as part of the population of each state, for as Nathaniel Gorham explained, "The number of blacks and whites, with some regard to supposed wealth, was the general guide" to the initial numbers of representatives in the committee's recommendation. The legislature would presumably follow the same guide in later adjustments.

The Convention accepted the committee's proposal to leave future reapportionment to the legislature, but the suggested composition of the first lower house appeared to please nobody. It was referred to yet another grand committee of the states. But the discussion made it clear that more than a few delegates were not happy with the idea of including the wealth of a state as a factor in determining representation. Hugh Williamson thought it would be necessary to return to the rule of numbers, though he made an exception in the case of new Western states. If their property was as valuable as that of the Atlantic states, he felt, they should have equal representation.

And William Paterson of New Jersey said bluntly, "I consider the proposed estimate for the future according to the combined rule of numbers and wealth as too vague. For this reason, New Jersey is against it." But a return to representation based on population should not, Paterson insisted, include *any* proportion of the slaves. "I can regard Negro slaves in no light but as property," he said. "They are not free agents, have no personal liberty, no faculty of acquiring property, but on the contrary are themselves property, and like other property, entirely at the will of the master.

"Has a man in Virginia a number of votes in proportion to the number of his slaves?" he asked. "And if Negroes are not represented in the states to which they belong, why should they be represented in the general government? What is the true principle of representation? It is an expedient by which an assembly of certain individuals chosen by the people is substituted in place of the inconvenient meeting of the people themselves. If such a meeting of the people were actually to take place, would the slaves vote? They would not. Why then should they be represented?"

It was a moment James Madison could not resist. "I would remind Mr. Paterson," he said, "that his doctrine of representation, which is in its principle the genuine one, must forever silence the pretensions of the small states to an equality of votes with the large ones. They ought to vote in the same proportion in which their citizens would do if the people of all the states were collectively met. I suggest as a proper ground of compromise that in the first branch, the states should be represented according to their number of free inhabitants, and in the second, which has for one of its primary objects the guardianship of property, according to the whole number, including slaves."

Rufus King had yet another idea. "I have always expected,"

he said, "that as the Southern states are the richest, they will not league themselves with the Northern unless some respect is paid to their superior wealth. If the latter expect those preferential distinctions in commerce and other advantages which they will derive from the connection, they must not expect to receive them without allowing some advantages in return. Eleven out of thirteen of the states have agreed to consider slaves in the apportionment of taxation, and taxation and representation ought to go together."

When the new grand committee of the states reported the next day with still another apportionment of the first lower house, there were again objections. John Rutledge and General Pinckney of South Carolina wanted to reduce New Hampshire's representation from three to two seats. Rufus King of Massachusetts, who had chaired the new grand committee, defended New Hampshire's right to three seats and went on to reveal some of what had gone into the committee's thinking. "The four Eastern states," he said, referring to New England, "having 800,000 souls, have one-third fewer representatives than the four Southern states, having not more than 700,000 souls, rating the blacks as five for three. The Eastern people will advert to these circumstances and be dissatisfied. I believe them to be very desirous of uniting with their Southern brethren, but I do not think it prudent to rely so far on this disposition as to subject them to any gross inequality."

And then, reverting to James Madison's argument, King said, "I am fully convinced that the question concerning a difference of interests does not lie where it has hitherto been discussed, between the great and small states." It lay instead, he said, "between the Southern and Eastern." For this reason, he had been ready to yield something in the proportion of representation for the security of the Southern states. But no principle would justify giving them a majority. "They are brought as near an equality as is possible," he concluded.

A quick calculation by any delegate would have revealed

King's meaning. Considering Pennsylvania and all of the states to the north of it as Northern states and Delaware and the states to its south as Southern, the North, in the committee's apportionment, would have thirty-five seats to the South's thirty. Reducing New Hampshire's seats from three to two would narrow that already slender margin.

But General Pinckney pointed out that the apportionment by the previous committee had been more favorable to the Southern states. There the proportions had been thirty seats to twenty-six in favor of the North, a four- rather than five-seat advantage. "I do not expect the Southern states to be raised to a majority of representatives," he said, "but wish them to have something like an equality."

Hugh Williamson of North Carolina agreed. "I am not for reducing New Hampshire from three to two, but for reducing some others," he said. "The Southern interest must be extremely endangered by the present arrangement. The Northern states are to have a majority in the first instance and the means of perpetuating it."

Jonathan Dayton of New Jersey saw it differently. "The line between the Northern and Southern interest has been improperly drawn," he said. "Pennsylvania is the dividing state, there being six on each side of her."

But General Pinckney was not to be distracted. Pointing to the superior wealth of the Southern states, he insisted it should have its due weight in the government.

Gouverneur Morris took the floor to note his regret at the turn the debate was taking. "I think the Southern states have, by the report, more than their share of representation. Property ought to have its weight but not all the weight." What Pinckney meant by wealth and Morris by property was, of course, slaves.

The motion to reduce New Hampshire's representation lost, with only the two Carolinas voting for it. And on three successive attempts by Southern delegates to accomplish the same end by increasing the representation of, first, North

Carolina, then South Carolina and, finally, Georgia, the Convention held firm. In the end, the recommendation of the committee was accepted. There would be sixty-five seats in the first lower house. Delaware and Rhode Island would each have one; New Hampshire and Georgia, three; New Jersey, four; Connecticut and the two Carolinas, five; New York and Maryland, six; Massachusetts and Pennsylvania, eight; and Virginia, ten.

When the delegates left the State House after adjournment on Tuesday, July 10, two of them left for good. Robert Yates and John Lansing, Jr., who had outvoted Alexander Hamilton to ally New York with the small states, returned to Albany determined to oppose whatever the Convention eventually decided. Their attempt to defeat the plan for a new national government had failed, and in their report to Governor George Clinton, they made it clear that they would have opposed any system "which had in object the consolidation of the United States into one government."

It may have been only a coincidence, but on the very day that Yates and Lansing left Philadelphia, Washington wrote to the third New York delegate, Alexander Hamilton. "When I refer you to the state of the councils which prevailed at the period you left this city," he wrote, "and add that they are now, if possible, in a worse train than ever, you will find but little ground on which the hope of a good establishment can be formed. In a word, I *almost* despair of seeing a favorable issue to the proceedings of the Convention and do therefore repent having had any agency in the business.

"The men who oppose a strong and energetic government are, in my opinion, narrow-minded politicians or are under the influence of local views. The apprehension expressed by them that the *people* will not accede to the form proposed is the *ostensible*, not the *real* cause of the opposition. But admitting that the *present* sentiment is as they prognosticate, the question ought nevertheless to be, is it, or is it not, the best form?"

In a more personal vein, he added, "I am sorry you went away. I wish you were back. The crisis is equally important and alarming, and no opposition under such circumstances should discourage exertions till the signature is fixed."

Three days later, Hamilton was back in Philadelphia, though New York's rules requiring a quorum of two delegates prevented him from voting.

8

The Great Compromise

"Had we not better keep the government up a little longer, hoping that another convention will supply our omissions, than abandon everything to hazard?"

JOHN RUTLEDGE to the Convention
July 16, 1787

July 11–17, 1787

On Wednesday, July 11, the Convention took up a motion made the previous day by Edmund Randolph of Virginia. It would require the legislature to provide for both a census and an estimate of the wealth of each state within a year after its first meeting and periodically thereafter and to adjust future apportionment of the lower house according to the results.

Gouverneur Morris had opposed the motion on two grounds: first, that it fettered the legislature by *requiring* both the census and the reapportionment, and second, that it might someday give Western states a majority in the lower house. "In time," he had said, "the Western people will outnumber the Atlantic states. I wish, therefore, to put it in the power of the latter to keep a majority of votes in their own hands."

Now, Roger Sherman of Connecticut agreed with Morris's first objection. "I am against shackling the legislature too much," he said. "We ought to choose wise and good men and then confide in them."

But George Mason saw dangers in Sherman's approach.

"The greater the difficulty we find in fixing a proper rule of representation," he said, "the more unwilling ought we to be to throw the task from ourselves on the general legislature. I do not object to the conjectural ratio which is to prevail at the outset, but I consider a revision from time to time according to some permanent and precise standard as essential to the fair representation required in the first branch.

"According to the present population of America," he continued, "the Northern part of it has a right to preponderate, and I cannot deny it. But I wish it not to preponderate hereafter when the reason no longer continues. From the nature of man, we may be sure that those who have power in their hands will not give it up while they can retain it. On the contrary, we know they will always, when they can, rather increase it.

"If the Southern states, therefore, should have three-fourths of the people of America within their limits, the Northern states will hold fast the majority of representatives. One-fourth will govern the three-fourths. The Southern states will complain, but they may complain from generation to generation without redress. Unless some principle, therefore, which will do justice to them hereafter is inserted in the constitution, disagreeable as the declaration is to me, I must declare I could neither vote for the system here nor support it in my state."

But Mason's insistence on democratic representation was not based solely on his concern for the South. "Strong objections have been drawn from the danger to the Atlantic interests from new Western states," he noted. "Ought we to sacrifice what we know to be right in itself lest it should prove favorable to states which are not yet in existence? If the Western states are to be admitted into the Union as they arise, they must, I will repeat, be treated as equals and subjected to no degrading discriminations.

"They will have the same pride and other passions which we have and will either not unite with, or will speedily revolt from the Union if they are not in all respects placed on an equal footing with their brethren. It has been said they will be poor and unable to make equal contributions to the general treasury. I do not know but that in time they will be both more numerous and more wealthy than their Atlantic brethren."

Turning finally to a subject that had presumably been decided, Mason urged the Convention to consider that population, while not always a precise standard of wealth, "was sufficiently so for every substantial purpose."

Hugh Williamson agreed with Mason about requiring the legislature to reapportion the lower house on the basis of a census. "I am," he said, "for making it the duty of the legislature to do what is right and not leaving it at liberty to do or not to do it." He then moved to amend Randolph's proposal to specify that the census should be "of the free white inhabitants and three-fifths of those of other descriptions," his euphemism for slaves.

Randolph accepted the amendment, but Pierce Butler and General Pinckney, obviously smarting from the defeat of the Southern attempt to increase its representation in the first lower house, now moved that slaves be counted equally with whites in any census used for reapportionment. This precipitated a whole new North-South argument.

Elbridge Gerry of Massachusetts said, "Three-fifths of them is, to say the least, the full proportion that can be admitted." But Pierce Butler defended his proposal vigorously. "The labor of a slave in South Carolina is as productive and valuable as that of a freeman in Massachusetts," he told Gerry. And since wealth was the great means of defense and utility to the nation, slaves "are equally valuable to it with freemen. Consequently, an equal representation ought to be allowed for them in a government which is instituted principally for the protection of property and is itself to be supported by property."

George Mason, who worked his Virginia plantation with the labor of some three hundred slaves, could not agree. Though it was favorable to Virginia, he said, "I think it unjust. It is certain that the slaves are valuable, as they raise the value of land, increase the exports and imports, and, of course, the revenue will supply the means of feeding and supporting an army." Slaves, he suggested, "might in cases of emergency become themselves soldiers." Since they were therefore useful to the community at large, they ought not to be excluded from consideration. "I cannot, however, regard them as equal to freemen," he concluded, "and cannot vote for them as such."

The Butler-Pinckney motion that slaves be counted equally with whites was defeated, and the Convention turned back to Hugh Williamson's proposal to specify that three-fifths of them be included in censuses used for reapportionment. Gouverneur Morris opposed it chiefly, he said, because it threatened the previously approved resolution for reapportionment based on both population and wealth. "If slaves are to be considered as inhabitants, not as wealth," he said, "then the previous resolution will not be pursued; if as wealth, then why is no other wealth but slaves included?" His great objection, he said, "is that the number of inhabitants is not a proper standard of wealth."

John Rutledge of South Carolina also insisted that wealth should be counted in reapportionment and seemed willing to drop the three-fifths requirement in favor of representation "according to the principles of wealth and population."

Roger Sherman disagreed. "I think the number of people alone is the best rule for measuring wealth as well as representation," he said. James Wilson concurred. "Wealth," he said, "is an impracticable rule."

The problem was to some degree a semantic one. Most of the delegates acknowledged, as Rufus King had put it, that the Southern states were the richest. The cash value of their slaves made that clear. In any apportionment of representation based solely on *white* population, therefore, their superior wealth would not be taken into account. Hence the proposal to count three-fifths of the slaves as well. But in an apportionment based on population and wealth, the slaves would be counted as part of the Southern states' wealth, and wealth in other kinds of property would be counted for all the states. It was largely Gouverneur Morris's insistence that wealth be considered along with population in reapportionment that led to the prolonged and tangled argument.

And still he persisted. "I can not persuade myself that numbers alone would be a just rule at any time," he said. Then, referring to George Mason's belief that new Western states ought to be admitted on the same terms as the original states, he expanded on his own earlier statement that the rule of representation should be fixed in such a way that the Atlantic states could prevent their ever being outvoted by the new Western states. "It must be apparent," he said of future Western states, "that they will not be able to furnish men equally enlightened to share in the administration of our common interests. The busy haunts of men, not the remote wilderness, are the proper school of political talents. If the Western people get the power into their hands, they will ruin the Atlantic interests. The back members are always the most averse to the best measures."

Turning finally to the three-fifths question, he revealed that at least part of his opposition was based on the way such a provision would appear to his own constituents. "The people of Pennsylvania," he said, "would revolt at the idea of being put on a footing with slaves. They would reject any plan that is to have such an effect."

Rufus King again expressed himself as "much opposed to fixing numbers as the rule of representation, particularly so on account of the blacks." He agreed with Morris that "the admission of them along with whites at all, will excite great discontents among the states having no slaves," and he once again pointed out that in the temporary allotment of representatives for the first lower house, "the Southern states have received more than the number of their white and three-fifths of their black inhabitants entitle them to."

James Wilson wanted to know on what principle the three-fifths proportion of blacks was based. "Are they admitted as citizens?" he asked. "Then why are they not admitted on an equality with white citizens? Are they admitted as property? Then why is not other property admitted in the computation?" These might have seemed odd questions for Wilson to raise since he, himself, had first introduced the three-fifths formula exactly a month earlier. Then, it had presumably been a tactic to attract Southern votes to his proposal that proportional representation in the lower house be based on population. And it had succeeded.

But Wilson was not actually suggesting that the proportion be abandoned, for he continued by saying that the questions he had raised "were difficulties, however, which I think must be overruled by the necessity of compromise." And he reaffirmed his belief that population was a valid measure of wealth.

Just before the vote on including three-fifths of the slaves in censuses used for reapportionment, Gouverneur Morris spoke yet again. "I am," he said, "compelled to declare myself reduced to the dilemma of doing injustice to the Southern states or to human nature, and I must therefore do it to the former. For I can never agree to give such encouragement to the slave trade as will be given by allowing them a representative for their Negroes, and I do not believe those states will ever confederate on terms that will deprive them of this trade."

Finally, in a series of votes on various parts of the motion before them, the delegates rejected the addition of three-fifths of the slaves, approved requiring a census within a year of the first meeting of the legislature, agreed to a census every fifteen years thereafter, and agreed that the legislature *must* use the census as the basis for reapportionment of the lower house. And then, having wrapped the proposal in a neat package, the Convention voted unanimously to reject it. The work of the entire day was undone, and once again, the Convention had ground to a halt.

When the delegates assembled again on Thursday, July 12, Gouverneur Morris attempted to cut through at least some of the problems that had plagued them the day before. Reverting to Rufus King's idea that taxation and representation ought to go together, he proposed that "direct taxation ought to be proportioned to representation." If the Southern states demanded extra representation for their slaves, let them also be subject to extra taxes in the same proportion. It was a formula designed to curb the Southern appetite for excessive representation.

Direct taxes, as the delegates understood them, were taxes levied either on land or on individuals. And in sharp contrast to the indecisiveness of the previous day, this proposal was unanimously accepted by the Convention.

That still left open the question of what proportion of the slaves should be counted. Pierce Butler of South Carolina held out for all of them. William R. Davie of North Carolina took the floor. "It is high time now," he said, "to speak out. I see that it is meant by some gentlemen to deprive the Southern states of any share of representation for their blacks. I am sure that North Carolina will never confederate on any terms that do not rate them at least as three-fifths. If the Eastern states mean therefore to exclude them altogether, the business is at an end."

William Samuel Johnson of Connecticut, perhaps surprisingly, agreed with Pierce Butler. "I think that wealth and population are the true, equitable rule of representation," he said, "but I conceive that these two principles resolve themselves into one. Population is the best measure of wealth. Therefore, the number of people ought to be established as the rule, and all descriptions, including blacks equally with the whites, ought to fall within the computation."

Gouverneur Morris, not surprisingly, disagreed. "It has been said that it is high time to speak out," he began. "As one member, I will candidly do so. I came here to form a compact for the good of America. I am ready to do so with all the states. I hope and believe that all will enter into such a compact. If they will not, I am ready to join with any states that will. But as the compact is to be voluntary, it is in vain for the Eastern states to insist on what the Southern states will never agree to.

The Delegates

Abraham Baldwin, Georgia

Richard Bassett, Delaware

Gunning Bedford, Jr., Delaware

John Blair, Virginia

William Blount, North Carolina

Pierce Butler, South Carolina

Daniel Carroll, Maryland

George Clymer, Pennsylvania

Jonathan Dayton, New Jersey

William Richardson Davie,
North Carolina

John Dickinson, Delaware

Oliver Ellsworth, Connecticut

William Few, Georgia

Benjamin Franklin, Pennsylvania

Elbridge Gerry, Massachusetts

Nicholas Gilman, New Hampshire

Nathaniel Gorham, Massachusetts

Alexander Hamilton, New York

Jared Ingersoll, Pennsylvania

William Samuel Johnson,
Connecticut

Rufus King, Massachusetts

John Langdon, New Hampshire

John Lansing, Jr., New York

William Livingston, New Jersey

James McHenry, Maryland

James McClurg, Virginia

James Madison, Virginia

Alexander Martin, North Carolina

Luther Martin, Maryland

George Mason, Virginia

John Francis Mercer, Maryland

Thomas Mifflin, Pennsylvania

Gouverneur Morris, Pennsylvania

Robert Morris, Pennsylvania

William Paterson, New Jersey

Charles Pinckney, South Carolina

Charles Cotesworth Pinckney,
South Carolina

Edmund Randolph, Virginia

George Read, Delaware

John Rutledge, South Carolina

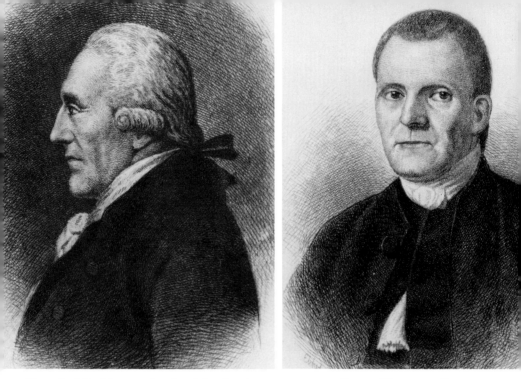

Daniel of St. Thomas Jenifer, Maryland

Roger Sherman, Connecticut

Richard Dobbs Spaight, North Carolina

Caleb Strong, Massachusetts

George Washington, Virginia

Hugh Williamson, North Carolina

James Wilson, Pennsylvania

George Wythe, Virginia

We are unable to locate portraits of the following delegates:

David Brearly, New Jersey
Jacob Broom, Delaware
Thomas Fitzsimons, Pennsylvania
William Churchill Houston, New Jersey
William Houstoun, Georgia
William Pierce, Georgia
Robert Yates, New York.

The author and the publishers gratefully acknowledge permission to reproduce the following photographs supplied by the following collections.

American Philosophical Society: Baldwin, Bassett, Bedford, Carroll, Ellsworth, Gerry, Gilman, Gorham, Hamilton, Johnson, Langdon, Lansing, Luther Martin, Gouverneur Morris, Randolph, Sherman, Strong, Williamson, Wilson, Wythe.

Independence National Historical Park Collection: Clymer, Dayton, Davie, Dickinson, Few, Ingersoll, King, Livingston, McHenry, Madison, Alexander Martin, Mason, Mercer, Mifflin, Robert Morris, Charles Cotesworth Pinckney, Read, Spaight.

The New York Historical Society: Jenifer.

The New York Public Library, Print Division: Blair, Blount, Butler, McClurg, Paterson, Rutledge.

New York State Office of Parks, Recreation and Historic Preservation, Phillips Manor State Site: Charles Pinckney.

The Pennsylvania Academy of Fine Arts, Joseph and Sarah Harrison Collection: Franklin, Washington.

It is equally vain for the latter to require what the other states can never admit, and I verily believe the people of Pennsylvania will never agree to a representation of Negroes. What can be desired by these states more than has been already proposed: that the legislature shall from time to time regulate representation according to population and wealth?"

General Pinckney answered the question directly. "I desire that the rule of wealth be ascertained and not left to the pleasure of the legislature, and that property in slaves shall not be exposed to danger under a government instituted for the protection of property."

Governor Randolph favored the three-fifths ratio, and he wanted it stated explicitly and not left up to the legislature. "Express security ought to be provided for including slaves in the ratio of representation," he said. "I lament that such a species of property exists. But as it does exist, the holders of it will require this security."

Charles Pinckney held out for counting all the slaves. "This," he said, "is nothing more than justice. The blacks are the laborers, the peasants of the Southern states. They are as productive of pecuniary resources as those of the Northern states. They add equally to the wealth, and considering money as the sinew of war, to the strength of the nation."

By the end of the day, the Convention had agreed only that representation in the lower house ought to be proportioned according to direct taxation and that direct taxation would be altered by the legislature from time to time in accordance with a census, including three-fifths of the slaves, to be taken within six years of the first meeting of the legislature and every ten years thereafter. This still left wealth as a consideration in determining representation.

On Friday, Edmund Randolph moved to strike out wealth, leaving population, including three-fifths of the slaves, as the sole guide to reapportionment of the lower house. As he must have anticipated, Gouverneur Morris rose immediately to oppose the change.

"If Negroes are to be viewed as inhabitants and the revision is to proceed on the principle of numbers of inhabitants," he said, "they ought to be added in their entire number and not in the proportion of three-fifths. If they are to be viewed as property, the word 'wealth' is right, and striking it out will produce the very inconsistency which it is meant to get rid of."

The debates, Morris added, and the recent turn they had taken, had led him to deep meditation, and he would candidly state the result of these thoughts. "A distinction has been set up and urged between the Northern and Southern states. I have hitherto considered this doctrine as heretical. I still think the distinction groundless. I see, however, that it is persisted in and that the Southern gentlemen will not be satisfied unless they see the way open to their gaining a majority in the public councils." The consequences of such a transfer of power, Morris said, from the maritime interest of the Northern states to the interior and landed interest of the Southern states, would be such an oppression of commerce that he would be forced to vote for the vicious principle of an equality of votes in the Senate to provide some defense for the Northern states against it.

"But to come more to the point," he said, "either this distinction is fictitious or real. If fictitious, let it be dismissed and let us proceed with due confidence. If it be real, instead of attempting to blend incompatible things, let us at once take friendly leave of each other. There can be no end of demands for security if every particular interest is to be entitled to it. The Eastern states may claim it for their fishery and for other objects as the Southern states claim it for their peculiar objects.

"In this struggle between the two ends of the Union, what part ought the Middle States in point of policy to take? To join their Eastern brethren, according to my ideas?"

Morris then made explicit what he had only hinted at in his brief earlier reference to a danger that new Western states might carelessly involve the country in war. No one at the Convention could have misunderstood his meaning, for the issue had divided Northerners and Southerners at least since 1784, when Spain had closed the Mississippi River to American navigation and trade and thereby denied the Southern states a future outlet to the sea in the West.

Sectional jealousies between North and South had been exacerbated by a treaty negotiated by John Jay, as Secretary of Foreign Affairs, with the Spanish Minister to the United States in 1785–86. Jay had been instructed by the Confederation Congress to obtain a repeal of the Spanish closing of the Mississippi. When it appeared that a liberal commercial agreement could be reached with Spain by an American renunciation of its right to navigate the Mississippi for several decades, Jay asked Congress to revise his instructions and allow this concession.

Southern members of Congress saw the request as a deliberate attempt to sacrifice their interests to benefit Northern commerce, and when the seven most Northern states, from New Hampshire to Pennsylvania, voted to approve Jay's request, the Southern states killed any possibility of a treaty by denying it the necessary nine-state majority. The issue had produced not only bitter debate in Congress but the starkest sectional division thus far experienced by Congress.

Now Gouverneur Morris raised the whole hotly contested question again, this time in the new context of the Convention debate between North and South over representation in the lower house of the new legislature. "If the Southern states get the power into their hands and be joined as they will be with the interior country," he said flatly, "they will inevitably bring on a war with Spain for the Mississippi. This language is already held. The interior country, having no property or interest exposed to the sea, will be little affected by such a war. I wish to know what security the Northern and Middle states will have against this danger."

Pierce Butler of South Carolina rose to respond. "The security the Southern states want," he said bluntly, "is that their Negroes may not be taken from them, which some gentlemen within or without doors have a very good mind to do."

James Wilson took the floor in an obvious attempt to quell the gathering storm. "Conceiving that all men wherever placed have equal rights and are equally entitled to confidence, I view without apprehension the period when a few states should contain the superior number of people," he said. "The majority of people, wherever found, ought in all questions to govern the minority. If the interior country should acquire this majority, they will not only have the right but will avail themselves of it whether we will or no."

Then, reminding the delegates of recent history, he continued, "This jealousy mislead the policy of Great Britain with regard to America. The fatal maxims espoused by her were that the colonies were growing too fast and that their growth must be stinted in time. What were the consequences? First, enmity on our part, then actual separation. Like consequences will result on the part of the interior settlements if like jealousy and policy be pursued on ours.

"Further, if numbers be not a proper rule, why is not some better rule pointed out? No one has yet ventured to attempt it. Congress has never been able to discover a better. No state, as far as I have heard, has suggested any other. In 1783, after elaborate discussion of a measure of wealth, all were satisfied then as they are now that the rule of numbers does not differ much from the combined rule of numbers and wealth.

"Again, I cannot agree that property is the sole or the primary object of government and society. The cultivation and improvement of the human mind is the most noble object. With respect to this object, as well as to other personal rights, numbers are surely the natural and precise measure of representation."

Whether because of Wilson's measured plea for democracy or not, the Convention voted unanimously to strike out wealth as a consideration in reapportionments of the lower house.

After adjournment that afternoon, as Benjamin Franklin sat under a mulberry tree in his garden with several men and women, Elbridge Gerry brought a visitor, the Reverend Manasseh Cutler, to meet him. Cutler, who lived in Massachusetts, was a versatile man who practiced medicine and had undertaken the first systematic account of New England botany. A founder of the Ohio Company, he was currently lobbying the Confederation Congress for a grant of land in what would become Ohio, where he planned to settle a colony of pioneers. Cutler presented Franklin with letters of introduction, and Franklin, in turn, introduced him to his other guests. Most of the men were delegates to the Convention.

Recording the visit later in his journal, Cutler wrote: "The Doctor showed me a curiosity he had just received, and with which he was much pleased. It was a snake with two heads, preserved in a large vial. . . . The Doctor mentioned the situation of this snake, if it was traveling among bushes, and one head should choose to go on one side of the stem of a bush and the other head should prefer the other side, and that neither of the heads would consent to come back or give way to the other. He was then going to mention a humorous matter that had that day taken place in Convention, in consequence of his comparing the snake to America, for he seemed to forget that everything in Convention was to be kept a profound secret; but the secrecy of Convention matters was suggested to him, which stopped him, and deprived me of the story he was going to tell."

By Saturday, July 14, a Convention very like Dr. Franklin's two-headed snake had been immobilized by debate on the compromise report for nine days. Now Elbridge Gerry returned to what he called "the dangers apprehended from Western states." He was, he said, "for admitting them on liberal terms, but not for putting ourselves into their hands. They will, if they acquire power, like all men, abuse it. They will oppress commerce and drain our wealth into the Western country.

"To guard against these consequences," he continued, "I

think it necessary to limit the number of new states to be admitted into the Union in such a manner that they shall never be able to outnumber the Atlantic states." He then offered a motion to that effect. His colleague, Rufus King, seconded it.

Roger Sherman spoke against the motion. "I think," he said, "there is no probability that the number of future states will exceed that of the existing states. If the event should ever happen, it is too remote to be taken into consideration at this time. Besides, we are providing for our posterity, for our children and grandchildren, who will be as likely to be citizens of new Western states as of the old states. On this consideration alone, we ought to make no such discrimination as is proposed by the motion."

But Gerry was not persuaded. "If some of our children should remove," he said, "others will stay behind, and I think it incumbent on us to provide for their interests. There is a rage for emigration from the Eastern states to the Western country, and I do not wish those remaining behind to be at the mercy of the emigrants." The Convention apparently took Roger Sherman's more generous attitude, for it defeated Gerry's motion, five states to four.

While the lengthy debate on apportionment in the lower house had been going on, the Convention had taken up the provision of the compromise committee requiring money bills to originate in the lower house of the legislature. Though it had been presented as a concession to the larger states, it was opposed by Madison of Virginia, Gouverneur Morris and James Wilson of Pennsylvania, Hugh Williamson of North Carolina, and Pierce Butler and the two Pinckneys of South Carolina, all large-state delegates. Despite their opposition, the Convention chose to retain it as part of the committee's report by a vote of five states to three, with three states divided and thus not voting. The report as a whole would be voted on later.

The compromise committee's provision for a single vote for

each state in the Senate had also been taken up, and with almost no debate, it, too, had been retained as part of the report by a vote of six states to three, with two states divided. As Madison noted, however, several of the affirmative votes and some that resulted in dividing two states were tentative, since a vote would be taken later on the compromise report as a whole, after its various provisions had been subjected to debate and, perhaps, amendment. The real test would come on the final vote.

When Luther Martin of Maryland called for that vote on Saturday, July 14, John Rutledge of South Carolina proposed instead a reconsideration of both the money bill question and the provision for a single vote for each state in the Senate. Roger Sherman favored an immediate vote on the whole compromise, as amended. "It is," he said, "a conciliatory plan; it has been considered in all its parts; a great deal of time has been spent on it; and if any part should now be altered, it would be necessary to go over the whole ground again."

But James Wilson had other ideas, pointing out when the Convention had deadlocked, five states to five, on the question of a single vote for each state in the Senate, the states that had voted against it had represented two-thirds of the people of the United States. "This fact will ere long be known," he said, "and it will appear that this fundamental point has been carried by one-third against two-thirds. What hopes will our constituents entertain when they find that the essential principles of justice have been violated in the outset of the government? As to the privilege of originating money bills, it is not considered by any of us as of much moment and by many as improper in itself. I hope that both clauses will be reconsidered. The equality of votes in the Senate is a point of such critical importance that every opportunity ought to be allowed for discussing and collecting the mind of the Convention on it."

Luther Martin, who had all but anesthetized the Convention with his two-day speech on state sovereignty two weeks earlier, was now against delay, and he challenged Wilson's interpretation of the tie vote. Denying that there were two-thirds against the equality of votes in the Senate, he said, "The states that please to call themselves large are the weakest in the Union. Look at Massachusetts. Look at Virginia. Are they efficient states? I am for letting a separation take place if they desire it. I had rather there should be two confederacies than one founded on any other principle than an equality of votes in the second branch at least."

Wilson responded immediately. "I am not surprised that those who say that a minority does more than the majority should say that the minority is stronger than the majority," he said. "I suppose the next assertion will be that they are richer also, though I hardly expect it will be persisted in when the states shall be called on for taxes and troops."

Charles Pinckney moved that instead of an equality of votes, each state should be represented in the Senate by a specified number of Senators. Rhode Island and Delaware would each have one; New Hampshire, New Jersey, and Georgia, two; Connecticut, New York, Maryland, and the Carolinas, three; Massachusetts and Pennsylvania, four; and Virginia, five. James Wilson seconded the motion.

But Jonathan Dayton of New Jersey would have none of it. "The smaller states can never give up their equality," he said. "For myself, I would in no event yield that security for our rights."

And Roger Sherman said he favored an equality of votes in the Senate not so much as a security for the small states as for the state governments of all the states, which could not be preserved unless they were represented and had a voice in the general government.

Madison favored Pinckney's suggested compromise. Gerry said that he would also, but that it had no hope of success. Rufus King opposed it, favoring proportional representation in both houses. The argument consumed the entire day. When it ended, Pinckney's compromise was defeated, six states to four.

After adjournment and dinner, Washington went to the Opera House, where a play disguised as a concert was being presented. It was, appropriately enough, *The Tempest.*

As they made their way to the State House on Monday, July 16, the delegates knew they faced a final vote on the compromise. After a week and a half of debate, the critical moment had arrived. As amended, the compromise provided for a lower house of sixty-five members representing the states according to a rough approximation of their population and wealth. Future reapportionment would be required of the legislature on the basis of a census taken within six years of its first meeting and every ten years thereafter. Wealth having been abandoned in reapportionment, population, including three-fifths of the slaves, would be the determining factor. The proportion of a state's representation would also determine its share of any direct taxation. Money bills would originate in the lower house and could not be altered in the Senate. And in the Senate, each state would have a single vote.

When the vote was taken, the amended compromise passed, five states to four. The strong nationalists were stunned. The four states that had voted against it were all from the large-state bloc: Pennsylvania, Virginia, South Carolina, and Georgia. Massachusetts had divided, with King and Gorham against, and Gerry and Caleb Strong for the compromise. North Carolina, swayed by William R. Davie, who had served on the compromise committee, and Hugh Williamson, voted for the compromise. So did Connecticut, New Jersey, Delaware, and Maryland.

When the Convention attempted to proceed, Governor Randolph rose to voice the nationalists' concern. "The vote of this morning involving an equality of suffrage in the second branch has embarrassed the business extremely," he said. All the powers previously given to the legislature by the decisions of the Committee of the Whole, he explained, "were founded on the supposition that a proportional representation was to prevail in both branches of the legislature."

He had planned, he said, to offer the small states a compromise, giving them an equal vote in the Senate on specific matters about which they had expressed concern. "But finding from the preceding vote that they persist in demanding an equal vote in all cases, that they have succeeded in obtaining it, and that New York, if present, would probably be on the same side, I cannot but think we are unprepared to discuss this subject further.

"It will probably be in vain to come to any final decision with a bare majority on either side," he added. "For these reasons, I wish the Convention might adjourn, that the large states might consider the steps proper to be taken in the present solemn crisis of the business, and that the small states might also deliberate on the means of conciliation."

William Paterson of New Jersey took the floor. "I think with Mr. Randolph," he said caustically, "that it is high time for the Convention to adjourn, that the rule of secrecy ought to be rescinded, and that our constituents should be consulted. No conciliation can be admissible on the part of the smaller states on any other ground than that of an equality of votes in the second branch. If Mr. Randolph will reduce to form his motion for an adjournment sine die, I will second it with all my heart."

An adjournment sine die would have ended the Convention. General Pinckney asked if that was what Randolph intended. If so, he said, "it differs much from my idea. I cannot think of going to South Carolina and returning again to this place." Besides, he added, it was visionary to suppose that the states, if consulted, would ever agree separately and beforehand.

"I never entertained an idea of an adjournment sine die," Randolph replied, "and I am sorry that my meaning has been so readily and strangely misinterpreted. I have in view merely an adjournment till tomorrow in order that some conciliatory experiment might, if possible, be devised and that in case the smaller states continue to hold back, the larger might then take such measures—I will not say what—as might be necessary."

At that, Paterson seconded the motion to adjourn for the day. But even this presented problems. The vote on adjournment was a tie, five states to five. Elbridge Gerry then announced that Massachusetts, which had voted against adjournment, would now agree to it, and the Convention adjourned in confusion and disarray.

It is difficult to imagine a happy face on any of the delegates as they left the State House. Determined nationalists, like Madison, King, and Wilson, had tasted defeat on what, to them, was a vital principle of simple justice. The four states voting against equal state representation in the Senate outnumbered the rest in population by a large margin, however slaves might be counted. But determined small-staters, like Paterson and Dayton of New Jersey and Gunning Bedford, Jr., of Delaware, who had won their point, were no more satisfied with the outcome. They had already swallowed the principle of proportional representation in the lower house, and Paterson, at least, clearly resented the reluctance of the large states to accept defeat in the case of the Senate.

Still, between these two groups, there were men from both large and small states who, however unsatisfied with the outcome so far, were more than ready after seven weeks of debate to find some accommodation that would keep the shaky Union from disintegrating. John Rutledge of South Carolina presumably spoke for them when he said just before the adjournment that he could see no chance of a further compromise.

"The little states are fixed," he added. "They have repeatedly and solemnly declared themselves to be so. All that the large states then have to do is to decide whether they will yield or not. For my part, I conceive that although we cannot do what we think best in itself, we ought to do something. Had we not better keep the government up a little longer, hoping that another convention will supply our omissions, than abandon everything to hazard? Our constituents will be little satisfied with us if we take the latter course."

The next morning, Tuesday, July 17, a number of large-state delegates met to attempt to find some common ground on which to proceed. Several small-state delegates sat in on the meeting. Madison, who must have hoped for a decision by the large states to go it alone, was sorely disappointed. "The time was wasted in vague conversation on the subject," he noted glumly, "without any specific proposition or agreement. It appeared, indeed, that the opinions of the members who disliked the equality of votes differed much as to the importance of that point and as to the policy of risking a failure of any general act of the Convention by inflexibly opposing it. . . . It is probable that the result of this consultation satisfied the smaller states that they had nothing to apprehend from a union of the larger in any plan whatever against the equality of votes in the second branch."

Still, when the Convention itself resumed, Gouverneur Morris moved to reconsider the previous day's vote. His motion was not even seconded. It was clear, then, that the Great Compromise, as it would be called, would endure. Stripped to its essence, it was a joining of the confederate principles of the Articles of Confederation with the nationalist principles of the Virginia Plan. It made clear that the states would be states and not sovereign nations and that the Union, a sovereign nation, would be made up of separate and indestructible parts. It helped to create a new kind of compound nation out of elements already present. The fact that it resulted from the clash of so many separate interests that a majority was found only through compromise was in a strange way a confirmation of James Madison's earlier insistence that a large heterogeneous democracy might turn out to be the safest kind.

9

We the People

*"The true idea, in my opinion, is that every
man having evidence of attachment to, and permanent common interest with the society ought
to share in all its rights and privileges."*
GEORGE MASON to the Convention
August 7, 1787

July 18–August 7, 1787

With their most divisive problem behind them, the delegates settled down to complete their consideration of the resolutions they had adopted in the Committee of the Whole.
Almost immediately, it became clear that small-state intransigence on the issue of representation in the Senate had not necessarily implied opposition to a strong national government.
Indeed, small-state nationalists, released from the fear of having nothing of special value to take home to their constituents,
now concentrated their attention on giving the new government the powers it would need for success. Some quickly became leaders in the building of national power.

In the main, the work of the next nine days consisted of
confirming decisions already made, though there were some
significant changes. After agreeing that the legislature should
inherit the legislative rights of the Confederation Congress,
the discussion turned to the new legislative powers it would
acquire.

The Committee of the Whole had agreed that it should have

power "to legislate in all cases to which the separate states are incompetent or in which the harmony of the United States may be interrupted by the exercise of individual legislation." Gunning Bedford, Jr., whose fears of large-state domination of the national government had obviously disappeared, now moved successfully to give the national legislature power "to legislate in all cases for the general interests of the Union," an expansion of national power so great that Edmund Randolph himself called it "a formidable idea indeed."

Next to be considered was Madison's cherished provision that the national legislature could veto state laws in conflict with the Constitution or national treaties. Accepted and even broadened by the Committee of the Whole more than six weeks earlier, it now came under attack. "This power," said Gouverneur Morris, "is likely to be terrible to the states and not necessary if sufficient legislative authority is given to the general government."

"It is unnecessary," Roger Sherman agreed, "as the courts of the states would not consider as valid any law contravening the authority of the Union and which the legislature would wish to be negatived."

Luther Martin considered the power improper and inadmissible. "Shall all the laws of the states be sent up to the general legislature before they shall be permitted to operate?" he asked.

But Madison persisted. "I consider the negative on the laws of the states as essential to the efficacy and security of the general government," he said. The very necessity for a general government, he maintained, proceeded directly from "the propensity of the states to pursue their particular interests in opposition to the general interest. This propensity will continue to disturb the system unless effectively controlled. Nothing short of a negative on their laws will control it."

Nor could confidence be placed in the state courts, as Sherman had suggested. "In all the states," Madison said, "these are more or less dependent on the legislatures."

Both Gouverneur Morris and Roger Sherman spoke again in opposition, and only Charles Pinckney supported Madison. When a vote was taken, the legislative veto lost, seven states to three. Madison had lost again.

Immediately after the vote, Luther Martin, who must have enjoyed Madison's defeat, offered a resolution to make all legislative acts and treaties of the United States the supreme law of the states. It came almost word for word from the rejected New Jersey Plan. And it passed unanimously.

Turning then to the earlier decisions on the executive, the Convention first reaffirmed that it would consist of a single person and then fell into endless confusion and debate over how to elect him. The Committee of the Whole had agreed on election by the national legislature for a single seven-year term. By now, though, many delegates had come to oppose the executive's election by the legislature because, in Gouverneur Morris's words, it would make him "the mere creature of the legislature." It had been to reduce the executive's dependence on the legislature that he had been made ineligible for reelection. But Morris and others felt this was not enough.

An additional problem with restricting the executive to a single term was that it would rule out a second term for the man most delegates were convinced would be the first executive, the man now presiding over their deliberations: George Washington. And that, to most of them, was simply shortsighted.

All of these considerations—length of term, reeligibility, and means of election—were, in fact, so interrelated and so bound up with the expectation that Washington would be the first to occupy the office that to change one of them required, in the minds of many delegates, revision of others. And the obvious importance of an executive who remained independent of the legislature and responsible to the people injected a new question into the conundrum: How and for what reasons might an executive be impeached?

It was again the sort of problem that required stepping back to see the growing mosaic of the government as a whole as well as the interrelations of its various parts. Yet whenever someone did that, a whole new arrangement was often suggested. It was proposed, for example, that the executive should be chosen by the people, by the state legislatures, by electors chosen by the state legislatures, by the governors of the states, by electors chosen by the governors, by fifteen members of the national legislature chosen by lot, and, of course, by the national legislature, as decided earlier.

Terms of six, seven, eight, eleven, fifteen, and twenty years were proposed for the executive, along with one proposal that he serve "during good behavior," which meant, of course, for life. With each new combination of means of election and term of office, delegates swung back and forth between an executive who would be reeligible or restricted to a single term and one who would or would not be subject to impeachment.

In the end, the Convention returned to the decisions of the Committee of the Whole. A single executive, chosen by the national legislature for a single seven-year term, would be removable on impeachment and conviction of malpractice or neglect of duty. But if anyone believed the question had been finally resolved, he was badly mistaken.

When the earlier decisions about the national judiciary were reconsidered, Madison succeeded in extending its jurisdiction to "all cases arising under the national laws." And without too much debate, the delegates decided that the Senate would consist of two members from each state who would vote as individuals, a significant change in their Great Compromise decision that in the Senate, each state would have a single vote.

By Tuesday, July 24, the Convention had completed its consideration of the resolutions adopted in the Committee of the Whole and had chosen a Committee of Detail to draft a constitution from its decisions. The five-man committee elected by the Convention gave geographical representation to all regions of the Union: Gorham of Massachusetts, from central New England; Ellsworth of Connecticut, from lower New England; Wilson of Pennsylvania, from the Middle States; Randolph of Virginia, from the upper South; and Rutledge of South Carolina, from the Deep South. But if it had geographical balance, the committee's composition made no concessions to either the small states (Connecticut being the only one represented) or the diehard antinationalists (all but Ellsworth being strong nationalists). All five of the members had had extensive political experience, and all but Gorham were lawyers.

To the Committee of Detail were referred not only the resolutions adopted by the Convention but the plan that Charles Pinckney had presented two months earlier, the New Jersey Plan presented by William Paterson and rejected by the Committee of the Whole five weeks before, and a last-minute resolution offered by George Mason in favor of property and citizenship qualifications for officeholders in the new government. And General Pinckney of South Carolina issued a warning: "If the committee should fail to insert some security to the Southern states against an emancipation of slaves and taxes on exports, I shall be bound by duty to my state to vote against their report."

Thus burdened, the Committee of Detail was given ten days to do its work, and the Convention adjourned until Monday, August 6.

Four days before this adjournment, two of the four elected delegates from New Hampshire finally arrived—two months late. John Langdon and Nicholas Gilman had made the long journey to Philadelphia to represent a state that had refused even to pay their expenses. Langdon, a wealthy merchant, had eventually decided to pay them out of his own pocket. Elected as delegates in January, their arrival in Philadelphia more than six months later must have seemed to them a triumph of perseverance. For a Convention that nine days earlier had finally settled the long conflict between the small and large states by adopting the Great Compromise, it was a barely noted anti-climax.

When the Convention adjourned for ten days on Thursday, July 26, the delegates scattered. General Pinckney headed north to Bethlehem, Pennsylvania, his carriage drawn by two bay geldings purchased some weeks earlier for fifty-five pounds each from Jacob Hiltzheimer. Hiltzheimer, a prominent Philadelphia farmer and stock breeder, provided the general with a list of the best public houses along the route.

A second South Carolinian, Pierce Butler, made for New York, where, as a recent appointee to Congress, he had left his family. Roger Sherman and William Samuel Johnson made it all the way to Connecticut and back during the recess. The New Jersey delegates also went home, and David Brearley wrote to Jonathan Dayton, who had apparently left earlier, to inform him of the adjournment and make tentative plans to return with him on the stagecoach.

Washington, after a weekend in Philadelphia, set off along the Schuylkill River on a fishing trip with Gouverneur Morris. One day, as Morris stumped along on his wooden leg casting for trout in a nearby stream, Washington rode on to Valley Forge, where he and his troops had spent their bitterest winter of the Revolutionary War ten years earlier. As he noted in his diary: "I rid over the whole old Cantonment of the American Army of the Winter 1777 and 8, visited all the Works wch. were in Ruins; and the Incampments in woods where the grounds had not been cultivated." Whatever grim memories were stirred in him by the visit must have been tempered somewhat by the lush green on every hand, for Washington had never seen Valley Forge in summer.

During the recess, newspapers throughout the country copied a story from the *Pennsylvania Herald*: "The Federal Convention, having resolved upon the measures necessary to discharge their important trust, adjourned in order to give a committee, appointed for the purpose, time to arrange and systematize the materials which that honorable body have collected. The public curiosity will soon be gratified, and it is hoped, from the universal confidence reposed in this delegation, that the minds of the people throughout the United States are prepared to receive with respect and to try with a fortitude and perseverance the plan which will be offered to them by men distinguished for their wisdom and patriotism."

It may have been this story that led Madison's cousin, the Reverend James Madison, President of William and Mary, to write from Virginia: "We are here, and I believe everywhere, all impatience to know something of your Conventional deliberations. If you cannot tell us what you are doing, you might at least give us some information of what you are not doing."

While the rest of the delegates traveled or gave themselves over to the pleasures of Philadelphia, the five-man Committee of Detail pored over the Convention's resolutions. They also looked closely at the Articles of Confederation, the best of the state constitutions, the Pinckney and New Jersey plans— anything that might prove useful in drafting a new constitution. During the committee's deliberations, Edmund Randolph wrote: "In the draft of a fundamental constitution, two things deserve attention: 1. To insert essential principles only, lest the operations of government should be clogged by rendering those provisions permanent and unalterable which ought to be accommodated to times and events; and 2. To use simple and precise language and general propositions according to the example of the constitutions of the several states." This was in fact the spirit in which the Constitution would be written.

Because there was no James Madison busily taking notes, the work of the committee can only be reconstructed from surviving manuscripts. A rough draft by Edmund Randolph was apparently discussed point by point, with changes inserted by John Rutledge, who had been chosen the committee's chairman. The corrected draft was then turned over to James Wilson, the most learned and experienced member of the committee, who produced a more fluent and detailed version. Reviewed again by the full committee, a clear copy was finally given to the Philadelphia printers, John Dunlap and David Claypoole, publishers of the *Pennsylvania Packet.* Under a strict injunction of secrecy, Dunlap and Claypoole printed enough copies for the delegates only.

On Monday morning, August 6, the Convention reconvened. Each delegate was handed the printed report of the Committee of Detail, a pamphlet of seven numbered pages with broad margins for notes. The draft constitution produced by the committee contained a preamble and twenty-three articles divided into forty-one sections. From twelve hundred words of disjointed resolutions adopted by the Convention, the committee had constructed an integrated plan of government of thirty-seven hundred words. The executive had become the "President," the legislature, "Congress," its lower house, the "House of Representatives." The "supreme tribunal of the national judiciary" had been transformed into the "Supreme Court."

But besides giving new names to institutions, the Committee of Detail had earned its name, for there were now specifics to replace earlier generalities. For the first time, the jurisdiction of the courts, the powers of the President and Congress, and the restrictions on state governments were spelled out. In a few instances, where the Convention had made no decision, the committee had filled the gap. In others, decisions had been left to future Congresses.

And in euphemistic but well-understood language, the committee had heeded the threat by General Pinckney about slaves and export duties. John Rutledge, who read the report to the Convention, may have glanced at his fellow South Carolinian as he read: "No tax or duty shall be laid by the legislature on articles exported from any state; nor on the migration or importation of such persons as the several states shall think proper to admit; nor shall such migration or importation be prohibited." "Such persons," of course, were slaves.

When Rutledge had finished, the Convention adjourned for the day, and the delegates dispersed to study the report.

Maryland delegate James McHenry, who had arrived in Philadelphia on the second day of the Convention, had been called to Baltimore four days later by news of the serious illness of his brother. Now, after an absence of more than two months, he returned in time to hear the report of the Committee of Detail. What he heard moved him to action. Leaving the State House with his copy of the report, he urged his fellow Maryland delegates to meet that afternoon to confer on the report and prepare to act as a united delegation.

They met in the lodgings of Daniel Carroll, a wealthy tobacco planter. Besides McHenry and Carroll, there was Daniel of St. Thomas Jenifer, the moderate nationalist whose late arrival at the State House a month earlier had helped produce the tie vote on representation in the Senate. Luther Martin, the state's attorney general, who had cast Maryland's vote for equality in the Senate in Jenifer's absence, was also there, along with John Francis Mercer, a young former Virginian who had served with distinction during the war. Mercer had married the daughter of a rich Maryland family and moved to her estate two years earlier. He had arrived at the Convention for the first time this very day.

McHenry, who had urged the meeting, was Irish-born and not quite thirty-four. He had served as a surgeon in the Revolution before inheriting money and going into Maryland politics. Now he suggested that the delegates go through the committee report paragraph by paragraph. Mercer asked him if he thought Maryland would accept the system of government it described. "I don't know," McHenry replied, "but I presume the people will not object to a wise system."

When Mercer asked the others the same question, Luther

Martin said flatly that the people of Maryland would not accept it. "I am against the system," he said, adding that its promoters had succeeded in bringing it this far only by compromise. "Had Mr. Jenifer voted with me," he said accusingly, "things would have taken a different turn."

"I voted with you until I saw it was in vain to oppose its progress," Jenifer replied.

Pleading for order, McHenry suggested they agree to offer a motion to postpone consideration of the report in order to turn the Convention back to an attempt to amend the Articles of Confederation. Carroll didn't think amending the Articles would meet the country's needs, and Mercer and Jenifer agreed with him. Luther Martin most decidedly did not. Finally, at McHenry's urging, four of them agreed to meet again the next day. Martin, who was leaving to spend a few days in New York, would be unable to join them.

After the meeting broke up, McHenry picked out the three provisions of the draft constitution that bothered him most. He would try to unite his delegation in opposing them at the meeting the next day.

The next morning, Tuesday, August 7, the Convention began a clause-by-clause consideration of the draft constitution. It would continue for the next five weeks. It began with deceptive ease when the preamble and the first two articles were accepted unanimously.

The preamble was noteworthy chiefly for its first three words, "We the people," which made clear at the outset that what followed was not a confederation of states. Article I simply confirmed the government's name: "The United States of America." Article II specified what everyone had agreed was the minimum necessary to strengthen the Articles of Confederation: that the new government would "consist of supreme legislative, executive, and judicial powers."

Article III placed the legislative power in a Congress of two houses which would meet on the first Monday in December each year. This produced comments from no fewer than eleven delegates before it was amended to require at least one meeting a year on the first Monday of December unless a different day were chosen by Congress. It was a foretaste of things to come.

The next disputed point was the qualifications of voters for members of the House of Representatives. The Committee of Detail had qualified anyone eligible to vote for members of the most numerous branch of his own state's legislature. Gouverneur Morris moved immediately to require that voters be freeholders—owners of land. James Wilson explained that the committee had given careful consideration to this provision. "It is difficult," he said, "to form any uniform rule of qualifications for all the states." But it would be "very hard and disagreeable for the same persons at the same time to vote for representatives in the state legislature and to be excluded from a vote for those in the national legislature."

It was not an easy question to resolve. Ten states had property qualifications for voting, and they varied from fifty pounds worth of property of any kind to the ownership of fifty acres of land. Three states required only that a voter be a taxpayer. What Morris was urging was not only a property qualification but one restricted to property in land.

Oliver Ellsworth, who had served on the Committee of Detail with Wilson, defended the Committee's solution. "The right of suffrage is a tender point," he warned, "and strongly guarded by most of the state constitutions. The people will not readily subscribe to the national constitution if it should subject them to be disfranchised."

Pierce Butler agreed wholeheartedly. "There is no right of which the people are more jealous than that of suffrage," he said. "Abridgements of it tend to the same revolution as in Holland, where they have at length thrown all power into the hands of the Senates, who fill up vacancies themselves and form a rank aristocracy."

John Dickinson of Delaware supported Gouverneur Morris's proposal that only freeholders be permitted to vote. "I consider them," he said, "as the best guardians of liberty and the restriction of the right to them as a necessary defense against the dangerous influence of those multitudes without property and without principle with which our country, like all others, will in time abound."

But Oliver Ellsworth was concerned about men of wealth who might not own land. "How shall the freehold be defined?" he asked. "Ought not every man who pays a tax to vote for the representative who is to levy and dispose of his money? Shall the wealthy merchants and manufacturers, who will bear a full share of the public burdens, be not allowed a voice in the imposition of them? Taxation and representation ought to go together."

Gouverneur Morris, clearly irked by Pierce Butler's suggestion that restricting the vote to freeholders would lead to an aristocracy, persisted. "I have," he said, "long learned not to be the dupe of words. The sound of 'aristocracy' therefore has no effect on me. It is the thing, not the name, to which I am opposed, and one of my principal objections to the Constitution as it is now before us is that it threatens this country with an aristocracy. The artistocracy will grow out of the House of Representatives.

"Give the votes to the people who have no property, and they will sell them to the rich," he declared. Foreseeing a day when a growth in manufacturing would produce a large new class of wage earners, Morris warned, "We should not confine our attention to the present moment. The time is not distant when this country will abound with mechanics and manufacturers who will receive their bread from their employers. Will such men be the secure and faithful guardians of liberty? Will they be the impregnable barrier against aristocracy?"

Turning then to Ellsworth's linking of taxation and representation, he added, "I am as little duped by the association of the words 'taxation' and 'representation.' The man who does not give his vote freely is not represented. It is the man who dictates the vote. Children do not vote. Why? Because they want prudence. Because they have no will of their own. The ignorant and the dependent can be as little trusted with the public interest. I do not conceive the difficulty of defining 'freeholders' to be insuperable. Still less that the restriction could be unpopular. Nine-tenths of the people are at present freeholders, and they will certainly be pleased with it." As for wealthy merchants and manufacturers with no land, he said, "If they have wealth and value the right, they can acquire it. If not, they don't deserve it."

George Mason, ever the staunch republican, rose to disagree. "We all," he said, "feel too strongly the remains of ancient prejudices and view things too much through a British medium. A freehold is the qualification in England, and hence it is imagined to be the only proper one. The true idea, in my opinion, is that every man having evidence of attachment to, and permanent common interest with the society ought to share in all its rights and privileges. Is this qualification restrained to freeholders? Does no other kind of property but land evidence a common interest in the proprietor? Does nothing besides property mark a permanent attachment? Ought the merchant, the monied man, the parent of a number of children whose fortunes are to be pursued in their own country to be viewed as suspicious characters and unworthy to be trusted with the common rights of their fellow citizens?"

James Madison was inclined to go along with Gouverneur Morris's views. Benjamin Franklin was not. "It is of great consequence," he said, "that we should not depress the virtue and public spirit of our common people, of which they displayed a great deal during the war and which contributed principally to the favorable issue of it." He did not think "that the elected have any right in any case to narrow the privileges of the electors." He was, he said, "persuaded also that such a restriction as is proposed will give great uneasiness in the populous states. The sons of a substantial farmer, not being themselves freeholders, will not be pleased at being disfranchised, and there are a great many persons of that description."

When a vote was finally taken, Gouverneur Morris's attempt to permit only freeholders to vote in the election of members of the House of Representatives was defeated, seven states to one, with Maryland divided. Only Delaware, swayed perhaps by John Dickinson's arguments, voted for it. Later, the Committee's provision was approved. That settled the question of property qualifications for voters at least by the national government. The states, in deciding who might vote for members of the largest branch of their own legislatures, would by that act decide also the qualifications for voters for the new House of Representatives.

*   *   *

It was a decision that would endure without change for eighty-three years. Then, in 1870, in the aftermath of the Civil War, the ratification of the Fifteenth Amendment would add the declaration that "the right of citizens of the United States to vote shall not be denied or abridged by the United States or by any State on account of race, color, or previous condition of servitude." Fifty additional years would pass before the Nineteenth Amendment guaranteed the right of women to vote.

In 1964, the Twenty-fourth Amendment eliminated both the "white primaries" and the "poll tax" by which many Southern states had prevented blacks from voting in national elections. Finally, in 1971, with Americans under the age of twenty-one being drafted to fight in Vietnam, the ratification of the Twenty-sixth Amendment lowered the voting age to eighteen.

*   *   *

When the Convention adjourned that Tuesday, August 7, the Maryland delegates met once again, and James McHenry outlined his proposals to the others. The delegation, he urged, should resolutely oppose the provision giving the House of Representatives the exclusive right to originate money bills. It would, he maintained, give "that branch an inordinate power in the Constitution." The others, aware that Maryland would have only six of the sixty-five seats in the first House of Representatives, agreed.

McHenry then turned to a provision dealing with navigation acts, which meant, in general, acts regulating commerce. The subject had not been discussed by the Convention, but the Committee of Detail had inserted in its report a requirement for a two-thirds majority in both Houses of Congress to pass such acts. It was, as every delegate knew, a concession to the South.

From the Southern point of view, the immediate danger was that the Northern states, which controlled shipping and would hold a majority in both Houses of Congress, might push through an act requiring that American products be shipped in American vessels. Such an act would greatly stimulate Northern shipbuilding and commerce. But since the Southern states were the major producers of commodities that were shipped, their interests would be better served by unrestricted trade.

Nor were Southern fears of navigation acts merely theoretical. The British had infuriated all the American colonies by restricting American trade to British vessels. And the New England states had passed similar statutes in 1784 and 1785 for their own benefit. Requiring a two-thirds majority for such acts was an attempt to provide at least a measure of protection to the South.

McHenry thought even more was needed. He favored a provision to require the votes of two-thirds of the representatives of *each state* for the passage of navigation acts. Once again, his fellow Maryland delegates agreed.

Finally, McHenry expressed his fears about the ratification procedure proposed by the Committee of Detail. Under it, conventions in each state would have the power to ratify the new Constitution, and ratification by a number of them yet to be decided would put the new government into effect. It seemed clear that that number might be as few as nine. Since the Articles of Confederation required a unanimous vote of all the states for amendments, it seemed to McHenry that a unanimous vote should be required to replace it.

Daniel Carroll seemed less concerned about this final point than McHenry, but all four delegates agreed to act together. John Francis Mercer wanted it understood, however, that he did not like the plan of government as a whole.

10

Amendment and Revision

"We grow more and more skeptical as we pro-
ceed. If we do not decide soon, we shall be un-
able to come to any decision."
OLIVER ELLSWORTH to the Convention
August 15, 1787

August 8–18, 1787

The next morning, Wednesday, August 8, on his third day
in attendance at the Convention, twenty-eight-year-old John
Francis Mercer delivered his verdict to the Convention. "I dislike the whole plan," he said, "and in my opinion, it can never
succeed." If there was a response, neither Madison, Rufus
King, nor James McHenry, the three delegates taking notes
that day, recorded it. Yet since Luther Martin had already
made clear his vigorous opposition to a strong national government, this new and unsolicited declaration may well have
given nationalists in the Convention some uneasiness about
Maryland.

In fact, things were not quite as bad as they may have
seemed. Luther Martin was not without opposition in his delegation. As James McHenry reported later, when Martin said of
the Constitution, "I'll be hanged if ever the people of Maryland agree to it," Daniel of St. Thomas Jenifer replied, "I ad-
vise you to stay in Philadelphia lest you should be hanged."

The Convention slogged its way forward. That day it considered a provision in the Committee of Detail's draft consti-

tution requiring members of the House of Representatives to be twenty-five years old, citizens of the United States for three years, and residents of the state they were chosen to represent. Even so simple a matter as this brought thirteen delegates from seven states to their feet. Six amendments were proposed and two passed before the delegates were ready to move on. The citizenship requirement was raised from three to seven years, and the word "resident" was changed to "inhabitant."

When they reached the provision for counting three-fifths of a state's slaves in apportioning future representation in the House, Rufus King of Massachusetts rose to object. The admission of slaves into the rule of representation was, he said, "a most grating circumstance to my mind, and I believe it will be so to a great part of the people of America. I have not made a strenuous opposition to it heretofore because I hoped that this concession would produce a readiness, which has not been manifested, to strengthen the general government and to mark a full confidence in it." The Committee's report, he said, had "put an end to all these hopes."

In the background of some of the previous discussions of slavery had been the question of slave insurrections. King now brought it into the open. "In two great points," he said, "the hands of the legislature are absolutely tied. The importation of slaves cannot be prohibited; exports cannot be taxed. Is this reasonable? What are the great objects of the general system? 1. Defense against foreign invasion. 2. Defense against internal sedition. Shall all the states then be bound to defend each? And shall each be at liberty to introduce a weakness which will render defense more difficult? Shall one part of the United States be bound to defend another part and that other part be at liberty not only to increase its own danger, but to withhold the compensation for the burden? If slaves are to be imported, shall not the exports produced by their labor supply a revenue the better to enable the general government to defend their masters?"

He had hoped, he said, that some accommodation would

have taken place on this subject, "that at least a time would have been limited for the importation of slaves. I can never agree to let them be imported without limitation and then be represented in the national legislature." At all events, he added, "either slaves should not be represented or exports should be taxable."

Gouverneur Morris went further. "I never will concur in upholding domestic slavery," he declared. "It is a nefarious institution. It is the curse of heaven on the states where it prevails."

Upon what principle is it, he asked, "that the slaves shall be computed in the representation? Are they men? Then make them citizens and let them vote. Are they property? Why, then, is no other property included? The houses in this city of Philadelphia are worth more than all the wretched slaves which cover the rice swamps of South Carolina. The admission of slaves into the representation when fairly explained comes to this: that the inhabitant of Georgia and South Carolina who goes to the coast of Africa and in defiance of the most sacred laws of humanity tears away his fellow creatures from their dearest connections and damns them to the most cruel bondage shall have more votes in a government instituted for protection of the rights of mankind than the citizen of Pennsylvania or New Jersey who views with a laudable horror so nefarious a practice.

"I would add," he said, "that domestic slavery is the most prominent feature in the aristocratic countenance of the proposed constitution. The vassalage of the poor has ever been the favorite offspring of aristocracy. And what is the proposed compensation to the Northern states for a sacrifice of every principle of right, of every impulse of humanity? They are to bind themselves to march their militia for the defense of the Southern states—for their defense against those very slaves of whom they complain."

The Southern states, he continued, "are not to be restrained from importing fresh supplies of wretched Africans, at once to increase the danger of attack and the difficulty of defense; nay, they are to be encouraged to it by an assurance of having their votes in the national government increased in proportion and are, at the same time, to have their exports and their slaves exempt from all contributions for the public service."

Yet for all the strength of their objections, King and Morris apparently changed no one's mind. As Roger Sherman put it, "I regard the slave trade as iniquitous, but the point of representation having been settled after much difficulty and deliberation, I do not think myself bound to make opposition." The three-fifths rule remained.

Madison spotted another problem. The stipulation that the House would be reapportioned in the future with one Representative for every 40,000 inhabitants of a state could, with a large increase in population, lead to a very large House of Representatives. Nathaniel Gorham was not disturbed. "It is not to be supposed," he said, "that the government will last so long as to produce this effect. Can it be supposed that this vast country, including the Western territory, will a hundred and fifty years hence remain one nation?" The vast country of which Gorham spoke ended, of course, at the Mississippi.

Still, on a motion by Sherman and Madison, the words "not exceeding" were inserted before the proportion of one Representative for every 40,000 inhabitants. And at the suggestion of John Dickinson, the words "provided that each state shall have one representative at least" were added at the end. That took care of Dickinson's state of Delaware, which was believed to have a population of just 37,000.

Feeling their way slowly through the Committee of Detail's draft, the delegates, after a brief debate, struck out the provision requiring money bills to originate in the House of Representatives. And that, of course, pleased James McHenry and his Maryland colleagues.

When the Convention reached the requirement that Senators must have been citizens of the United States for at least four years, Gouverneur Morris moved to increase the period to fourteen years. After listening to the arguments for and against the motion, James Wilson rose to address the delegates in his soft Scottish burr. "I rise," he said, "with feelings which are perhaps peculiar since I am not a native, and the possibility exists, if the ideas of some gentlemen are pursued, of my being incapacitated from holding a place under the very constitution which I have shared in the trust of making. I must point out the illiberal complexion which the motion will give to the system, the effect which a good system will have in inviting meritorious foreigners among us, and the discouragement and mortification they will feel from the degrading discrimination now proposed.

"I have myself experienced this mortification," he continued. "On my removal into Maryland, I found myself, from defect of residence, under certain legal incapacities which never ceased to produce chagrin, though I assuredly did not desire and would not have accepted the offices to which they related. To be appointed to a place may be a matter of indifference. To be incapable of being appointed is a circumstance grating and mortifying."

Gouverneur Morris's motion lost, but after further debate, the Convention voted to require nine years of citizenship for Senators.

It took a week for the Convention to work its way through the sections of the draft that dealt with the rules governing Congress. Two were postponed. And when, toward the end of the week, there was a motion to postpone decision on a third, the irritation of some delegates became vocal. Nathaniel Gorham complained, "I see no end to these difficulties and postponements. Some cannot agree to the form of government before the powers are defined. Others cannot agree to the powers till it is seen how the government is to be formed."

John Rutledge concurred. "I am strenuously against postponing. The proceedings are becoming very tedious."

Oliver Ellsworth added his voice to the chorus. "We grow more and more skeptical as we proceed. If we do not decide soon, we shall be unable to come to any decision."

When the question of the executive veto of legislation came

up, Hugh Williamson moved to require a three-fourths vote of each House of Congress to override it instead of the two-thirds previously agreed on. James Wilson, who had earlier pushed for an absolute veto, seconded the motion, and it passed, six states to four.

Earlier, Charles Pinckney had objected strongly to the way the Committee of Detail had dealt with the Convention's last-minute resolution in favor of property qualifications for officeholders. The Committee had simply left the question open to be decided by Congress. Pinckney moved instead that the President, judges, and members of Congress be required to swear to clear, unencumbered estates of specific amounts in each case. He suggested $100,000 for the President, $50,000 for judges, and a somewhat lesser amount for legislators.

Dr. Franklin responded. "I must express my dislike of everything that tends to debase the spirit of the common people," he said. "If honesty is often the companion of wealth and if poverty is exposed to peculiar temptation, it is not less true that the possession of property increases the desire of more property. Some of the greatest rogues I was ever acquainted with were the richest rogues."

The Constitution, he reminded them, "will be much read and attended to in Europe, and if it should betray a great partiality to the rich, it will not only hurt us in the esteem of the most liberal and enlightened men there but discourage the common people from removing to this country."

Madison noted: "The motion of Mr. Pinckney was rejected by so general a *no* that the states were not called." And in the end, as it had with property qualifications for voting, the Convention rejected all such qualifications throughout its deliberations.

Ironically, at the very time that the Convention was deliberately erecting barriers against even a monied aristocracy, some Americans were apparently promoting the idea of a monarchy. On Monday, August 13, a Philadelphia newspaper published a dispatch from New Haven, Connecticut: "A circular letter is handing about the country recommending a kingly Government for these States. The writer proposes to send to England for the Bishop of Osnaburgh, second son of the King of Great Britain, and have him crowned King over this continent. We have found by experience, says he, that we have not wit enough to govern ourselves—that all our declamation and parade about Republicanism, Liberty, Property and the Rights of Man are mere stuff and nonsense, and that it is high time for us to tread back the wayward path we have walked in these twelve years."

When the story had made the rounds of newspapers throughout the country and questions were raised about what the Convention itself might propose, the delegates decided to act. Unofficially, members of the Convention authorized a public statement, which appeared in the *Pennsylvania Gazette* on August 15. "We are well informed," the *Gazette* reported, "that many letters have been written to the members of the Federal Convention from different quarters, respecting the reports, idly of circulating, that it is intended to establish a monarchical government to send for the Bishop of Osnaburgh, etc. etc.—to which it has been uniformly answered, 'Tho we cannot affirmatively tell you what we are doing; we can, negatively tell you what we are not doing—we never once thought of a King."

By Thursday, August 16, the delegates were ready to consider the legislative powers of Congress. Here, they faced the most fundamental and important change made by the Committee of Detail, for the Convention's general statement of broad and indefinite authority had been replaced by a long list of specified powers. With little difficulty, the delegates agreed to a number of them, granting Congress power to lay and collect taxes, duties, imposts, and excises; to regulate commerce; to establish a uniform rule of naturalization; to coin money; to regulate the value of foreign money; and to fix the standard of weights and measures. They agreed to the power to establish post offices and added post roads.

When they reached a clause granting Congress power to "emit bills on the credit of the United States," which meant, of course, to issue paper money, Gouverneur Morris moved to strike it out. "If the United States has credit," he said, "such bills will be unnecessary; if they have not, it will be unjust and useless." Pierce Butler seconded the motion.

In his first presentation of the Virginia Plan, Edmund Randolph had referred to "the havoc of paper money" as one of the defects of the Confederation. Few of the delegates would have contested that description. In seven states—Rhode Island, New York, New Jersey, Pennsylvania, the Carolinas, and Georgia—paper money had been introduced during the 1780s in varying amounts and for different reasons, and in three other states—New Hampshire, Massachusetts, and Maryland—it had become the subject of angry controversy. John Jay had denounced its issuance as "the doctrine of the political transsubstantiation of paper into gold and silver," and Washington had written to a citizen of Rhode Island, "Paper money has had the effect in your State that it ever will have, to ruin commerce, oppress the honest, and open a door to every species of fraud and injustice."

Still, paper money had an almost irresistible appeal to men in great debt with unpopular taxes to pay and little in coin with which to pay them. And as cheap and inflated paper money became the preferred way of paying debts, it tended to drive hard money, or specie, out of the market. The havoc to which Randolph had referred had been described by Governor William Livingston of New Jersey as "cheating according to law." William Grayson of Virginia had written to Madison in 1786, "Congress should have the power of preventing States from cheating one another, as well as their own citizens."

In the draft constitution now before the delegates, the right to issue paper money was forbidden to the states without the consent of Congress. What Gouverneur Morris and Pierce

Butler now proposed was to deny the right to the national government as well. Madison suggested simply prohibiting Congress from making paper money a legal tender and thereby permitting creditors to refuse it in the payment of debts. But Morris replied, "The monied interest will oppose the plan of government if paper emissions are not prohibited."

Nathaniel Gorham of Massachusetts suggested striking out the power without specifically prohibiting it, but George Mason thought Congress would not have the power if it were not expressed. "Though I have a mortal hatred of paper money," he said, "yet as I cannot foresee all emergencies, I am unwilling to tie the hands of the legislature. The late war could not have been carried on had such a prohibition existed."

John Francis Mercer spoke up. "I am a friend to paper money," he said, "though in the present state and temper of America, I would neither propose or approve of such a measure. Consequently, I am opposed to a prohibition of it altogether." People of property, he felt sure, would favor the plan of government in any case, and it made no sense to excite the opposition of those like himself who favored paper money.

Oliver Ellsworth disagreed completely. "This," he said, "is a favorable moment to shut and bar the door against paper money. The mischiefs of the various experiments which have been made are now fresh in the public mind and have excited the disgust of all the respectable part of America. By withholding the power from the new government, more friends of influence will be gained to it than by almost anything else."

Edmund Randolph, though he was against paper money, was against striking out the power to emit it. James Wilson disagreed. And George Read of Delaware thought the words "emit bills on the credit of the United States," if not struck out, "will be as alarming as the mark of the beast in Revelation." John Langdon of New Hampshire felt even more strongly. "I would rather reject the whole plan," he said, "than retain the three words 'and emit bills.' "

In the end, Morris's motion carried, nine states to two, but the precise effect of striking out the power to emit bills remained in some doubt. Some delegates clearly believed they were prohibiting paper money. Others, like Madison, assumed that by neither granting nor prohibiting it, the door would be, if not exactly open, at least not shut and barred, as Ellsworth preferred.

Ambiguity, in this and other instances, was thus a conscious policy of many of the Convention delegates. By striking out potentially offensive words ("emit bills," "slavery") and by leaving the Constitution silent on controversial issues like this one, they sought to make the Constitution "as palatable as possible," as Gouverneur Morris later explained.

On Friday, August 17, after tinkering with some of the specified powers of Congress and approving others, the Convention reached "to make war." Charles Pinckney objected on the grounds that the proceedings of Congress would be too slow for it to properly exercise this power. Congress, he pointed out, "would meet but once a year. The House of Representatives," he added, "would be too numerous for such deliberations. The Senate would be the best depositary, being more acquainted with foreign affairs and most capable of proper resolutions."

Pinckney's colleague Pierce Butler pointed out that all of the objections against Congress as a whole applied in a great degree to the Senate as well. "I am," he said, "for vesting the power in the President, who will have all the requisite qualities and will not make war but when the nation will support it."

Madison and Gerry moved to change the wording from "make war" to "declare war," leaving the power in Congress while leaving to the President the power to repel sudden attacks. Roger Sherman thought the clause was fine as it was. And Elbridge Gerry, responding to Pierce Butler's suggestion, said, "I never expected to hear in a republic a motion to empower the executive alone to declare war."

George Mason agreed. "I am against giving the power of war to the executive," he said, "because he is not safely to be trusted with it. Or to the Senate, because it is not so constructed as to be entitled to it. I am for clogging, rather than facilitating, war."

When the question came to a vote, the Convention substituted "declare" for "make" and left the power where the Committee of Detail had placed it, with Congress. Assuming, apparently, that the President, as commander in chief of the army and navy, would have the inherent power, as Madison had put it, to repel sudden attacks, the delegates made no attempt, either now or later, to include that power specifically in the Constitution.

* * *

Almost two hundred years later, in 1973, Congress faced similar questions when it debated and finally passed the War Power Resolution over President Richard Nixon's veto. A reaction to America's undeclared entry into the Vietnam War, the Resolution required the President to report to Congress within forty-eight hours after committing armed forces to combat abroad. Combat action could not continue beyond sixty days unless authorized by Congress. Within the sixty-day period, Congress could order an immediate removal of the forces by adopting a concurrent resolution not subject to an executive veto. The 1973 War Power Resolution marked the first time that Congress had spelled out the war-making powers of Congress and the President.

* * *

On Saturday, August 18, James Madison submitted a list of additional powers he felt should be given to Congress. Charles Pinckney, Elbridge Gerry, John Rutledge, and George Mason added others, and all were referred to the Committee of Detail. Rutledge then moved for a grand committee of the states to consider having the United States assume the debts of the states. The Convention agreed, and the new committee was chosen.

Rutledge then took the floor once more. More than three months had passed since the official date of the Convention's opening. Rutledge noted the probable impatience of the public and the extreme anxiety of many delegates to bring the business to an end. He moved that the Convention begin its meetings at ten o'clock sharp each morning and that at precisely four in the afternoon, the President adjourn the session without waiting for a motion. No motion to adjourn earlier than four o'clock would be permitted. The motion carried.

Turning back, then, to the powers of Congress, the Convention considered the clause, "to raise armies." At the suggestion of Nathaniel Gorham, the delegates changed it to "raise and support armies." But Elbridge Gerry was unhappy with that. Expressing concern that no limit had been placed on standing armies in peacetime, he said, "The people are jealous on this head, and great opposition to the plan will spring from such an omission." He proposed a limit of two or three thousand troops.

At this, General Washington, who as presiding officer could not offer a motion, turned to another delegate. In a whisper, he facetiously suggested an amendment providing that no foreign enemy be permitted to invade the United States with more than three thousand troops. Others undoubtedly had the same thought, for Gerry's idea was unanimously rejected.

11

The Slave Trade

"If slavery be wrong, it is justified by the example of all the world. . . . In all ages, one-half of mankind have been slaves."
CHARLES PINCKNEY to the Convention
August 22, 1787

August 19–24, 1787

The next day, August 19, was a Sunday. Washington rode the fourteen miles to White Marsh, Pennsylvania, with a friend. Here, ten years earlier, he and the Continental Army had been encamped after the British, under General William Howe, captured Philadelphia. It had been from White Marsh that the Americans had set out to surprise Howe at Germantown in a battle that cost the Americans a thousand men. Now, as he noted in his diary, Washington "traversed my old Incampment, and contemplated on the dangers which threatened the American Army at that place."

Two days earlier, he had contemplated more immediate dangers in a letter to his wartime colleague Lafayette. "There are seeds of discontent in every part of the Union," he wrote, "ready to produce other disorders if the wisdom of the present Convention should not be able to devise, and the good sense of the people be found ready to adopt, a more vigorous and energetic government."

On Monday, August 20, Charles Pinckney submitted to the Convention a list of proposals for referral to the Committee of

Detail. Calling for such protections of individual rights as habeas corpus—the right to be brought before a court—freedom of the press, and a ban on religious tests for national office, the list amounted to a partial bill of rights. Pinckney's proposals, along with some from Gouverneur Morris, dealing chiefly with a presidential cabinet, were referred to the committee.

George Mason then moved to enable Congress to enact sumptuary laws: acts designed to regulate personal behavior on moral and religious grounds. "No government can be maintained," Mason said, "unless the manners be made consonant to it."

Connecticut's great consumer of snuff, Oliver Ellsworth, begged to differ. "The best remedy," he said, "is to enforce taxes and debts. As far as the regulation of eating and drinking can be reasonable, it is provided for in the power of taxation." After Gouverneur Morris and Elbridge Gerry added their own words of opposition, the Convention rejected Mason's motion.

* * *

One hundred and thirty-two years later, in 1919, the United States would return to George Mason's idea with a vengeance. With the ratification of the Eighteenth Amendment, the manufacture, sale, transportation, importation, and exportation of intoxicating liquors was prohibited. As Americans quickly divided into "drys," who saw Prohibition as a keystone of American morality, and "wets," who made a joke of the new law, the country entered an era of unprecedented lawlessness. An army of smugglers, rum-runners, moonshiners, and bootleggers sprang up in cities and towns across the land. In the larger cities, armed gangs staked out territorial claims to control the sale and distribution of illegal and sometimes lethal whiskey, and gang wars quickly became a recognized feature of American life.

The continuing battle between wets and drys produced predictable extremes. In New York City, "speakeasies" made illegal drinking chic; in Michigan, conviction of a fourth offense against the Prohibition law meant life imprisonment. The "noble experiment" lasted only fourteen years, but it left in its wake a generation of Americans for many of whom disrespect for the law had become a daily reality. Prohibition ended in 1933 with the ratification of the Twenty-first Amendment, which unceremoniously repealed the Eighteenth.

*   *   *

When the Convention delegates reached the final and sweeping power granted to Congress in the report of the Committee of Detail, they approved it unanimously. In addition to all of its specified powers, Congress would have the power "to make all laws which shall be necessary and proper for carrying into execution the foregoing powers, and all other powers vested by this Constitution in the Government of the United States, or in any department or officer thereof."

*   *   *

The precise meaning of this clause would eventually be decided in the notable case of *McCulloch versus Maryland* in 1819, thirty-two years later. The case involved a conflict between the state of Maryland and the Bank of the United States, which had been chartered by Congress. Much to the annoyance of state officials and the officers of banks chartered by Maryland itself, the Bank of the United States maintained a branch office in Baltimore. To get rid of it, Maryland enacted a prohibitive tax and then tried to collect it. When the Bank's cashier, James W. McCulloch, refused to pay the tax, the issue quickly moved into the courts.

By the time the case reached the Supreme Court, the basic questions were clear-cut: Were the federal law chartering the Bank and the state law taxing it in conflict? If so, which was constitutional and hence overruled the other? Maryland argued that because the Constitution did not expressly grant Congress power to create a bank, chartering the Bank of the United States had been an unconstitutional act. Attorneys for the United States held, on the contrary, that the chartering of the Bank was an act "necessary and proper for carrying into execution" powers that had been expressly granted to Congress: to lay and collect taxes, to borrow money, to regulate commerce, and the like.

Maryland's answer to that was that the "necessary and proper" clause, far from extending the powers of Congress to the passage of laws designed to execute its expressly granted powers, was intended simply to make it clear that Congress could make laws. Among the counsel representing the state of Maryland in this disingenuous argument was none other than the former Convention delegate, Luther Martin, now serving his state for a second time as Attorney General.

In a unanimous decision, the Supreme Court found for the United States. The act of Congress chartering the Bank was declared to be constitutional; the act of Maryland taxing the bank, unconstitutional. Most important, however, was the Court's ruling that the "necessary and proper" clause gave Congress the implied power to carry its expressed powers into execution. In the words of Chief Justice John Marshall, who wrote the opinion of the Court, "Let the end be legitimate, let it be within the scope of the Constitution, and all means which are appropriate, which are plainly adapted to that end, which are not prohibited, but consist with the letter and spirit of the Constitution, are constitutional."

*   *   *

Turning without pause from their unanimous acceptance of the "necessary and proper" clause, the Convention delegates took up the Committee of Detail's recommendations on the subject of treason. After much discussion and several amendments, they approved a section that read: "Treason against the United States shall consist only in levying war against them, or in adhering to their enemies, giving them aid and comfort. The legislature shall have power to declare the punishment of treason. No person shall be convicted of treason, unless on the testimony of two witnesses to the same overt act, or on confession in open court. No attainder of treason shall work corruption of blood, nor forfeiture, except during the life of the person attainted." Simply put, this last provision meant that whatever loss of civil rights or forfeiture of property might be levied against a convicted traitor, the penalties would not be passed on to his heirs.

On Tuesday, August 21, after some discussion and minor amendments, the Convention agreed to a section that regulated the proportions of direct taxation of each state in precisely the same manner as its representation in the House of Representatives: by its free population plus three-fifths of its slaves. Gouverneur Morris had suggested this formula on July 12 as a way of assuring that if the Southern states were to benefit from the ownership of slaves in their representation in the House of Representatives, they would suffer to the same degree in direct taxation. Two weeks later, when the three-fifths rule had been accepted by both Northern and Southern states, Morris expressed the hope that the Committee of Detail would strike out this provision. "I meant it only as a bridge to assist us over a certain gulf," he explained. "Having passed the gulf, the bridge may be removed." As it turned out, the Committee of Detail had retained Morris's bridge, and the Convention kept it as well.

In the course of discussion of this section, Rufus King of Massachusetts asked, "What is the precise meaning of *direct* taxation?" As Madison indicated in his notes, "No one answered." We can assume, however, that most of the delegates understood direct taxes to mean taxes on land or individuals.

*   *   *

For all of the attention paid by the Convention to direct taxation, Congress would levy direct taxes on real estate only twice, in 1798 and 1861, and when it attempted, in 1894, to levy an income tax, the Supreme Court struck it down as a direct tax which was not, according to the constitutional provision, apportioned among the states according to population. Eighteen years later, in 1913, the Sixteenth Amendment, which authorized an income tax without apportionment among the states, was ratified.

*   *   *

Finally, the Convention reached the section written by the Committee of Detail in response to General Pinckney's warning nearly a month earlier. Pinckney had insisted on "some security to the Southern states against an emancipation of slaves and taxes on exports." He got even more. The section read: "No tax or duty shall be laid by the legislature on articles exported from any state; nor on the migration or importation of such persons as the several states shall think proper to admit; nor shall such migration or importation be prohibited." As anyone could have predicted, it brought yet another angry argument. This one lasted most of two days.

After extended debate, the ban on taxing exports was upheld, seven states to four, and the argument turned to the injunctions against prohibiting and taxing the importation of slaves. Luther Martin of Maryland was opposed to both. "As five slaves are to be counted as three free men in the apportionment of Representatives," he said, "such a clause will leave an encouragement to this traffic. Secondly, slaves weaken one part of the Union which the other parts are bound to protect. The privilege of importing them is therefore unreasonable. And thirdly, it is inconsistent with the principles of the revolution and dishonorable to the American character to have such a feature in the Constitution."

That brought John Rutledge of South Carolina to his feet. "I do not see how the importation of slaves could be encouraged by this section," he said flatly. "I am not apprehensive of slave insurrections, and I would readily exempt the other states from the obligation to protect the Southern states against them." Then, in an allusion to statements by other delegates on the immorality of slavery, he continued, "Religion and humanity have nothing to do with this question. Interest alone is the governing principle with nations. The true question at present is whether the Southern states shall or shall not be parties to the Union. If the Northern states consult their interest, they will not oppose the increase of slaves which will in-

crease the commodities of which they will become the car-
riers."

Oliver Ellsworth favored leaving the clause as it stood. "Let
every state import what it pleases," he said. "The morality or
wisdom of slavery are considerations belonging to the states
themselves. What enriches a part enriches the whole, and the
states are the best judges of their particular interest. The old
confederation did not meddle with this point, and I do not see
any greater necessity for bringing it within the policy of the
new one."

Roger Sherman agreed with his Connecticut colleague. "I
disapprove of the slave trade," he said. "Yet as the states are
now possessed of the right to import slaves, as the public good
does not require it to be taken from them, and as it is expedient to have as few objections as possible to the proposed
scheme of government, I think it best to leave the matter as we
find it. The abolition of slavery seems to be going on in the
United States," he added, "and the good sense of the several
states will probably by degrees complete it."

Young Charles Pinckney added his warning to that of his
colleague John Rutledge. "South Carolina," he declared, "can
never receive the plan if it prohibits the slave trade. In every
proposed extension of the powers of Congress, the state has
expressly and watchfully excepted that of meddling with the importation of Negroes. If the states are all left at liberty on this
subject, South Carolina may perhaps by degrees do herself
what is wished, as Virginia and Maryland have already done."

But none of this satisfied Virginia's slave-owning George
Mason. "This infernal traffic," he said, "originated in the ava-
rice of British merchants. The British Government constantly
checked the attempts of Virginia to put a stop to it. The present question concerns not just the importing states but the
whole Union. The evil of having slaves was experienced during the late war," he added, reminding his fellow Southerners
how the British had encouraged slaves to run away and join
their forces.

"Maryland and Virginia have already prohibited the importation of slaves expressly," he said. "North Carolina has done the same in substance. All this will be in vain if South Carolina and Georgia are at liberty to import them. The Western people are already calling out for slaves for their new lands and will fill that country with slaves if they can be got through South Carolina and Georgia.

"Slavery," he continued, "discourages arts and manufacturing. The poor despise labor when it is performed by slaves. Slaves prevent the immigration of whites, who really enrich and strengthen a country. They produce the most pernicious effect on manners; every master of slaves is born a petty tyrant." Slaves, Mason insisted, bring the judgment of heaven on a country. "I lament," he added, "that some of our Eastern brethren have, from a lust of gain, embarked in this nefarious traffic.

"As to the states being in possession of the right to import slaves, this is the case with many other rights now to be properly given up. I hold it essential in every point of view that the general government should have power to prevent the increase of slavery."

Oliver Ellsworth was not persuaded. "As I have never owned a slave," he said, "I cannot judge of the effects of slavery on character. If it is to be considered in a moral light, however, we ought to go farther and free those already in the country." Slaves, he said, multiply so rapidly in Virginia and Maryland, "that it is cheaper to raise than import them, whilst in the sickly rice swamps, foreign supplies are necessary." To give Congress power to end the slave trade, he said, would "be unjust towards South Carolina and Georgia.

"Let us not intermingle. As population increases, poor laborers will be so plentiful as to render slaves useless. Slavery, in time, will not be a speck in our country. Provision is already made in Connecticut for abolishing it, and the abolition has already taken place in Massachusetts. As to the danger of insurrections from foreign influence, that will become a motive to kind treatment of the slaves."

Charles Pinckney said, "If slavery be wrong, it is justified by the example of all the world," and he cited Greece, Rome, and other ancient states as well as the sanction given to it by France, England, Holland, and other modern states. "In all ages," he continued, "one-half of mankind have been slaves." Then having defended the institution, he suggested again that the slave trade might well be ended by those states now engaged in it. "If the Southern states are let alone, they will probably of themselves stop importations. I would myself, as a citizen of South Carolina, vote for it. An attempt to take away the right," however, would "produce serious objections to the Constitution which I wish to see adopted."

General Pinckney rose to support his young cousin. "South Carolina and Georgia cannot do without slaves," he said bluntly. "As to Virginia, she will gain by stopping the importations. Her slaves will rise in value, and she has more than she wants." The slave trade, he contended, was in the interest of the whole Union. "The more slaves, the more produce to employ the carrying trade. The more consumption also, and the more of this, the more of revenue for the common treasury."

Abraham Baldwin, the recent transplant from Connecticut, took the floor to declare that his new state of Georgia was decided on this point. "If left to herself," he added, "she may probably put a stop to the evil."

James Wilson of Pennsylvania spotted an inconsistency. "If South Carolina and Georgia are themselves disposed to get rid of the importation of slaves in a short time, as has been suggested, they will never refuse to unite because the importation might be prohibited," he said. "As the section now stands, all articles imported are to be taxed. Slaves alone are exempt. This is, in fact, a bounty on that article."

Elbridge Gerry thought the Convention should not interfere with slavery in any state but should be careful not to sanction it. John Dickinson of Delaware disagreed. "It is inadmissible on every principle of honor and safety that the importation of slaves should be authorized to the states by the Constitution," he said. "The true question is whether the national happiness will be promoted or impeded by the importation, and this question ought to be left to the national government, not to the states particularly interested."

Turning then to Charles Pinckney's arguments, he said, "If England and France permit slavery, slaves are at the same time excluded from both those kingdoms. Greece and Rome were made unhappy by their slaves." Nor did he believe that the Southern states would refuse to join the others simply to preserve the slave trade.

Hugh Williamson of North Carolina assured him that they would. Rufus King responded that if South Carolina and Georgia would not accept the Constitution without the clause, other states would be equally opposed to accepting it with it. John Langdon wondered if the Southern states would, in fact, give up importing slaves, and General Pinckney replied, "I think myself bound to declare candidly that I do not think South Carolina will stop her importations of slaves in any short time, but only stop them occasionally as she now does." Then, admitting that he thought it was right that slaves be taxed equally with other imports, he moved to refer the clause to a committee.

John Rutledge rose. "If the Convention thinks that North Carolina, South Carolina, and Georgia will ever agree to the plan unless their right to import slaves is untouched," he said, "that expectation is vain. The people of those states will never be such fools as to give up so important an interest. I am strenuously against striking out the section." He then seconded his colleague's motion.

Gouverneur Morris saw an opportunity for compromise, and he urged that a committee consider not only the clause in question but also a number of other questions at issue between the Northern and Southern states, including export taxes and navigation acts. "These things," he suggested, "may form a bargain among the Northern and Southern states." After a brief argument, the Convention agreed to refer all of these questions except the prohibition on export taxes, which, as Roger Sherman pointed out, had already been approved, to still another committee of the states.

The debate over the slave trade had been one of the angriest of the summer. Nineteen delegates, from ten of the eleven states then represented on the Convention floor, had taken part in it. Only New Jersey had stayed out of it. James Madison, who had carefully noted the arguments of the others but had made none of his own, must surely have seen the debate as a vindication of his statements nearly two months earlier that the great division of interests in the United States was not between the small and large states but between those with slaves and those without them.

With the controversy over the slave trade safely in the hands of a committee, the Convention adopted a motion by Elbridge Gerry to add to the restrictions on the powers of Congress a clause reading: "The legislature shall pass no bill of attainder nor any ex post facto law." A bill of attainder was a legislative act that punished certain crimes by forfeiture of property and loss of civil rights—all without trial. An ex post facto law inflicted penalties retroactively.

That afternoon, Wednesday, August 22, most of the delegates left the State House after adjournment and proceeded to the bank of the Delaware River to witness the trial run of a steamboat invented by John Fitch. The most famous inventor in America, Benjamin Franklin, was not among them, mostly because of the difficulty of getting there. But Franklin doubted the practicality of the invention even if it proved to work. It was, he thought, too expensive to be useful.

As it turned out, the steamboat's twelve oars, wheeling through the water, moved the boat successfully against the current. For Convention delegates who had been paddling hard upstream for nearly three months, anything that did the job with speed and efficiency must have seemed almost miraculous.

On Thursday, August 23, after much discussion, the Convention gave Congress power to make laws to organize the state militia. The delegates then affirmed their republican principles by unanimously adopting a section reading: "The United States shall not grant any title of nobility. No person holding any office of profit or trust under the United States shall, without the consent of the legislature, accept of any present, emolument, office, or title of any kind whatever from any king, prince, or foreign state." On some matters, at least, the delegates were in complete agreement.

They agreed, also unanimously, that Congress should have the power "to provide for calling forth the militia to execute the laws of the Union, suppress insurrections, and repel invasions."

More than a month earlier, Luther Martin had succeeded in a move to make all acts of Congress and treaties of the United States the supreme law of the states. Now, at the suggestion of John Rutledge, the provision was enlarged. As the Convention unanimously approved it, *the Constitution and* the laws and treaties of the United States would be the supreme law of the states and superior to the state constitutions as well.

That, apparently, was the last straw for Luther Martin, "a total and unconditional surrender" by the states to the national government, he called it later. And it was at about this time, according to Martin, that Elbridge Gerry of Massachusetts and George Mason of Virginia began holding evening meetings aimed at protecting the rights of the states. The meetings, which Martin said he had attended, also included delegates from New Jersey, Connecticut, Delaware, South Carolina, and Georgia. Precisely what took place at them, Martin never revealed. Their "sole object," he said, was "to protect and preserve, if possible, the existence and essential rights of all the states, and the liberty and freedom of their citizens."

When the Convention reached the portion of the draft constitution that dealt with the Senate, there was deadlock. The first section, giving the Senate power to make treaties and appoint ambassadors and judges of the Supreme Court, caused such argument that it was sent back to the Committee of Detail.

The other two sections, which were reached the next day, proposed a highly complicated way of dealing with disputes between states. When John Rutledge assured them that the national judiciary could handle such problems, the delegates happily dropped both sections.

That brought them to the executive, where they almost immediately struck the same snag on which they had all but foundered earlier. They had spent ten days debating how to choose the President before agreeing to election by the legislature. Faced now with that decision, they faltered. Motions to substitute other methods came fast and furious, and for a while, it seemed they might devote another ten days to the question. In the end, they postponed a decision.

Before they had worked their way through the section that dealt with the President's powers and duties, the now compulsory adjournment hour of four o'clock had arrived. It had been a week since they agreed to work an extra hour each day. Now they voted unanimously to return to their earlier practice of quitting at three, an hour that made it possible for them to dine with the rest of Philadelphia.

12

The North-South Bargain

*"I had myself prejudices against the Eastern
states before I came here, but I will acknowledge that I have found them as liberal and candid as any men whatever."*

CHARLES COTESWORTH PINCKNEY
to the Convention
August 29, 1787

August 25–30, 1787

When the delegates gathered in the State House chamber on
Saturday, August 25, it was three months to the day since the
Convention had begun its work. Before continuing their discussion of the President's powers and duties, they turned to a
reconsideration of a decision already made.

A week earlier, John Rutledge of South Carolina had moved
successfully for the appointment of a grand committee of the
states "to consider the necessity and expediency of the United
States assuming all the state debts." Three days later, the
committee had recommended giving the legislature "power to
fulfill the engagements which have been entered into by Congress, and to discharge as well the debts of the United States
and the debts incurred by the several states during the late war
for the common defense and general welfare."

That hadn't satisfied Elbridge Gerry, who had speculated
heavily in both government securities and paper money during the Revolution. If he was not the largest holder of conti-

nental securities among the delegates, he was surely one of them. "I consider giving the power only, without adopting the obligation," he said, "as destroying the security now enjoyed by the public creditors of the United States."

Roger Sherman disagreed, feeling the clause left the status of such creditors unchanged. On the motion of his Connecticut colleague Oliver Ellsworth, the committee's report had been tabled.

When the Convention returned to the question on August 22, it had adopted an amendment by Gouverneur Morris requiring the legislature to "discharge the debts and fulfill the engagements of the United States." The second part of the clause, relating to state debts, was simply dropped.

Now, at the behest of Pierce Butler of South Carolina, the Convention took another look. Every delegate knew the importance of the question, and some, like Gerry, had a personal interest in how it would finally be worded. Butler, for his part, had said earlier, "I am dissatisfied, lest it should compel payment as well to the blood-suckers who speculated on the distresses of others as to those who fought and bled for their country."

The problem, like many the Convention was attempting to resolve, went back to the Revolution and the Continental Congress. Faced with war against the British and no money to pay for it, the Continental Congress had borrowed against various kinds of securities and had issued its own continental paper money, which it made a legal tender for all transactions. The value of both securities and money had fluctuated wildly. Paper money had dropped in value to the point where "not worth a continental" became a proverbial way of describing worthlessness.

The Continental Congress, lacking both the money and the power to tax the states, had not paid its debts. The Confederation Congress, which inherited those debts—to foreign and domestic creditors as well as to the veterans of the Continental Army—immediately faced additional financial problems of its own. The future credit of the country and the demands of simple honesty now required some kind of action by the Convention.

But the question was complicated, as Pierce Butler had indicated, by the fact that it was not simply honest investors in the Revolutionary government who stood to lose money. Many, by selling government securities in times of need, had already suffered severe losses. Speculators, who had bought them up at distress prices, stood to reap enormous profits if the securities were redeemed by the new government at their original value.

George Mason of Virginia was opposed to requiring Congress to pay off its debts. "The use of the term *shall*," he said, "will beget speculations and increase the pestilent practice of stock-jobbing. There is a great distinction between original creditors and those who purchased fraudulently of the ignorant and distressed."

John Langdon of New Hampshire thought the creditors should be left precisely as they were. Elbridge Gerry did not. "For myself," he said, "I have no interest in the question, not being possessed of more of the securities than would, by the interest, pay my taxes." Since, however, the country had received the value of the exact amount of the securities, the full value ought to be paid to someone. "The frauds on the soldiers ought to have been foreseen," he said. And as for stock-jobbers, "I see no reason for the censures thrown on them. They keep up the value of the paper. Without them, there would be no market."

But Gerry's views did not prevail. Edmund Randolph of Virginia proposed to substitute a clause stating that "all debts contracted and engagements entered into by or under the authority of Congress shall be as valid against the United States under this Constitution as under the Confederation," and the Convention agreed. And that left creditors in precisely the same position as before.

The Convention turned next to the problems it had entrusted to a committee of the states three days earlier: the slave trade, import taxes on slaves, and navigation acts. As Gouverneur Morris had hoped it would, the committee proposed a compromise between North and South. Congress would be forbidden to end the slave trade before the year 1800 but could tax imported slaves at a rate no higher than the average of other import duties. All references to navigation acts would be dropped.

General Pinckney moved immediately to extend the prohibition on banning the slave trade from 1800 to 1808, more than twenty years hence. James Madison objected. "Twenty years," he said, "will produce all the mischief that can be apprehended from the liberty to import slaves. So long a term will be more dishonorable to the national character than to say nothing about it in the Constitution." But the Convention adopted General Pinckney's motion, seven states to four.

*   *   *

Nineteen years later, in December 1806, President Thomas Jefferson, reminding Congress that the time was nearing when it could prohibit the slave trade, urged that it be banned. Congress responded with an act outlawing the trade as of January 1, 1808, and Jefferson duly signed it into law. As the record of subsequent years would prove, however, outlawing the slave trade simply made it illegal. It would take the Civil War to end it.

*   *   *

There was a brief discussion in the Convention of whether to use the actual word "slaves" in the clause on the slave trade, but the delegates chose instead to retain the euphemism "such persons," and the words "slave," "slaves," and "slavery" were all kept out of the Constitution. Roger Sherman gave as his reason for favoring the euphemisms that the other terms "were not pleasing to some people."

When there were objections to the provision on taxing imported slaves, it was amended to permit a tax of no more than ten dollars for each "such person." Finally, in response to fears of the Maryland delegates that ships bound to or from Baltimore might be required to clear customs and pay duties in, say, Norfolk, Virginia, that problem was referred to yet another committee of the states. The questions were rapidly becoming more parochial.

On Sunday, as Washington noted in his diary, he "rode into the country for exercise 8 or 10 miles." We have been given a hint of the sort of houseguest he was in a letter by his hostess, Mrs. Robert Morris. He would come into the house so quietly, she said, that they would be wholly unaware of it until they discovered it by accident. He would go to his room and remain for hours, where they would eventually find him absorbed in his papers or sitting in silent meditation.

On Monday, August 27, the Convention returned to the remaining questions concerning the President. The Committee of Detail had included the sentence, "He shall be commander in chief of the Army and Navy of the United States, and of the militia of the several states." No one questioned the first part of the sentence, but Roger Sherman moved successfully to restrict the President's role as commander in chief of the militia to times when it was in the actual service of the United States.

Then came the question of how to fill a vacancy in the presidency. Gouverneur Morris objected to a provision that the President of the Senate, who would of course be a Senator, act temporarily as President in the event of the elected President's impeachment, death, resignation, or disability. He favored instead the Chief Justice.

Hugh Williamson of North Carolina felt that Congress should have the power to designate successors and moved that the clause be postponed. John Dickinson of Delaware seconded him, remarking that the clause was too vague. "What," he asked, "is the extent of the term 'disability,' and who is to be the judge of it?" The Convention voted to postpone the clause, and when it was accepted in amended form two weeks later, Dickinson's questions about the possible disability of a President remained unanswered.

*   *   *

The linking of disability with impeachment, death, and resignation would prove to be a special embarrassment, for it left unanswered an additional question. If the President was disabled by illness for a time, would his designated sucessor become President for the rest of his term in office?

All of these questions were still unanswered 132 years later when President Woodrow Wilson suffered a stroke in 1919. It was, of all people, his wife who effectively made the decision that he should continue to function as President. Some said that, for all practical purposes, Mrs. Wilson was President for the first two weeks after the stroke, and that for the next six weeks she exerted more influence over the office than Wilson himself. Wilson, of course, survived and served out his term of office. The memory of that episode remained an uneasy one, but it took another forty-eight years and the assassination of President John F. Kennedy for the country to answer Dickinson's questions with finality.

In 1967, the Twenty-fifth Amendment to the Constitution was ratified. It separated the problem of Presidential disability from those of impeachment, death, and resignation and set up procedures to determine when a President was disabled and when the disability no longer existed. And it specified that the Vice President would serve during those periods as Acting President.

* * *

Before moving on to the provisions concerning the judiciary, the delegates accepted a suggestion by George Mason and James Madison to add to the President's oath of office. The Committee of Detail had proposed simply: "I solemnly swear (or affirm) that I will faithfully execute the office of President of the United States of America." To that were now added the words, "and will to the best of my judgment and power preserve, protect, and defend the Constitution of the United States." Even this would later be changed to read "to the best of my ability."

Turning, then, to the judiciary, the Convention, with remarkably little discussion or debate and only a few amendments, accepted the recommendations of the Committee of Detail. The judiciary would consist of a Supreme Court and such inferior courts as Congress chose to create. By the Convention's failure to mention it, the size of the Supreme Court was left to Congress. Judges would be appointed for life.

The jurisdiction of the national courts was spelled out in detail, though the extent to which it would exclude the jurisdiction of the state courts was, by omission, left to Congress to decide. All crimes except impeachment would be tried by jury in the state where they were committed. And the privilege of habeas corpus—the right to be brought before a court—could not be suspended unless a rebellion or invasion required it for the public safety.

By Tuesday, August 28, the Convention had reached the part of the draft constitution that spelled out restrictions on the states. By the time they had finished with it, the states were forbidden to coin money, emit bills of credit, or make anything but gold and silver a legal tender in payment of debts. The threat of state paper money was effectively crushed. In addition, states could not grant letters of marque and reprisal—licenses to private persons to plunder an enemy. They could not enter into treaties, alliances, or confederations, or grant titles of nobility. The Convention had previously forbidden the passing of bills of attainder and ex post facto laws by Congress. The states were now included in those bans.

Besides these outright prohibitions, the delegates agreed on a list of acts forbidden to the states without the consent of Congress. They could not, without such consent, tax imports or exports, keep troops or ships of war in time of peace, enter into agreements or compacts with other states or foreign powers, or engage in war unless invaded or threatened with invasion. Taken together, all of these provisions ended any question of the states acting as sovereign powers. They were, in effect, the Convention's substitute for James Madison's earlier plan for a congressional veto of state laws.

The next two provisions were quickly approved. The first gave citizens of each state all the privileges and immunities of citizens in other states. The second required states to return to each other fugitives from justice. Pierce Butler later moved to insert a clause requiring the return of fugitive slaves as well, and the Convention accepted it unanimously. With this provision, the bargain between the Northern and Southern states was sealed.

On Wednesday, the Convention struck several snags. First there was a provision of the draft constitution that read: "Full faith shall be given in each state to the acts of the legislatures and to the records and judicial proceedings of the courts and magistrates of every other state." Hugh Williamson wanted to know what it meant. James Wilson and William Samuel Johnson tried to explain. But when Charles Pinckney, James Madison, Edmund Randolph, and Gouverneur Morris all had ideas for changing it, both the provision and the various ideas were referred to a new committee for recommendations.

Next, the delegates returned to a committee recommendation made five days earlier that all references to navigation acts be dropped from the Constitution. Charles Pinckney immediately moved for a provision "that no act of the legislature for the purpose of regulating the commerce of the United States with foreign powers or among the several states shall be passed without the assent of two-thirds of the members of each House." This was, if anything, an expansion of the navigation act clause the committee had recommended dropping altogether. Since dropping it had been a part of the compromise over the slave trade and taxing imported slaves, Pinckney's motion, seconded by Luther Martin of Maryland, threatened the whole compromise.

Pinckney's colleague and cousin, General Pinckney, spoke against the motion. "It is the true interest of the Southern states to have no regulation of commerce," he admitted. "But considering the loss brought on the commerce of the Eastern states by the revolution, their liberal conduct toward the views of South Carolina, and the interest the weak Southern states have in being united with the strong Eastern states, I think it proper that no fetters should be imposed on the power of making commercial regulations. My constituents, though prejudiced against the Eastern states," he continued, "will be reconciled to this liberality. I had myself prejudices against the Eastern states before I came here, but I will acknowledge that I have found them as liberal and candid as any men whatever."

General Pinckney was for preserving the compromise. He was joined by his colleagues Pierce Butler and John Rutledge of South Carolina, Richard Spaight of North Carolina, and James Madison of Virginia. Only Edmund Randolph and George Mason of Virginia and Hugh Williamson of North Carolina, among the Southerners, spoke in favor of Charles Pinckney's motion.

Williamson acknowledged that he didn't think a two-thirds vote of both Houses of Congress to regulate commerce was necessary to protect Southern interests. He favored the proposal, however, because he knew the Southern people were apprehensive on the subject and would be pleased by the precaution.

But Mason and Randolph made it clear that they regarded the issue as a vital one. "If the government is to be lasting," Mason said, "it must be founded in the confidence and affections of the people and must be so constructed as to obtain these. The *majority* will be governed by their interests. The Southern states are the *minority* in both Houses. Is it to be expected," he asked, "that they will deliver themselves bound hand and foot to the Eastern states, and enable them to exclaim, in the words of Cromwell on a certain occasion, 'the lord hath delivered them into our hands'?"

Randolph went even further in his support of Charles Pinckney's motion. "There are," he said, "features so odious in the Constitution as it now stands that I doubt whether I shall be able to agree to it. A rejection of the motion will complete the deformity of the system."

When a vote was taken, Charles Pinckney's motion was defeated, and the Convention went on to drop all mention of navigation acts from the Constitution. Congress could regulate commerce by a simple majority of both Houses.

It took the rest of that day and all of the next to deal with the next four sections of the draft constitution. After much argument and a number of amendments, the delegates agreed that Congress could admit new states and would have power over territory belonging to the United States. With considerably less difficulty, the states were guaranted a republican form of government and protection against invasions. At the request of a state's legislature or executive, the Convention agreed, the United States would protect it against domestic violence as well.

Without debate, the delegates accepted a provision that "on the application of the legislatures of two-thirds of the states in the Union for an amendment of this Constitution, the legislature of the United States shall call a convention for that purpose."

Members of the legislatures and the executives and judges of the United States and of the states, the Convention agreed, would be bound by an oath or affirmation to support the Constitution. An amendment offered by Charles Pinckney and approved by the Convention added the provision that no religious test could ever be required as a qualification for holding national office.

Pinckney's amendment caused little discussion. Roger Sherman thought it was unnecessary, given the prevailing liberality of the people. Yet it represented a distinct change from the practice of the states. Every state constitution except those of New York and Virginia contained some kind of religious qualification for representatives in its state legislature. Thus, for example, in New Hampshire, New Jersey, both Carolinas, and Georgia, state representatives were required to be Protestants; in Massachusetts and Maryland, Christians; in Pennsylvania, Protestants with a belief in God and the divine inspiration of the Old and New Testaments; and in Delaware, believers in the Trinity and the divine inspiration of the Bible.

Nor was this a matter of concern to the Convention delegates alone. For on September 7, a week and a day after they adopted Charles Pinckney's proposal, Jonas Phillips, a Philadelphia Jew, wrote the Convention delegates urging them to do precisely what they had already done.

Finally, on that Thursday, August 30, the Convention took up a provision that read simply: "The ratifications of the conventions of——states shall be sufficient for organizing this Constitution." There was immediate argument over the number of states to be required, and the Convention adjourned without filling in the blank.

If the pace was quickening—and it was—it reflected the fact that the major compromises of the Convention were behind it. Now, there was impatience to finish the work and get home. And it was not just the delegates who were impatient. The *Pennsylvania Gazette* had carried a story the day before that suggested how the country at large was reacting: "Every enterprize, public as well as private, in the United States (says a correspondent) seems suspended till it is known what kind of Government we are to receive from our National Convention. The States neglect their roads and canals, till they see whether these necessary improvements will not become the objects of a National Government. Trading and manufacturing companies suspend their voyages and manufactures, till they see how far their commerce will be protected and promoted by a National system of commercial regulations. The lawful usurer locks up or buries his specie, till he sees whether the new Frame of Government will deliver him from the curse or fear of paper money and the tender laws. The wealthy farmer views a plantation with desire for one of his sons, but declines to empty his chest of his hard dollars for it, till he is sure it will not in a few years be taken from him by the enormous weight of State Governments and taxes. The public creditor, who, from the deranged state of finances in every State, and their total inability to support their partial funding systems, has reason to fear that his certificates will perish in his hands, now places all his hope of justice in an enlightened and stable National Government. The embarrassed farmer and the oppressed tenant, who wish to become free and independent by emigrating to a frontier county, wait to see whether they shall be protected by a National force from the Indians and by a National system of taxation from the more terrible pest of State and county tax gatherers. In short, the pulse of industry, ingenuity, and enterprize in every occupation of man now stands still in the United States, and every look and wish and hope is only *to* and every prayer to Heaven that has for its object the safety of your country is only *for*, the present august National Convention."

If the *Gazette's* correspondent was to be believed, the country was almost literally holding its breath.

13

The Presidency

*"We have in some revolutions of this plan
made a bold stroke for monarchy."*
EDMUND RANDOLPH to the Convention
September 5, 1787

August 31–September 7, 1787

On Friday, August 31, the Convention returned to the question of the ratification of the nearly completed Constitution. Before adjournment the day before, James Wilson had proposed that ratification by seven states should be sufficient to begin government under the new Constitution. Gouverneur Morris had thought there should be a smaller number if the ratifying states were contiguous than if they were dispersed. Roger Sherman opted for a minimum of ten states before considering the Constitution as having been adopted. Edmund Randolph suggested nine. Wilson, who moments before had proposed seven, now suggested eight. Pierce Butler was in favor of nine. Daniel Carroll of Maryland moved to require all thirteen, and Rufus King of Massachusetts seconded his motion. That was where the matter had stood at adjournment.

Now King moved successfully to add the words "between the said states" so that no matter what number of states was required to ratify the Constitution, they alone would be governed by it.

Gouverneur Morris moved to strike out ratification by state conventions, leaving the states to decide what means to use.

King declared that would be "equivalent to giving up the business altogether. Conventions alone, which will avoid all the obstacles from the complicated formation of the legislatures, will succeed."

Madison, who also strongly favored conventions, pointed out that "the powers given to the general government being taken from the state governments, the legislatures will be more disinclined" to ratify the Constitution than conventions. "The people," he said, "are in fact the fountain of all power, and by resorting to them all difficulties are got over. They can alter constitutions as they please."

Luther Martin, who had left no doubt where he stood on the Constitution, insisted on referring it to the state legislatures. "Think of the danger of commotions from a resort to the people," he said, in which the state "governments might be on one side and the people on the other." Then, to make sure no one felt he was concerned about his own state, he added, "I am apprehensive of no such consequences, however, in Maryland, whether the legislature or the people should be appealed to. Both of them will be generally against the Constitution."

When the vote was taken on Morris's motion to strike out the requirement of ratification by conventions, it was defeated, and the delegates eventually agreed that ratification by nine states would be sufficient to begin the new government.

Then, nearing the end of the draft constitution, the Convention took up a provision that the Constitution be placed before the existing Congress "for their approbation." Gouverneur Morris and Charles Pinckney moved to strike out the words "for their approbation." The motion carried, eight states to three. Without debate, the Convention that had begun by defying the injunction of Congress to meet "for the sole and express purpose of revising the Articles of Confederation" had now voted almost three to one to deny Congress even the right to approve a government designed to replace it.

Morris and Pinckney then moved to include a phrase urging the state legislatures to provide for the calling of conventions "as speedily as circumstances will permit." "My object," Morris said, "is to impress in stronger terms the necessity of calling conventions in order to prevent enemies to the plan from giving it the go-by. When it first appears, with the sanction of this Convention, the people will be favorable to it. By degrees, the state officers and those interested in the state governments will intrigue and turn the popular current against it."

Luther Martin, who as Attorney General of Maryland was of course a state officer, rose to reply. "I believe Mr. Morris is right," he said, "that after a while the people will be against it, but for a different reason from the one alleged. I believe they will not ratify it unless they are hurried into it by surprise."

Elbridge Gerry agreed. "The system is full of vices," he said. "We ought not to destroy the existing Confederation without the unanimous consent of the parties to it."

When Morris's and Pinckney's motion for speed was defeated, Gerry moved to postpone a vote on the whole provision to place the Constitution, first, before Congress, and next, before state conventions for ratification.

George Mason seconded him. "I would sooner chop off my right hand than put it to the Constitution as it now stands," Mason said. "I wish to see some points not yet decided brought to a decision before being compelled to give a final opinion on this article. Should these points be improperly settled, my wish would then be to bring the whole subject before another general convention."

That brought Gouverneur Morris to his feet. "I am ready for a postponement," he said sharply. "I have long wished for another convention that will have the firmness to provide a vigorous government, which we are afraid to do."

And that, in turn, brought a reply from Edmund Randolph, who had presented the Virginia Plan to the Convention in the first place. "My idea is," he said, "in case the final form of the Constitution should not permit me to accede to it, that the state conventions should be at liberty to propose amendments to be submitted to another general convention, which may reject or incorporate them as shall be judged proper."

If there was a groan from the delegates at the thought of yet another convention, James Madison did not record it. Yet the bitter complaints of Martin, Gerry, and Mason, and the equivocation of Randolph were not just grousings about specific provisions of the Constitution. They were, as the delegates were soon to learn, portents of trouble ahead.

Still, the Convention refused to postpone a vote on the amended section, and it was accepted, ten states to one. The sole vote against it was Maryland's. The Constitution would be submitted to Congress for transmittal to the states, which would then consider it in conventions.

At last, the Convention reached the final section, which suggested a means by which the Constitution might be put into operation. With a minor amendment, it was adopted.

Turning back, then, to the Maryland proposals to protect the port of Baltimore that had been referred to a committee of the states, the committee's proposal was accepted with a minor amendment. Added to the restrictions on the power of Congress, it now read: "Nor shall any regulation of commerce or revenue give preference to the ports of one state over those of another, or oblige vessels bound to or from any state to enter, clear, or pay duties in another. And all duties, imposts, and excises laid by the legislature shall be uniform throughout the United States."

Finally, on a motion by Roger Sherman, the Convention ducked the rest of its postponed problems by referring them to a new committee of the states. The committee was chosen, and the Convention adjourned for the day.

The new Committee on Postponed Matters must have gone to work at once, for by the next morning, Saturday, September 1, its chairman, New Jersey's David Brearley, had one item to report. After hearing that and a brief report from a committee headed by John Rutledge, the Convention adjourned for the weekend.

On Monday, September 3, the delegates went to work on two recommendations from a committee appointed on August

29. After minor amendments, they agreed that "full faith and credit shall be given in each state to the public acts, records, and judicial proceedings of every other state." They accepted also a proposal giving Congress power to establish uniform laws on bankruptcies.

Turning then to the first recommendation of the Committee on Postponed Matters, they put the final touches on a provision that had been debated and amended for weeks. As finally accepted, it prohibited members of Congress from simultaneously holding any other office in the national government, thereby ruling out any possibility of a parliamentary cabinet like those in Britain.

On Tuesday, September 4, the Committee on Postponed Matters reported nine recommendations, and the Convention scrambled to deal with them. Some involved minor changes or a tidying up of language, but the bulk of them dealt with the questions involving the President that had caused so much trouble.

Under the Committee's new plan, the President and a Vice President would serve four-year terms and be eligible for re-election. That much was simple and straightforward. The method devised by the Committee for electing them was neither.

Each state would appoint electors equal in number to its combined representation in both Houses of Congress. The state legislatures would decide how these electors were to be chosen. Each elector would then vote for two persons, only one of whom could be a resident of his own state. Finally, lists of all candidates thus nominated, together with the number of votes cast for each, would be sent from each state to the President of the Senate, who would supervise the count.

The person with the most votes, if they constituted a majority, would become President. If two or more candidates, each with a majority, were tied, the Senate would choose the President from among them. If no candidate had a majority, the Senate would choose the President from among the five candidates with the largest number of votes. Once the President had been selected, the person with the next highest number of votes would become Vice President. Here again, a tie would be settled by the Senate.

The complexity of the scheme, as every delegate surely understood, stemmed in part from the Convention's rejection of such simpler methods as direct election of the President by the people or by a joint session of Congress. But the Committee on Postponed Matters had also attempted, by involving the Senate in the process, to steer a political course midway between the interests of the large and small states. And as any delegate might have predicted, the Convention argued over virtually every aspect of the complicated proposal.

The debate continued for three entire days. Much of it was based on the assumption that electors would invariably vote for candidates from their own states, an assumption that had led the Committee to require electors to vote for two persons, one of whom came from another state. But that assumption, if correct, meant also that there would inevitably be a large number of candidates and hence a relatively slight chance that any of them would achieve a majority of the votes cast.

Nathaniel Gorham of Massachusetts had this in mind when he objected that, by this method, the Vice President might well turn out to be "a very obscure man with very few votes." Madison feared that by requiring both President and Vice President to be chosen from the five candidates with the most votes, the electors would tend to select candidates rather than genuine choices for the two offices.

George Mason was sure that nineteen times out of twenty the President would be chosen by the Senate, "an improper body for the purpose." Charles Pinckney agreed and added, "The electors will be strangers to the several candidates and of course unable to decide on their comparative merits." He also opposed a President eligible for reelection, which, he said, "will endanger the public liberty."

Abraham Baldwin thought the plan looked better the more

he considered it. "The increasing intercourse among the people of the states will render important characters less and less unknown, and the Senate will consequently be less and less likely to have the eventual appointment thrown into their hands." James Wilson and Edmund Randolph thought that eventual appointment ought to be by the entire legislature rather than just the Senate.

With nothing decided, the delegates took copies of the Committee's report to study when they adjourned.

The next day, Wednesday, September 5, the debate continued. Charles Pinckney again objected that electors would not know the men most fit to be President and "will be swayed by an attachment to the eminent men of their respective states." That, he said, would leave the appointment to the Senate, making the President "the mere creature of that body." As such, Pinckney predicted, the President would combine with the Senate against the House of Representatives. The proposed change in the method of electing the President, he said, had been intended to make it possible for him to be reelected without leaving him dependent on the legislature. Instead, Pinckney charged, "he will become fixed for life under the auspices of the Senate."

Pinckney's South Carolina colleague, John Rutledge, agreed and moved to return to the Convention's previous decision for election of the President by both Houses of Congress for a single seven-year term. When the delegates rejected this motion, eight states to two, the four-year term and eligibility for reelection became part of the Constitution.

*   *   *

And so it would remain for 164 years. The movement for change began on January 3, 1947, the opening day of the first Republican-controlled Congress since the initial election of Franklin D. Roosevelt to the presidency in 1932. On that day, with what many Americans felt was unseemly haste, Republican leaders in both Houses introduced a joint resolution calling for an amendment to the Constitution that would limit future Presidents to two terms in office.

A patently partisan reaction to Roosevelt's unprecedented election to four successive terms, the joint resolution received the unanimous vote of Republican members of both Houses. A House Democrat called it "a pitiful victory over a great man now sleeping on the banks of the Hudson." Though the joint resolution permitted seven years for ratification, the required three-fourths of the state legislatures had, by 1951, ratified what then became the Twenty-second Amendment to the Constitution.

*   *   *

The Convention, having decided the President's term of office and eligibility for reelection, turned again to the question of how to elect him. George Mason and Hugh Williamson, convinced that under the Committee's proposal the Senate would almost always make the final selection, moved to elect the candidate with the highest vote without requiring a majority. Their proposal was rejected.

Edmund Randolph, who three months earlier had opposed the very idea of a single executive as "the foetus of monarchy," rose now to oppose the entire proposal. "We have in some revolutions of this plan made a bold stroke for monarchy," he warned. "We are now doing the same thing for an aristocracy." Giving the Senate such an influence over the election of the President, in addition to its other powers, would tend, he said, "to convert that body into a real and dangerous aristocracy."

George Mason had calculated that with an initial Senate of twenty-six members and a quorum of only fourteen, it could take as few as eight Senators to prevail, and he now put his objections even more strongly. "As the mode of appointment is now regulated," he said, "I cannot forebear expressing my opinion that it is utterly inadmissible. I would prefer the Government of Prussia to one which will put all power in the hands of seven or eight men and fix an aristocracy worse than absolute monarchy."

The sole note made by Maryland's James McHenry provides an accurate summary of the day's progress: "The greatest part of the day spent in desultory conversation on that part of the report respecting the mode of choosing the President. Adjourned without coming to a conclusion."

On Thursday, September 6, they tried again. And finally, after much debate, Roger Sherman offered a solution. He moved that a tie or lack of a majority be settled, not by the Senate, but by the House of Representatives, with the Representatives of each state casting a single vote. With what must have been an audible sigh of relief, the Convention adopted the idea. The choice of the Vice President under similar circumstances would continue to be made by the Senate.

*   *   *

As it happened, there was a tie vote in the fourth presidential election in 1800, with Thomas Jefferson and Aaron Burr each receiving seventy-three electoral votes. And though both men had planned from the outset that Burr would be Jefferson's Vice President, voting in the House of Representatives went through thirty-six ballots before that outcome was finally achieved. Four years later, in 1804, the Twelfth Amendment to the Constitution was ratified, making such a tie impossible in the future. Electors would henceforth vote for President and Vice President in separate ballots.

*   *   *

On Friday, September 7, having finally decided how to elect the President, the delegates added a provision permitting Congress to decide what official would act as President in the event of the death, resignation, or disability of both the President and Vice President. They agreed that the President should be at least thirty-five years old, a resident of the United States for fourteen years, and either born in the United States or a citizen at the time the Constitution was adopted.

When they turned to the recommendation of the Committee on Postponed Matters that the Vice President serve as President of the Senate with the right to vote only to break a tie, Elbridge Gerry declared himself opposed. "We might as well put the President himself at the head of the legislature," he said. "The close intimacy that must subsist between the President and Vice President makes it absolutely improper. I am against having any Vice President." Ironically, Gerry would himself run successfully for that office in 1812, to serve until he died in 1814 as Vice President under James Madison.

Gouverneur Morris tried to disabuse Gerry of the notion that there would necessarily be a close intimacy between a President and his Vice President. If so, he said, the Vice President "will be the first heir apparent that ever loved his father." Roger Sherman also saw no such danger. And he saw an advantage. "If the Vice President were not to be President of the Senate, he would be without employment."

Hugh Williamson, who had served as a member of the committee that had made the recommendation, explained why the office of Vice President had been invented in the first place. "Such an officer as Vice President was not wanted," he said. "He was introduced only for the sake of a valuable mode of election of the President, which required two to be chosen at the same time." In the end, the Convention adopted the committee's recommendation, and a vice presidency was born out of all but thin air.

* * *

Many who would eventually occupy the office would come to agree with Roger Sherman's assessment that the Vice President was virtually "without employment." In 1960, when Democratic presidental candidate John F. Kennedy offered the second spot on his ticket to Lyndon Johnson, Johnson turned to a fellow Texan, John Nance Garner, for advice. Garner, who had served as Vice President under Franklin Roosevelt during his first two terms, had a pungent reply. "The Vice Presidency," he said, "isn't worth a pitcher of warm spit."

* * *

Moving on to the powers of the President, the Convention agreed that, by and with the advice and consent of the Senate, the President would have power to make treaties, appoint ambassadors and other public ministers and consuls, judges of the Supreme Court, and all other officers whose appointments were not provided for elsewhere in the Constitution. But there was a brief argument about a provision that no treaty could be made without the consent of two-thirds of the Senators present.

James Wilson objected to the two-thirds requirement, which, he said, "puts it in the power of a minority to control the will of a majority." Only Rufus King of Massachusetts spoke in agreement with him, and the delegates voted to retain the two-thirds requirement.

*　　*　　*

In 1919, 132 years later, this two-thirds requirement would figure dramatically in an angry confrontation between Senator Henry Cabot Lodge of Massachusetts and President Woodrow Wilson over the Treaty of Versailles and the League of Nations. Lodge, who was Majority Leader of the Senate when Wilson submitted the treaty for ratification, insisted on adding reservations to it. Wilson refused to compromise, and since Lodge controlled more than the number of votes needed to defeat ratification, the United States neither ratified the treaty nor joined the League of Nations.

*　　*　　*

With the end of their work in sight, it was inevitable that many of the delegates would begin to feel a kind of letdown. As the final shape of the Constitution became clear, there was also certain to be disillusionment. No delegate had won all that he wanted, and many had lost what they considered crucial points. Luther Martin, for one, had made no bones about his displeasure with the whole plan of government. He had left for Maryland three days earlier. Elbridge Gerry, George Mason, and Edmund Randolph had been equally outspoken.

Now, James Madison, in a letter to Thomas Jefferson in Paris, revealed his own gloomy feelings. "I hazard an opinion," he wrote, that the plan, "should it be adopted, will neither effectively answer its National object, nor prevent the local mischiefs which everywhere excite disgusts against the State Governments."

14

Last-Minute Changes

"After spending four or five months in the laborious and arduous task of forming a government for our country, we are ourselves at the close throwing insuperable obstacles in the way of its success."

JAMES WILSON to the Convention
September 10, 1787

September 8–12, 1787

On Saturday, September 8, the Convention turned to the proposal of the Committee on Postponed Matters for impeachment of the President. With little argument and only minor amendments, the delegates agreed that "He shall be removed from his office on impeachment by the House of Representatives and conviction by the Senate for treason or bribery or other high crimes and misdemeanors against the United States."

With no discussion at all, the Vice President and other civil officers of the United States were made subject to the same impeachment process. The Senate was given power to try all impeachments with the provision that "no person shall be convicted without the concurrence of two-thirds of the members present, and every member shall be on oath."

The Committee on Postponed Matters had also grappled with the much-argued provision on money bills, and, with a minor alteration, it was finally agreed that "All bills for raising revenue shall originate in the House of Representatives, but the Senate may propose or concur with amendments as in other bills."

* * *

For all the discussion of this provision and its inclusion as a presumed concession by the small states in the Great Compromise, it would in its final form prove to have a negligible effect in actual practice. Since the Senate can amend revenue bills of the House by substituting entirely new measures, its presence in the Constitution serves as little more than a reminder of a teapot tempest.

* * *

Finally, after providing that the President might convene either or both Houses of Congress on extraordinary occasions, the Convention chose a committee to revise the style and arrange the articles of the Constitution and adjourned for the weekend.

Whatever they thought individually about the Constitution they had turned over to the new Committee of Style, there was probably not a delegate who wasn't relieved that the work of creating it was all but over. On Sunday, September 9, young Jonathan Dayton of New Jersey wrote his father, General Elias Dayton, in words that undoubtedly echoed the feelings of many. "We have happily so far finished our business," he wrote, "as to be employed in giving it its last polish and preparing it for the public inspection. This, I conclude, may be done in three or four days, at which time the public curiosity and our desire of returning to our respective homes will be equally gratified."

But the work was not quite over. On Monday, September 10, while the Convention waited for the Committee of Style to complete its work, the delegates reconsidered the method of amending the Constitution they had adopted a week and a half earlier. It required Congress, on the request of two-thirds of the state legislatures, to call a convention for that purpose.

Elbridge Gerry was concerned that such a convention might act in such a way as to subvert the state constitutions. Alexander Hamilton felt, on the contrary, that the state legislatures would never apply for such a convention except to increase their powers. Congress, he thought, "will be the first to perceive and will be most sensible to the necessity of amendments and ought also to be empowered, whenever two-thirds of each branch should concur, to call a convention."

But the very idea of calling a convention to amend the Constitution worried James Madison, for a new convention might easily undo all of the laborious work of this one. Perhaps recalling the ease with which he and others had diverted this Convention from merely amending the Articles of Confederation, he expressed his concern about the vagueness of the terms "call a convention for that purpose." "How," he asked, "is a convention to be formed? By what rule will it decide? What will be the force of its acts?"

After efforts by Roger Sherman and James Wilson at drafting new language, Madison himself proposed what was in fact an entirely new provision—and one that eliminated any possibility of a new convention. Under it, Congress, by a two-thirds vote of both Houses or on the application of two-thirds of the state legislatures, would propose amendments. Ratification by three-fourths of the states would then render the amendments part of the Constitution.

At the insistence of John Rutledge of South Carolina, a clause was added forbidding amendments that would end the slave trade before 1808. That appeared to satisfy nearly everyone, and the provision was accepted, nine states to one. Madison had succeeded in eliminating any possibility of a new convention. Or so he thought.

Then, at the urging of Elbridge Gerry, Alexander Hamilton, and Edmund Randolph, the Convention agreed to reconsider the provision requiring ratification by only nine states to adopt the Constitution as well as the absence of any requirement for its approval by the Confederation Congress. Thomas

Fitzsimons of Pennsylvania pointed out that the requirement of approval by the Confederation Congress had been dropped, at least in part, to save its members from having to act against the very Articles under which they and the Congress held their authority. But Edmund Randolph was adamantly opposed to the way the provision stood.

"If no change is made in this part of the plan," he declared, "I shall be obliged to dissent from the whole of it. I have from the beginning been convinced that radical changes in the system of the Union are necessary. Under this conviction, I brought forward a set of republican propositions as the basis and outline of a reform. These republican propositions have, however, much to my regret, been widely and, in my opinion, irreconcilably departed from. In this state of things, it is my idea, and I accordingly mean to propose, that the state conventions should be at liberty to offer amendments to the plan and that these should be submitted to a second general convention with full power to settle the Constitution finally. I do not expect to succeed in this proposition, but the discharge of my duty in making the attempt will give quiet to my own mind."

Alexander Hamilton proposed submitting the Constitution to Congress and, if they approved it, to state conventions, which, if they also approved it, would then be asked to declare their approval of permitting nine assenting states to form a new Union. James Wilson had heard enough of this.

"It is necessary now," he said, "to speak freely." And so he did. "It is worse than folly to rely on the concurrence of the Rhode Island members of Congress in the plan," he pointed out. "Maryland voted on this floor for requiring the unanimous assent of the thirteen states to the proposed change in the federal system. New York," he continued, "has not been represented for a long time past in the Convention.

"Many individual deputies from other states have spoken much against the plan. Under these circumstances can it be safe to make the assent of Congress necessary? After spending four or five months in the laborious and arduous task of forming a government for our country, we are ourselves at the close throwing insuperable obstacles in the way of its success."

George Clymer agreed with his Pennsylvania colleague. So did Rufus King. "If the approbation of Congress be made necessary and they should not approve," King said, "the state legislatures will not propose the plan to conventions. Or if the states themselves are to provide that nine states shall suffice to establish the system, that provision will be omitted, everything will go into confusion, and all our labor will be lost."

John Rutledge agreed with King, and when Hamilton's proposal was put to a vote, it lost, ten states to one. The provision to require the ratification of only nine states was then unanimously approved. A motion to require the approval of Congress was unanimously defeated.

At that, Edmund Randolph rose to list his objections to the Constitution as it stood. He was opposed, he said, to the Senate's being made the court of impeachment of the President, to the need for three-fourths instead of two-thirds of each House of Congress to override a presidential veto, to the smallness of the House of Representatives, to the lack of a limit on the size of a standing army, to the power of Congress to pass "necessary and proper" laws.

He opposed the lack of a restraint on navigation acts, the power of the national government to put down domestic violence on the application of state executives. The list went on and on. "With these difficulties in my mind," he asked finally, "what course am I to pursue? Am I to promote the establishment of a plan which I verily believe will end in tyranny?

"I am unwilling to impede the wishes and judgment of the Convention, but I must keep myself free, in case I should be honored with a seat in the convention of my state, to act according to the dictates of my judgment. The only mode in which my embarrassments can be removed is that of submitting the plan to Congress, to go from them to the state legislatures, and from these to state conventions having the power to adopt, reject, or amend; the process to close with another gen-

eral convention with full power to adopt or reject the alterations proposed by the state conventions and to establish, finally, the government. Accordingly, I propose a resolution to
this effect."

Benjamin Franklin seconded Randolph's proposal. Before it
could be put to a vote, George Mason successfully urged that
it be tabled for a day or two to see what steps might be taken
to deal with Randolph's objections. For a Convention nearing
its end, it had been an exhausting and aggravating day.

On Tuesday, September 11, the delegates gathered at the
State House to learn that the Committee of Style had as yet
nothing to report. They adjourned until the next day. When
they returned on Wednesday, William Samuel Johnson, the
Committee chairman, presented the revised Constitution.
After it had been read, printed copies were ordered from
Dunlap and Claypoole, and the Convention settled down to
reconsider more of its earlier decisions.

Hugh Williamson, who had originally proposed that a
three-fourths vote of each House of Congress be required to
override a presidential veto, now felt it gave the President too
much power. He thought it should be changed to two-thirds.
That, of course, was one of the points Edmund Randolph had
made in listing his objections to the Constitution. Roger Sherman, Elbridge Gerry, George Mason, and Charles Pinckney
favored the change, while Gouverneur Morris, Alexander
Hamilton, and James Madison—all strong nationalists—opposed it. After a brief but vigorous debate, the change was
agreed to, six states to four, with one state divided.

Williamson next suggested a provision for jury trials in civil
cases. That led George Mason to express his wish that the plan
had been prefaced by a complete bill of rights. Since Mason
had been the author of Virginia's famous Declaration of
Rights, it must have been a matter of some curiosity to the
other delegates why he had waited so long to call for a national
equivalent. Even his way of suggesting it now was oddly dif-

fident. "I would second a motion if made for the purpose," he said. "It would give great quiet to the people, and with the aid of the state declarations, a bill might be prepared in a few hours."

When Elbridge Gerry moved for a committee to prepare a bills of rights, Mason, as promised, seconded the motion. Roger Sherman pointed out that the state declarations of rights were not repealed by the Constitution. He felt they were sufficient.

"The laws of the United States are to be paramount to the state bills of rights," Mason answered. Still, the vote against Gerry's motion was unanimous.

Mason might have been correct that it would take only a few hours to draw up a bill of rights, but no one who had been through the argument, bargaining, and compromise that had greeted far less controversial subjects could have believed that acceptance of the *language* of a bill of rights by the Convention would be an easy matter.

It was not as though the Convention had ignored the rights of individuals. The delegates had rejected property qualifications for voting and holding office. They had accepted the most liberal state qualifications for voting for members of the House of Representatives. They had prohibited religious tests for holding national office and had provided for jury trials in criminal cases, safeguards in the law of treason, a guarantee of the privilege of habeas corpus, and a guarantee to the states of a republican form of government. They had outlawed bills of attainder and ex post facto laws for both the national and state governments.

But there was another reason for the lack of interest in a formal bill of rights. The Constitution created a government of limited powers, and as Alexander Hamilton would put it later, "Why declare that things shall not be done, which there is no power to do?" It may well have been for all of these reasons that Mason's suggestion of a formal bill of rights was so tardy and so tentative.

* * *

In the end, though, George Mason would prove to be right about the American people's feelings on the subject. So strong was the sentiment for a bill of rights that five of the state conventions that ultimately ratified the Constitution did so with recommendations that amounted in some cases almost to demands that a bill of rights be added.

Thomas Jefferson, writing to Madison from Paris after receiving a copy of the Constitution, listed first the things he liked about it. "I will now add what I do not like," he wrote. "First the omission of a bill of rights . . . a bill of rights is what the people are entitled to against every government on earth, general or particular, and what no just government should refuse, or rest on inference."

Madison, who had been skeptical of the need for a bill of rights, was eventually persuaded, as he put it, that "the political truths declared in that solemn manner acquire by degrees the character of fundamental maxims of free government, and as they become incorporated with the national sentiment, counteract the impulses of interest and passion." Jefferson, whose arguments had been most effective in changing Madison's mind, suggested an additional reason for a bill of rights: "the legal check which it puts into the hands of the judiciary," to protect individual rights.

It would be Madison, as a member of the first House of Representatives, who was most responsible for the passage and ratification of the first ten amendments to the Constitution: the Bill of Rights. They became a part of the Constitution on December 15, 1791.

15

Agreement and Dissent

> *"On the whole, Sir, I cannot help expressing a
> wish that every member of the Convention who
> may still have objections to it would with me,
> on this occasion, doubt a little of his own infal-
> libility and, to make manifest our unanimity,
> put his name to this instrument."*
>
> BENJAMIN FRANKLIN to the Convention
> September 17, 1787

September 13–18, 1787

On Thursday, September 13, the printed copies of the Constitution prepared by the Committee of Style were ready, and
the Convention began its final inspection of the work of nearly
four months. What had been twenty-three articles had been
reduced by the Committee to seven, with two resolutions at
the end on ratification and the beginning of the new government. Gouverneur Morris later took much of the credit for the
final language of the document, and he probably deserves it.

Serving with him on the Committee of Style were William
Samuel Johnson, Alexander Hamilton, James Madison, and
Rufus King. Together, they managed to place before the delegates a Constitution that was succinct, polished, and written
with grace and style. In two instances, it went beyond the expressed wishes of the Convention.

The first was in the preamble. The preamble of the Committee of Detail had begun, "We the people of the states of," and had then listed all of the states. Now, since as few as nine states might begin the new government, that wording had been changed. The new preamble read: "We the people of the United States, in order to form a more perfect Union, establish justice, insure domestic tranquillity, provide for the common defense, promote the general welfare, and secure the blessings of liberty to ourselves and our posterity, do ordain and establish this Constitution for the United States of America." It was accepted without comment.

The second addition was one that Rufus King of Massachusetts had failed to convince the Convention to make some days earlier. Since King was on the Committee, it is a fair assumption that he persuaded his fellow committee members to include it. The Convention accepted it with a slight change of wording, and the Constitution now forbade the states to pass laws impairing the obligation of contracts. This prohibition, together with the one against state issuance of paper money, summed up nicely the Convention's reaction to the recent chaotic economic history of the states.

Even as the Constitution was read and reviewed this final time—a process that took most of three days—a large number of fairly small changes were made. On Friday, for example, a provision for the appointment of a treasurer by Congress was dropped, leaving the treasurer to be appointed, along with other officers, by the President.

On Saturday, September 15, there was a significant change. The methods of amending the Constitution so carefully crafted by James Madison to eliminate new conventions caught George Mason's eye, and he objected. Congress, he pointed out, would be involved in proposing all amendments to the states, either on its own or at the request of two-thirds of the state legislatures. "No amendments of the proper kind will ever be obtained by the people if the government should become oppressive, as I verily believe will be the case."

Gouverneur Morris and Elbridge Gerry proposed a solution.

They moved that on the application of two-thirds of the state legislatures, Congress would be required to call a convention to propose amendments. It was the very thing Madison had sought to avoid, and once again he pointed out the dangers. This time, however, he lost, and the Convention adopted the proposal.

* * *

In practice, this alternate means of amending the Constitution has thus far been of little significance. In all the years since its ratification, the Constitution has been amended only twenty-six times. The first ten amendments—the Bill of Rights—were adopted in 1791. Of the sixteen adopted since then, two concerned Prohibition, the first adopting, the second repealing it. Apart from the Bill of Rights, then, only fourteen of these later amendments remain in the Constitution.

All twenty-six of the amendments adopted have been proposed by Congress. Every attempt to amend by the second method—a convention resulting from the application of two-thirds of the state legislatures—has thus far fallen short of endorsement by the required number of states. Yet as this book goes to press, thirty-two state legislatures—just two short of the necessary two-thirds—have voted for a convention to propose an amendment mandating a balanced federal budget.

The actual calling of such a convention would, of course, immediately raise all of the questions James Madison asked in 1787: "How is a convention to be formed? By what rule will it decide? What will be the force of its acts?"

In 1788, when a second federal convention was being urged by opponents of the Constitution, Madison stopped asking questions and, in a letter to a fellow Virginian, gave his reasons for opposing another convention. Some of them might be considered applicable today.

"If a General Convention were to take place for the avowed and sole purpose of revising the Constitution," Madison wrote, "it would naturally consider itself as having a greater latitude than the Congress appointed to administer and support as well as to amend the system; it would consequently give greater agitation to the public mind; an election into it would be courted by the most violent partizans on both sides; it would probably consist of the most heterogeneous characters; would be the very focus of that flame which has already too much heated men of all parties; would no doubt contain individuals of insidious views, who under the mask of seeking alterations popular in some parts but inadmissible in other parts of the Union might have a dangerous opportunity of sapping the very foundations of the fabric. Under all these circumstances it seems scarcely to be presumable that the deliberations of the body could be conducted in harmony, or terminate in the general good. Having witnessed the difficulties and dangers experienced by the first Convention which assembled under every propitious circumstance, I should tremble for the result of a second. . . ."

Madison's fears of a second convention in the months immediately following the first one are, of course, most persuasive in the context of those times. To the extent that they are applicable today, it is probably as a warning of potential pitfalls. There are, as there were in 1787, no rules by which a new convention would be governed. It is even doubtful whether such rules, passed presumably by Congress, would be upheld by the Supreme Court as constitutional. Each state, as in 1787, would certainly choose its own delegates and determine the quorum of its delegation. But how? By the state legislature? By a nominating convention? By public election?

And whatever rules might conceivably be agreed on in advance by Congress and upheld by the Supreme Court, there seems little to prevent the delegates from proceeding according to the doctrine expressed by James Wilson at the original Convention: "I conceive myself authorized to *conclude nothing* but to be at liberty to *propose anything.*"

There being no precedent, there can be no real answers to what a new convention might or might not do. The only near-precedent—the original Convention—is hardly reassuring.

Convened "for the sole and express purpose of revising the Articles of Confederation," it created instead the plan of an entirely new government. A second "runaway convention" could, if it chose, presumably do likewise.

If, as seems more likely, a new convention simply recommended amendments, including the one for which it was specifically called, these proposed amendments would, of course, be subject to ratification by the required three-fourths—or thirty-eight—of the fifty states. Yet even here, what precedent exists is not reassuring. If, for example, the ratification process resembled that of the proposed amendments that eventually became the Bill of Rights, the state legislatures would pick and choose from the amendments proposed which to ratify and which to reject. In that earlier case, Congress recommended twelve; the states ratified ten.

Assuming a new convention went beyond the specific question of a balanced budget amendment to recommend the other proposed amendments currently making the rounds of the state legislatures—and there is nothing to prevent it—the states would find themselves presented with a shopping list of constitutional amendments on such explosive issues as abortion, busing, school prayer, limiting the terms of federal judges, and abolishing the income tax as well as a balanced federal budget. To imagine all or even several of these issues being debated in all fifty states at the same time, with each having the potential of becoming part of the Constitution, is to envision a period of public agitation so divisive that the process itself would likely become, to use Madison's words, "the very focus of that flame which has already too much heated men of all parties."

* * *

There was one further change in the article on amending the Constitution made by the Convention that Saturday, September 15. As written by the Committee of Style, the provision contained the exception demanded by John Rutledge forbidding amendments to end the slave trade before 1808. A second exception was now added to it. No state could be deprived of its equal representation in the Senate without its consent. As Madison jotted down in his notes: "This motion being dictated by the circulating murmurs of the small states was agreed to without debate, no one opposing it, or on the question, saying no."

Finally, the same Edmund Randolph who had opened the Convention with his presentation of the Virginia Plan now rose to oppose the result. As Madison reported it: "Mr. Randolph, animadverting on the indefinite and dangerous power given by the Constitution to Congress, expressing the pain he felt at differing from the body of the Convention on the close of the great and awful subject of their labors, and anxiously wishing for some accommodating expedient which would relieve him from his embarrassments, made a motion importing 'that amendments to the plan might be offered by the state conventions, which should be submitted to and finally decided on by another general convention.' Should this proposition be disregarded, it would, he said, be impossible for him to put his name to the instrument."

George Mason seconded the motion, adding his own comments on the dangerous power and structure of the proposed government. "It will end," he said, "either in monarchy or a tyrannical aristocracy." It was, he added, "improper to say to the people, 'take this or nothing.'" If Governor Randolph's motion were passed, however, he could sign.

Charles Pinckney probably summarized the feelings of most of the delegates when he followed the two Virginians with a brief speech of his own. "These declarations from members so respectable at the close of this important scene," he said, "give a peculiar solemnity to the present moment." Turning then to the consequences of seeking amendments from the various states, he concluded, "Nothing but confusion and contrariety could spring from the experiment. The states will never agree in their plans. And the deputies to a second convention, coming together under the discordant impressions of their constituents, will never agree. Conventions are serious things," he said, "and ought not to be repeated."

Elbridge Gerry then rose to enumerate *his* objections to the Constitution. The list was long, but the three most important, he said, were the power of Congress "to make what laws they may please to call necessary and proper," to raise armies and money without limit, and in a reference to the lack of a guarantee of trial by jury in civil cases, "to establish a tribunal without juries, which will be a star-chamber as to civil cases." He, too, supported the Randolph motion.

Put to a vote, the motion was defeated unanimously, eleven states to none. A motion to agree to the Constitution as amended was then approved by the same unanimous vote. And as James Madison noted, "The Constitution was then ordered to be engrossed. And the House adjourned."

It was six o'clock when the delegates finally left the State House that evening. They had sat for eight hours without food or drink in the longest session of the Convention. It was now September 15, four months and a day since the first dozen or so had turned up for what was to have been the Convention's opening day. They had come, that dozen and the forty-odd more who followed, to save their country from ills that were obvious to all. They had stayed—those who had—to erect a new and as yet invisible nation in its place, a nation of articles and sections, phrases and clauses: a nation of words.

The question of whether—or to what extent—this nation might actually work was one each delegate had asked himself repeatedly. Washington is said to have told another delegate he didn't expect the Constitution, if approved, to last more than twenty years.

But what was more remarkable than their doubts was their unspoken belief that a nation founded on words—on a written constitution—*might* work, that a people with diverse interests spread over a country as large as most of Europe might conceivably accept these words in the way that older countries accepted centuries of shared experience: as a fundamental basis of unity.

When the Convention assembled for the last time on Monday morning, September 17, copies of the Constitution, printed once again by Dunlap and Claypoole, were available for the delegates to read. The official document, engrossed by an anonymous penman on four sheets of the finest parchment, lay on the table before Washington. Someone—most likely the secretary, Major Jackson—read the engrossed copy to the forty-one delegates who were there at the end.

When the reading of the now familiar words was over, Benjamin Franklin rose with a written speech in his hand. James Wilson read it for him. "Mr. President: I confess that there are several parts of this Constitution which I do not at present approve," Franklin began, "but I am not sure I shall never approve them. For having lived long, I have experienced many instances of being obliged by better information or fuller consideration to change opinions, even on important subjects, which I once thought right but found to be otherwise. It is therefore that the older I grow, the more apt I am to doubt my own judgment and to pay more respect to the judgment of others."

Lest the doubters and nay-sayers—Randolph, Mason, and Gerry—begin to squirm with resentment, Franklin had diplomatically included a light touch. "Most men, indeed, as well as most sects in religion," Wilson read, "think themselves in possession of all truth, and that wherever others differ from them, it is so far error. Steele, a Protestant, in a dedication, tells the Pope that the only difference between our churches in their opinions of the certainty of their doctrines is, the Church of Rome is infallible and the Church of England is never in the wrong. But though many private persons think almost as highly of their own infallibility as of that of their sect, few express it so naturally as a certain French lady who, in a dispute with her sister, said, 'I don't know how it happens, Sister, but I meet with nobody but myself that's always in the right'—'*Il n'y a que moi qui a toujours raison.*'

"In these sentiments, Sir, I agree to this Constitution with all its faults, if they are such, because I think a general government necessary for us, and there is no form of government but what may be a blessing to the people if well administered, and believe farther that this is likely to be well administered for a course of years and can only end in despotism, as other forms have done before it, when the people shall become so corrupted as to need despotic government, being incapable of any other.

"I doubt, too, whether any other convention we can obtain may be able to make a better constitution. For when you assemble a number of men to have the advantage of their joint wisdom, you inevitably assemble with those men all their prejudices, their passions, their errors of opinion, their local interests, and their selfish views. From such an assembly can a perfect production be expected?

"It therefore astonishes me, Sir, to find this system approaching so near to perfection as it does; and I think it will astonish our enemies, who are waiting with confidence to hear that our councils are confounded like those of the builders of Babel, and that our states are on the point of separation only to meet hereafter for the purpose of cutting one another's throats.

"Thus I consent, Sir, to this Constitution, because I expect no better and because I am not sure that it is not the best. The opinions I have had of its errors, I sacrifice to the public good. I have never whispered a syllable of them abroad. Within these walls they were born, and here they shall die. If every one of us in returning to our constituents were to report the objections he has had to it and endeavor to gain partisans in support of them, we might prevent its being generally received and thereby lose all the salutary effects and great advantages resulting naturally in our favor among foreign nations as well as among ourselves from our real or apparent unanimity.

"Much of the strength and efficiency of any government in procuring and securing happiness to the people depends on opinion, on the general opinion of the goodness of the government, as well as of the wisdom and integrity of its governors. I hope, therefore, that for our own sakes, as a part of the people, and for the sake of posterity, we shall act heartily and unanimously in recommending this Constitution (if approved by Congress and confirmed by the conventions) wherever our influence may extend, and turn our future thoughts and endeavors to the means of having it well administered.

"On the whole, Sir, I cannot help expressing a wish that every member of the Convention who may still have objections to it would with me, on this occasion, doubt a little of his own infallibility and, to make manifest our unanimity, put his name to this instrument."

It was, as James McHenry of Maryland noted about the speech, "plain, insinuating, persuasive" and whatever the ultimate fate of the Constitution, "guarded the Doctor's fame." It was also pure Franklin: witty, wise, and disarming. But the speech was merely a preface to another bit of ingenuity, this one devised by Gouverneur Morris, for Franklin now moved that the Constitution be signed under the words: "Done in Convention, by the unanimous consent of the States present the 17th of September, etc. In witness whereof we have hereunto subscribed our names." A signer of this statement would be testifying solely to the fact that the states represented on the day of signing were unanimous in their acceptance of the Constitution.

Before the Convention could vote on Franklin's motion, Nathaniel Gorham of Massachusetts had a final change to urge on the Convention: that the maximum ratio of one Representative in the House for every 40,000 people be altered to one for every 30,000, thus permitting a somewhat larger House of Representatives. Rufus King of Massachusetts and Daniel Carroll of Maryland supported the idea, and Washington rose to put the question to a vote. Or so everyone thought. Instead, he made his first speech since his acceptance of the presidency of the Convention, a role he referred to immediately. "Although," he said, "my situation has hitherto restrained me from offering my sentiments on questions depending in the House, and, it might be thought, ought now to impose silence on me, yet I cannot forebear expressing my wish that the alteration proposed might take place.

"It is much to be desired that the objections to the plan recommended might be made as few as possible," he continued. "The smallness of the proportion of Representatives has been considered by many members of the Convention an insufficient security for the rights and interests of the people. I acknowledge that it has always appeared to me among the exceptionable parts of the plan, and late as the present moment is for admitting amendments, I think this of so much consequence that it would give me much satisfaction to see it adopted."

Adopted it was, unanimously. And with that single change, the Convention voted unanimously to accept the Constitution for signing.

Once more Edmund Randolph rose to explain why he would not sign and even, with an allusion to Dr. Franklin's remarks, to apologize for his refusal. Gouverneur Morris, who had perhaps heard this speech once too often, was blunt in reply. "I, too, have objections," he said, "but considering the present plan as the best that is to be obtained, I shall take it with all its faults. The majority has determined in its favor, and by that determination, I shall abide. The moment this plan goes forth, all other considerations will be laid aside, and the great question will be, shall there be a national government or not? This must take place, or a general anarchy will be the alternative."

Hugh Williamson of North Carolina spoke up. "For myself," he said, "I do not think a better plan is to be expected and have no scruples against putting my name to it."

Alexander Hamilton was anxious that every delegate should

sign. "A few characters of consequence, by opposing or even refusing to sign the Constitution," he said, "may do infinite mischief by kindling the latent sparks which lurk under an enthusiasm in favor of the Convention which may soon subside. No man's ideas are more remote from the plan than my own are known to be, but is it possible to deliberate between anarchy and convulsion on one side and the chance of good to be expected from the plan on the other?"

William Blount of North Carolina, who had not opened his mouth during the Convention, spoke now to say that while he would not have signed otherwise, he would sign in the manner proposed by Franklin. And Franklin, speaking this time for himself, assured Edmund Randolph that he had not been alluding to him in his earlier remarks. "I profess a high sense of obligation to you," he added, "for having brought forward the plan in the first instance and for the assistance you have given in its progress, and I hope that you will still lay aside your objections and by concurring with your brethren, prevent the great mischief which the refusal of your name may produce."

But Randolph's signature was not to be had, and the form of signing made no difference. "In refusing to sign the Constitution," he said, "I take a step which may be the most awful of my life, but it is dictated by my conscience, and it is not possible for me to hesitate, much less to change."

And finally, Elbridge Gerry rose to reiterate his objections and express his fears that the Constitution in its present form would kindle what he saw as incipient civil war, if not in the country as a whole, at least in Massachusetts. "As for the remarks of Doctor Franklin," he said, "I cannot but view them as leveled at myself and the other gentlemen who mean not to sign."

Put to a vote, Franklin's form of signing was approved. The *Journal* of the Convention kept by Major Jackson was placed in Washington's custody, subject to the order of the new Congress if, as the resolution had it, "ever formed under the Constitution." The injunction of secrecy was then rescinded, and the delegates lined up to sign the Constitution they had created.

As they moved slowly forward to sign in the North to South order in which the many votes had been taken—New Hampshire, Massachusetts, Connecticut—those who had signed moved back to their places. When the last few were signing, Benjamin Franklin turned to the delegates nearest him. Indicating the painting of the sun on the back of the chair that Washington had occupied in presiding over the Convention, he said, "Painters have found it difficult to distinguish in their art a rising from a setting sun. I have often and often in the course of the session and the vicissitudes of my hopes and fears as to its issue, looked at that sun behind the President without being able to tell whether it was rising or setting. But now, at length," he added, "I have the happiness to know that it is a rising and not a setting sun."

With the ink still wet on the parchment, the delegates gave unanimous approval to a resolution drafted by the Committee of Style that the Constitution be presented to the Confederation Congress together with the opinion of the Convention that it should be submitted to state conventions for ratification. A second resolution, adopted with the first, recorded the Convention's opinion that, on ratification by nine states, the Confederation Congress should arrange for elections of the President and members of the House and Senate who should then "without delay proceed to execute this Constitution."

James Madison scribbled a final note: "The Constitution being signed by all the members except Mr. Randolph, Mr. Mason, and Mr. Gerry, who declined giving it the sanction of their names, the Convention dissolved itself by an adjournment sine die."

They left the State House for the last time at about four o'clock that afternoon. The thirty-eight who had signed—and most likely the three who had not—walked the few blocks to the City Tavern where a farewell dinner had been arranged.

There was, in fact, a thirty-ninth signature on the document left in the custody of Major Jackson. John Dickinson, tired and ill, had left Philadelphia over the weekend, but he had taken the precaution of asking his Delaware colleague, George Read, to sign for him. It was at dinner at the City Tavern that, as Washington noted in his diary, the delegates "took a cordial leave of each other."

That evening, Washington returned to his lodgings at Robert Morris's house. There, Major Jackson turned over the *Journal* to him. Later, Washington noted, he "retired to meditate on the momentous work which had been executed."

Early the next morning, Major Jackson left Philadelphia by stage to present the Constitution to Congress in New York. Accompanying it was a letter, addressed to the President of Congress and signed by George Washington, approved by the Convention the previous week. Drafted by a committee composed of Gouverneur Morris, Benjamin Franklin, and Jared Ingersoll, all members of the Pennsylvania delegation, it set forth in diplomatic and conciliatory language the reasons for the Convention's decision to draw up a plan for a whole new government:

"The friends of our country have long seen and desired that the power of making war, peace, and treaties, that of levying money and regulating commerce, and the correspondent executive and judicial authorities should be fully and effectually vested in the general government of the Union: but the impropriety of delegating such extensive trust to one body of men is evident. Hence results the necessity of a different organization.

"It is obviously impracticable in the federal government of these states to secure all rights of independent sovereignty to each, and yet provide for the interest and safety of all. Individuals entering into society must give up a share of liberty to preserve the rest. The magnitude of the sacrifice must depend as well on situation and circumstance as on the object to be obtained. It is at all times difficult to draw with precision the line between those rights which must be surrendered and those which may be reserved; and on the present occasion, this difficulty was increased by a difference among the several states as to their situation, extent, habits, and particular interests.

"In all our deliberations on this subject we kept steadily in our view that which appears to us the greatest interest of every true American: the consolidation of our Union, in which is involved our prosperity, felicity, safety, perhaps our national existence. This important consideration, seriously and deeply impressed on our minds, led each state in the Convention to be less rigid on points of inferior magnitude than might have been otherwise expected; and thus the Constitution which we now present is the result of a spirit of amity and of that mutual deference and concession which the peculiarity of our political situation rendered indispensable.

"That it will meet the full and entire approbation of every state is not perhaps to be expected; but each will doubtless consider that had her interest alone been consulted, the consequences might have been particularly disagreeable or injurious to others; that it is liable to as few exceptions as could reasonably have been expected, we hope and believe; that it may promote the lasting welfare of that country so dear to us all, and secure her freedom and happiness, is our most ardent wish."

16

Federalists and Antifederalists

". . . to say, as many do, that a bad govern-
ment must be established, for fear of anarchy,
is really saying, that we must kill ourselves, for
fear of dying."

RICHARD HENRY LEE
to EDMUND RANDOLPH
October 16, 1787

September 19–November 20, 1787

The fifty-five men who had taken part in the Convention had spent nearly four months doing what they could to create a plan of government suited, in the words of Charles Pinckney, "to the habits and genius of the people it is to govern." By avoiding offensive words and leaving the Constitution silent on some controversial issues, they had tried, as Gouverneur Morris said later, to make it "as palatable as possible" to those people. Now the time had come to find out what the American people thought of the result.

To help make sure it actually reached them, nine of the signers who were also members of Congress followed Major Jackson to New York to shepherd their creation through that body. The Constitution was laid before Congress on September 20, just three days after the Convention adjourned. By the time it came up for consideration on the twenty-sixth, the nine signers—Langdon and Gilman of New Hampshire, Gorham and King of Massachusetts, Johnson of Connecticut, Madison of Virginia, Blount of North Carolina, Butler of South Carolina, and Few of Georgia—had arrived and taken their seats in Congress. A tenth delegate-Congressman, William Pierce of Georgia, who had left the Convention early, was there to greet them.

Though the Philadelphia contingent would comprise almost a third of the thirty-three members of Congress in attendance, they expected trouble. They found it chiefly in the person of Richard Henry Lee of Virginia. Lee, who like Patrick Henry had declined to be a delegate to the Convention, had heard from George Mason about his objections to the Constitution, and he agreed with them.

In two days of debate, Lee first attempted to amend the Constitution before submitting it to the states. Only a small minority supported him. A majority sought a vigorous endorsement of the Constitution as it stood. Madison, knowing Virginia's prickly sensitivity to advice from Congress, hoped for a unanimous resolution, however mild its endorsement. The final compromise was a unanimous referral to the states with no endorsement whatever. On September 28, the Constitution went out from New York to the thirteen state legislatures.

Meanwhile it had reached the people through newspapers, pamphlets, and a flurry of excited discussion. Published first in the *Pennsylvania Packet* by Dunlap and Claypoole, who had become all but official printers to the Convention, it was rapidly reprinted throughout the country. The several hundred extra copies printed earlier for the delegates were also sent quickly on their way by post, packet boat, and transatlantic sailing ship to friends and correspondents everywhere. Washington sent copies off to Jefferson and Lafayette; Franklin, to friends in England, France, and Italy.

The argument began almost at once: first, and unofficially, in letters, pamphlets, newspapers, conversations, and even tavern harangues; next, and officially, in thirteen separate ratifying conventions held between November 21, 1787, and May 29, 1790, in thirteen still-sovereign states. To those engaged in it, it seemed a debate that could ultimately be decided either way.

Supporters of the Constitution entered the struggle with a number of distinct advantages. First, the Constitution came to the people from as distinguished a group of Americans as had ever met in one place. Signed by both of the country's preeminent heroes—Washington and Franklin—it carried endorsements of overwhelming potency.

The leadership of the proratification forces in every state was likewise drawn from what could only be called the continental elite. Prestigious and powerful Convention delegates like Madison, Hamilton, Wilson, Langdon, and Rutledge were joined by equally influential nationalists who had not attended, men like John Jay of New York, Edmund Pendleton of Virginia, and John Sullivan of New Hampshire.

Then, too, the supporters of ratification had the positive side of the argument; they had a proposal, a program to save the Union. It did not hurt that they had also determined the rules by which it would be settled: by state conventions that bypassed the state legislatures and could either accept or reject but not revise the plan. When the proponents managed to pre-empt the designation "Federalist" for themselves, they automatically left for their opponents the negative label of "Antifederalist."

The Federalists had the additional advantage of being united behind a single goal: ratification by nine states, including, if possible, Massachusetts, New York, Pennsylvania, and Virginia. Rejection by any one of these large states might well prove fatal. Antifederalists, on the other hand, differing widely in their objections to the Constitution, could at best unite only in demands for amendment, a second convention, or outright rejection.

Still, the Antifederalists were not without resources and their own cadre of leaders of integrity, ability, and character. As Madison himself wrote to a fellow Virginian, "I am truly sorry to find so many respectable names on your list of adversaries to the Federal Constitution." Among those adversaries would be Elbridge Gerry, James Winthrop, Samuel Adams, Benjamin Austin, James Warren, and Nathan Dane of Massachusetts; Governor George Clinton, John Lansing, Jr., John Lamb, Melancton Smith, and Robert Yates of New York; George Bryan of Pennsylvania; Luther Martin, John Francis Mercer, William Paca, Jeremiah T. Chase, and Samuel Chase of Maryland; Patrick Henry, Benjamin Harrison, George Mason, William Grayson, James Monroe, and Richard Henry Lee of Virginia; Willie Jones of North Carolina, Rawlins Lowndes, Patrick Calhoun, and Aedanus Burke of South Carolina. It was a formidable list.

On October 4, George Mason published his extensive objections to the Constitution in the *Pennsylvania Packet*. Six days later, Governor Edmund Randolph submitted a lengthy explanation of his refusal to sign to Virginia's House of Delegates. When Elbridge Gerry presented the Massachusetts legislature with a statement of his reasons for not signing, Americans in all thirteen states had been provided with reasons aplenty for delay, revision, or even rejection. While the objections of the three nonsigners differed from one another, both Mason and Gerry decried the lack of a bill of rights. All three insisted that without amendment before adoption, the Constitution threatened American liberties.

The major strategy of the Antifederalists quickly became an attempt to delay adoption. Maryland's Luther Martin had all but suggested this in the Convention itself when he said of the American people, "I believe they will not ratify it unless they are hurried into it by surprise."

Surprise—or at least haste—was precisely what Pennsylvania Federalists had in mind when, on September 28, before official word of the transmittal of the Constitution to the states had been received, former Convention delegate George Clymer pushed through the state assembly a motion for a vote to call a state ratifying convention. Antifederalists, outnumbered in the assembly, boycotted the afternoon session, when the vote was scheduled to be taken. Deprived of a quorum, the Federalists angrily adjourned until the next day.

The next morning, news of the action of Congress reached Philadelphia by express rider. With the Antifederalists still boycotting the assembly, the sergeant at arms located two of them. When they refused to attend, Federalist sympathizers dragged them through the streets to the State House. With a bare quorum, the assembly voted that delegates to the state ratifying convention would be elected on the first Tuesday in November. The Antifederalists promptly published an "Address of the Sixteen Seceding Members of the Legislature of Pennsylvania," which charged the majority with strong-arm tactics and criticized the Constitution for its lack of a bill of rights and of a prohibition of standing armies. The Federalists fired back on October 6 when James Wilson addressed a public meeting in the State House Yard in a speech widely distributed throughout the country.

Ten days later, on October 16, in a public letter to Governor Edmund Randolph, Richard Henry Lee in effect urged amendment. If the Constitution, he wrote, "be found good after mature deliberation, adopt it: if wrong, amend it at all events: for to say, as many do, that a bad government must be established, for fear of anarchy, is really saying, that we must kill ourselves, for fear of dying."

On October 27, the first of what would eventually be eighty-five letters over the pseudonym "Publius" was published in New York newspapers. Actually written by Alexander Hamilton, James Madison, and John Jay and known collectively as *The Federalist Papers*, the letters were in fact a series of essays explaining and defending the Constitution. Less than two weeks later, on November 8, the *New York Journal* advertised the first of two pamphlets, ultimately consisting of eighteen *Letters from the Federal Farmer* and later (and possibly wrongly) attributed to Richard Henry Lee.

Each publication, in its own way, became a classic: the

Letters from the Federal Farmer, as an able and moderate statement of the Antifederalist position; *The Federalist Papers*, as a masterpiece of thinking about federal government and the Constitution, which has become almost a companion piece to the Constitution itself. *The Federal Farmer* had the greater influence at the time, in part because the last of *The Federalist Papers* did not appear in newspapers until August 1788, with letters dealing with the most hotly contested parts of the Constitution appearing after most of the state conventions had already met. Nor did *The Federalist Papers* make for easy reading. As a correspondent wrote to North Carolina Federalist James Iredell of "Publius," "He is certainly a judicious and ingenious writer, though not well calculated for the common people."

There were, inevitably, less statesmanlike publications on both sides of the argument. Oliver Ellsworth, under the pseudonym "The Landholder," took to the press to impugn George Mason's motives in having opposed a continuation of the slave trade: "Mr. Mason has himself about three hundred slaves, and lives in Virginia, where it is found by prudent management they can breed and raise slaves faster than they want for their own use, and could supply the deficiency in Georgia and South Carolina; and perhaps Col. Mason may suppose it more humane to breed than import slaves."

Ellsworth attacked Elbridge Gerry for having moved in the Convention that the new government redeem old continental paper money. "As Mr. Gerry was supposed to be possessed of large quantitites of this species of paper," Ellsworth charged, "his motion appeared to be founded in such barefaced selfishness and injustice, that . . . the rejection of it by the Convention inspired the author with an utter rage and intemperate opposition to the whole system he had formerly praised." In fact, as Gerry replied, he had made no such motion.

When Luther Martin defended Gerry, Ellsworth, still in the disguise of "The Landholder," let fly at him. Describing Martin's rambling two-day convention speech as a "specimen of eternal volubility," Ellsworth charged among other things that "You, alone, advocated the political heresy, that the people ought not to be trusted with the election of representatives." In fact, of course, Ellsworth's Connecticut colleague, Roger Sherman, had been the first delegate in the Convention to speak against this provision, and Gerry, Butler, General Pinckney, and Rutledge had all opposed it at various times.

Martin, who had already urged the Maryland Assembly "to reject those chains which are forged for it" in a speech as voluble as anything the Convention had endured, now took on "The Landholder" in some ten thousand words. Since the entire three-cornered debate involving Gerry, Martin, and Ellsworth was widely reprinted, it was argued, in effect, with the entire country as an audience.

In the heat of the political battle that all but engulfed the United States in the aftermath of the Convention, two stereotypes quickly emerged. Antifederalists, according to the standard Federalist charge, were "men who have lucrative and influential state offices," "tories, debtors in desperate circumstances, or insurgents," believers in paper money and tender acts, to cite Oliver Ellsworth's descriptions. Washington himself wrote privately that acceptance of the Constitution by a great majority of the people was not to be expected "because the importance and sinister views of too many characters, will be affected by the change."

Federalists, in the typical Antifederalist characterization, were holders of public offices, bankers, lawyers, or members of the Society of Cincinnati bent on creating an American aristocracy. As with all stereotypes, the truth was more complex. Madison, for his part, saw the division as "a melancholy proof of the fallibility of the human judgment and of the imperfect progress yet made in the science of government." Nothing, he wrote from New York on October 30, was more common there "than to see companies of intelligent people equally divided and equally earnest in maintaining, on the one side, that the General Government will overwhelm the State Governments, and, on the other hand, that it will be a prey to their encroachments. . . ."

The *Federal Farmer* saw the political agitation as stemming from "two very unprincipled parties," one "composed of little insurgents, men in debt, who want no law, and who want a share of the property of others . . ." while the other was made up of "a few, but more dangerous men, with their servile dependents; these avariciously grasp at all power and property . . . dislike . . . free and equal government, and they go systematically to work to change, essentially, the forms of government in this country. . . ." Between the two parties, he maintained, was "the weight of the community: the men of middling property, men not in debt on the one hand, and men, on the other, content with republican governments, and not aiming at immense fortunes, offices and power." The two "unprincipled" parties were, he said, "really insignificant, compared with the solid, free, and independent part of the community."

Antifederalism had not simply appeared on the American scene as a result of opposition to the Constitution. The sentiments it represented had been growing ever since the Declaration of Independence. In essence, its roots were in the status quo, in the United States that had taken shape in the brief period that began with the Revolution and with the memory of what had led up to it.

In 1787, when the Constitution was laid before the American people, all of them above the age of eleven had spent some part of his life under a British King and Parliament, had been a British subject, or at least subject to British rule. They had lived through a war fought for freedom of the individual and of the states, for republican government, and against what they saw as the tyranny of rule by a distant, powerful, and highly centralized government in which they had no representation. Now, as many saw it, they were being asked after only the briefest of experiments with republican rule in an alliance of thirteen sovereign states to give it up for something "so new, it wants a name," as Patrick Henry put it. The nameless something, he charged "must be one great, consolidated, national government, of the people of all the states."

The older they were—the more adult experience they had had under British rule and their country's reaction to it—the more inclined Americans were to question the new plan of government. It is not insignificant that the leaders of the Antifederalist movement were generally older than their Federalist counterparts. Samuel Adams was sixty-five; George Mason, sixty-one; Richard Henry Lee, fifty-seven; George Bryan, fifty-six; Patrick Henry, fifty-one; Robert Yates, forty-nine; George Clinton, forty-eight; Samuel Chase, forty-six; and Elbridge Gerry and Luther Martin, both forty-three. James Madison, Rufus King, James McHenry, Alexander Hamilton, Charles Pinckney, William R. Davie, Gouverneur Morris, and Oliver Ellsworth—all Federalists and all Convention delegates—were all under thirty-eight.

Being in general older, it is not surprising that the Antifederalist leadership was also more conservative. Antifederalists often portrayed the issue as one of brash young Federalists jettisoning accepted forms and basic principles for innovations that threatened political stability, established law, the principles of the Declaration of Independence, and Federalism itself, as they had understood it. The ideas of the Antifederalists, in this view, were the accepted ideas of the times. It was the notions of the Federalists that were radical, new, untested, and potentially dangerous.

There were other basic divisions between the contending parties. One was geographical. Federalist power was located mostly in the settled, eastern sections of the states. Antifederalism was generally strongest in the backcountry and frontier areas, regions that had been underrepresented in the Convention. Far from the centers of political power in their own states, backcountry Americans saw themselves as certain to be even more remote from the seat of some new national government.

Independent, interested mostly in local affairs, inclined to be jealous of the more settled East and antagonistic to its cultural pretensions, far from the main sources of information, Westerners in many states were, not surprisingly, more likely to oppose than to favor the Constitution and the new government it described.

Antifederalists had at least one advantage over Federalists in the wide-ranging struggle over the Constitution. For while Federalists were forced to defend the plan as a whole, Antifederalists were free to pick and choose provisions they opposed. Planters in South Carolina and Georgia could point with alarm to the failure to give full and complete security to slavery. Opponents of the slave trade, North and South, could decry its legal extension for twenty years.

But if there was an overriding fear that united Antifederalists, it was of the imposition on the country of a powerful, centralized government. John Lansing, Jr., of New York was only one of hundreds who expressed the belief that "a consolidated government, partaking in a great degree of republican principles, and which had in object the control of the inhabitants of the extensive territory of the United States, by its sole operations could not preserve the essential rights and liberties of the people." It was, of course, the same doctrine Madison had argued against in the Convention, but it had a basis not only in Montesquieu's political preachments but in sectional fears and distrusts as well.

No one who had witnessed the clash of the small and large states, of the Northern and Southern states in the Convention; no one who had heard the debate over the terms of admission of new Western states, or who remembered the fears of Maryland's delegates that ships bound for Baltimore might be charged duties by Virginia—no one, in short, who had attended the Convention could doubt that Gunning Bedford, Jr.'s cry, "I do not, gentlemen, trust you," was a sentiment that lurked in many an American's heart when confronted by Americans of another state or section of the country. General

Pinckney had admitted as much for himself when he confessed to having harbored prejudices against New Englanders.

It was another South Carolinian, Christopher Gadsden, who in 1765, more than twenty years earlier, declared after the New York Stamp Act Congress, "There ought to be no New England man, no New Yorker . . . but all of us Americans." That this was a wish still unfulfilled in 1787 can be seen from just two of many similar comments made during the ratification struggle. Rawlins Lowndes, a South Carolina Antifederalist, characterized New Englanders as men "governed by prejudices and ideas extremely different from ours." Massachusetts Antifederalist James Winthrop spoke of "the idle and dissolute inhabitants of the South" in contrast to "the sober and active people of the North."

Sectional distrusts and prejudices were supplemented by the wild and reckless charges hurled between the contesting parties. A Philadelphia Antifederalist's letter widely circulated in newspapers listed as the blessings of the proposed Constitution: "1. The Liberty of the Press abolished. 2. A standing army. 3. A Prussian Militia. 4. No annual elections. 5. Fivefold taxes. 6. No trial by jury in civil cases. 7. General Search Warrants. 8. Excise laws, customs house officers, tide and land waiters, cellar rats, etc. 9. A free importation of negroes for one and twenty years. 10. Appeals to the Supreme Continental Court, where the rich may drag the poor from the furthermost parts of the continent. 11. Election for Pennsylvania held at Pittsburgh, or perhaps Wyoming. 12. Poll taxes for our heads, if we chose to wear them. 13. And *death* if we dare complain."

Federalists retorted with a parody of the accusations to be found in a typical Antifederalist essay, listing as the ingredients: "Well-born, nine times—Aristocracy, eighteen times—Liberty of the Press, thirteen times repeated—Liberty of Conscience, once—Negro slavery, once mentioned—Trial by Jury, seven times—Great Men, six times repeated—Mr. Wilson, forty times, and lastly George Mason's Right Hand in a Cutting box, nineteen times. Put them all together and dish them up at pleasure. These words will bear boiling, roasting or frying—and what is remarkable of them, they will bear being served, after being once used, a dozen times to the same table and palate."

17

Ratification

*"The people who are the authors of this bless-
ing must also be its guardians."*
JAMES MADISON in
the National Gazette
February 6, 1792

November 21, 1787–December 15, 1791

The fierce struggle over the adoption of the Constitution finally reached its climax in the ratification conventions of the
thirteen states. If the men who had drafted the document had
been among the most distinguished of those states, the men
who now gathered to consider their work included farmers,
craftsmen, preachers, tradesmen, and local politicians. Here, at
last, in thirteen open conclaves, the people, whose name had
been so often invoked during the Philadelphia Convention,
would make the ultimate judgment.

The Pennsylvania convention, with Federalists holding a
two-to-one majority, met on November 21, 1787, in the State
House chamber where the Constitution had been drafted. Perhaps because the result was never in doubt, the Federalists
made few attempts to rush a decision.

Pennsylvania Antifederalists opposed ratification chiefly on
the grounds that the Convention had exceeded its authority,
that the Constitution lacked a bill of rights, and that the sovereignty of the states would be destroyed. When news arrived
that Delaware, in a convention lasting only five days, had

unanimously ratified the Constitution on December 7, John Smilie, a leading Pennsylvania Antifederalist, said that Delaware had "reaped the honor of having first surrendered the liberties of the people." On December 12, the Pennsylvania convention followed Delaware's lead, ratifying the Constitution by a vote of 46 to 23. Pennsylvania Antifederalists, clearly hoping to influence the outcome in other states, promptly published their "Reasons for Dissent."

By January 9, 1788, when the Massachusetts convention began in Boston, three more states had ratified: New Jersey and Georgia, unanimously, and Connecticut, by a vote of 128 to 40. Massachusetts Federalists were slightly outnumbered when their convention opened, but before it had run its month-long course, two significant opponents had been won over and a formula for compromise on amendments had been found.

Samuel Adams, who at first opposed the Constitution, was convinced he should support it by a mass meeting of Federalist mechanics and tradesmen engineered by Paul Revere. Governor John Hancock, who had refused to commit himself, was persuaded to join the Federalist cause by hints that if Virginia did not ratify, which seemed possible, he would remain the "only fair candidate for President." Hancock, who had been elected president of the convention, then presented a Federalist formula of ratifying the Constitution without conditions but urging amendments. On February 6, 1788, when the convention voted for ratification by the thin margin of 187 to 168 and recommended amendments, Massachusetts became the sixth of the nine states necessary for adoption.

The Virginia convention met on June 2, 1788, with the knowledge that two additional states had ratified. In Maryland, the issue had been decided in the election of delegates to the convention. Voters, enthusiastically in favor of the Constitution, ignored the dire warnings of Luther Martin and John

Francis Mercer to elect a convention that took just five days to ratify by the lopsided vote of 63 to 11. South Carolina had devoted ten days to its deliberations and then ratified by a vote of 149 to 73 to become the eighth state to approve the Constitution.

New Hampshire had begun its convention in February, but when a large number of delegates showed up with instructions to reject the Constitution, the Federalists succeeded in adjourning until June 17. The Virginians, opening their convention two weeks before that date, were fully aware that a prior ratification by New Hampshire would fulfill the nine-state requirement for organizing the government under the new Constitution. Virginians being Virginians, however, were equally aware that a United States that excluded their powerful state would be as unworkable as it was, to them, unthinkable.

The Virginia convention was about evenly divided between friends and opponents of the Constitution. Antifederalists received a shock on the first day of actual debate when Governor Randolph, responding to a speech by Patrick Henry, announced his defection to the Federalist cause. Reviewing his reasons for refusing to sign the Constitution and maintaining that he would do it again under the same circumstances, he declared that its subsequent ratification by eight states had radically altered those circumstances. The question now was whether or not there would be a Union. The Union "is the anchor of our political salvation; and I will assent to the lopping of this limb," he said, indicating his arm, "before I assent to the dissolution of the Union."

The debate lasted until June 25, with Patrick Henry, at the height of his oratorical powers, contributing roughly a fifth of the words. His description of Randolph's apostasy as "strange and unaccountable," his assumption that "something extraordinary must have operated so great a change in his opinions," and a sharp exchange between the two men almost led to a duel. There were less acerbic words from George Mason, William Grayson, and James Monroe, on the Antifederalist side, and James Madison, George Nicholas, Henry Lee, and John Marshall, for the Federalists.

When the vote finally came, the Constitution was ratified, 89 to 79, and, following the Massachusetts model, amendments were recommended. It was only after the convention had adjourned that Virginians learned that theirs had been the tenth state to ratify. New Hampshire had become the ninth by a close vote of 57 to 47, four days earlier, on June 21. Like Massachusetts and Virginia, New Hampshire had recommended amendments.

If Virginia was essential to the new Union, New York was no less so, and in the New York convention, which began on June 17, Federalists were outnumbered, two to one. Earlier, Governor George Clinton had written his Virginia counterpart, Edmund Randolph, still presumed to be a fellow Antifederalist, stating his conviction that New York's convention would cordially "hold a communication with any sister State on the important subject" of a second federal convention. The broad hint that if Virginia would refuse to ratify without prior amendments, New York could be counted on to do likewise had not been lost on the now proratification Randolph, and he had suppressed the letter until it could no longer affect the Virginia convention.

The New York convention, which for the most part was an extended debate between Alexander Hamilton and Melancton Smith, an Antifederalist lawyer and merchant, was interrupted on June 24 by news of New Hampshire's ratification. On July 2 came the more crucial word of Virginia's. In the end, it was a combination of Virginia's action and Hamilton's suggestion that New York City and the southern counties of the state might well choose to join the new Union without upstate New York that brought Smith and ten other Antifederalists over to the side of ratification. For suddenly it seemed no longer a question of no Union without New York but instead one of no New York without Union. Still, New York's ratification on

July 26 by a vote of 30 to 27 was at best a grudging one. And with it came no fewer than thirty-two recommended amendments and a circular letter to the other states calling for a second general convention.

Grudgingly or not, New York became the eleventh state to ratify the Constitution. Now, only North Carolina and Rhode Island remained uncommitted. Rhode Island's intransigence surprised nobody; its members of the Confederation Congress had not even been present when the decision was made to transmit the Constitution to the states. But North Carolina had been expected by many to follow Virginia into the new Union. Instead, meeting on July 21, 1788, the North Carolina convention voted 184 to 84 on August 2 neither to ratify nor reject the Constitution until a second federal convention was held to consider a proposed bill of rights and other amendments.

In place of a new convention, North Carolinians were soon confronted by a new government, leaving them in the uncomfortable status of foreigners. For on February 4, 1789, five months after North Carolina adopted its wait-and-see posture, electors chosen by the eleven ratifying states unanimously elected George Washington President and John Adams Vice President of the United States. Two months later, on April 1, the duly elected members of the first Congress assembled in New York. On April 30, Washington was inaugurated.

North Carolina's foot-dragging ended on November 19, 1789, when a second state convention ratified the Constitution by a vote of 194 to 77. Six months later, after the United States Senate passed a bill breaking off commercial relations with Rhode Island, that tiny, fractious state finally saw the light. On May 29, 1790, by a paper-thin margin of 34 to 32, a Rhode Island convention ratified the Constitution. Three years to the month after the opening of the Convention in Philadelphia, the people of thirteen formerly sovereign states had voluntarily chosen membership in a new and sovereign nation.

With the ratification of the first ten amendments to the

Constitution on December 15, 1791, the new nation remedied the Convention's omission of a Bill of Rights. With its guarantees of free speech, a free press, religious freedom, and due process and its protection of the rights of the accused, a legal foundation had now been laid for the personal liberty of all Americans. Nearly five years of deliberate effort had gone into the creation of the new framework of government. Now that it was over, a new and infinitely more subtle process of shaping that framework to the changing needs of the times began.

From the beginning, the Constitution has grown and changed in the ways its creators foresaw that it would. In 1793, for example, a Supreme Court ruling in the case of *Chisholm versus Georgia* that a state could be sued in federal court by the citizens of another state provoked the Eleventh Amendment, reversing that judgment. And by these two methods—Supreme Court interpretation and constitutional amendment—the vitality of the Constitution has been preserved ever since. Of the two, interpretation by the Court has played by far the more frequent role. Indeed, in Woodrow Wilson's apt description, the Supreme Court has resembled a constitutional convention in continuous session.

As for amendment, Thomas Jefferson, writing in 1816, underscored the importance of that process. "Some men," he wrote, "look at Constitutions with sanctimonious reverence, and deem them, like the ark of the covenant, too sacred to be touched. They ascribe to the men of the preceding age a wisdom more than human, and suppose what they did to be beyond amendment. I knew that age well; I belonged to and labored with it. It deserved well of its country. It was very like the present, but without the experience of the present; and forty years of experience in Government is worth a century of book-reading; and this they would say themselves, were they to rise from the dead. I am certainly not an advocate for frequent and untried changes in laws and Constitutions. I think moderate imperfections had better be borne with; because, when once known, we accommodate ourselves to them, and find practical means of correcting their ill effects. But I know, also, that laws and institutions must go hand in hand with the progress of the human mind. As that becomes more developed, more enlightened, as new discoveries are made, new truths disclosed, and manners and opinions change with the change of circumstances, institutions must advance also and keep pace with the times."

Americans have been proud, possessive, and even reverent in their feelings about the Constitution over the years since its adoption. Washington once called it "that precious depository of American happiness," and Jefferson, "the result of the collected wisdom of our country." Martin Van Buren went so far as to describe it as "a sacred instrument." On the occasion of the one hundredth anniversary of its signing, President Grover Cleveland referred to it as "this ark of the people's covenant."

The Constitution has been described as "an experiment, as all life is an experiment," by Oliver Wendell Holmes and as "a cornerstone, not a complete building," by Woodrow Wilson. Franklin D. Roosevelt praised it as "so simple and practical that it is possible always to meet extraordinary needs by changes in emphasis and arrangement without loss of essential form."

So important a place has the Constitution assumed in the minds and hearts of Americans that to denigrate or disparage it produces outright shock. That is precisely what was intended by abolitionist William Lloyd Garrison when, in 1854 in protest against the Fugitive Slave Law, he denounced the Constitution as "a covenant with death, and an agreement with hell" and proceeded to burn a copy of it.

Yet Americans have argued long and loud about what its various provisions mean—or should mean. Ironically, these very differences and the vigor with which they are often pursued argue strongly for the central place the Constitution holds in our beliefs about ourslves as Americans. For with all its growth and change through court interpretation and amendment, the Consitution remains today, in the words of historian Gordon S. Wood, "our secular biblical authority, the supreme text against which we measure what we do or want to do. It is the final resting place for political disputes, the floor that keeps us from falling into a bottomless pit of democratic squabbling."

With the pivotal role the Constitution has come to play in our society, it is worth recalling the words of James Madison, who more than any other individual was responsible for it. Writing in 1792, when it was still new, he said, "The people who are the authors of this blessing must also be its guardians. Their eyes must be ever ready to mark, their voices to pronounce, and their arms to repel or repair, aggressions on the authority of their Constitutions."

18

Afterward

". . . there never was an assembly of men, charged with a great and arduous trust, who were more pure in their motives, or more exclusively or anxiously devoted to the object committed to them, than were the members of the Federal Convention of 1787. . . ."

JAMES MADISON, "Preface to the Debates in the Convention of 1787"

1787–1836

When the delegates who were there at the end of the Convention took leave of each other over dinner at Philadelphia's City Tavern, it would be, for many of them, a temporary farewell. Most of the fifty-five who had put in an appearance as delegates had come as political leaders of their own states, and it was thus inevitable that, for many, their lives would continue to intersect in the early years of the new government. In fact, between the first meeting of the new Congress and the death of the last surviving Convention delegate—James Madison, in 1836—thirty-nine of the fifty-five would serve in one capacity or another under the Constitution they had brought into being.

Two would be elected President of the United States, George Washington, as his colleagues had anticipated, by virtual acclamation. James Madison, who became the fourth President in 1809, served first in the House of Representatives, where he played the leading role in fashioning the Bill of Rights, and later as Secretary of State under Thomas Jefferson. Elected to two terms as President, Madison would begin his second, in 1813, with another former delegate, Elbridge Gerry, as Vice President.

The first session of Congress, which met in New York in 1789, saw eleven former Convention delegates sitting as United States Senators: John Langdon of New Hampshire; Caleb Strong of Massachusetts; Oliver Ellsworth and William Samuel Johnson of Connecticut; Rufus King, formerly of Massachusetts, now of New York; William Paterson of New Jersey; Robert Morris of Pennsylvania; George Read and Richard Bassett of Delaware; Pierce Butler of South Carolina; and William Few of Georgia. Eight of their former Convention colleagues sat in the new House of Representatives: Nicholas Gilman of New Hampshire; Elbridge Gerry of Massachusetts; Roger Sherman of Connecticut; George Clymer and Thomas Fitzsimons of Pennsylvania; Daniel Carroll of Maryland; James Madison of Virginia; and Abraham Baldwin of Georgia.

Serving under Washington in the executive branch were Alexander Hamilton, the first Secretary of the Treasury, and Edmund Randolph, the first Attorney General. Before Washington's second term ended, Randolph would serve as his second Secretary of State, and James McHenry of Maryland would become his third Secretary of War. In 1796, Rufus King would accept Washington's appointment as Minister to Great Britain and then stay on in that post until 1803 to serve under John Adams and Thomas Jefferson as well.

Washington also appointed two former Convention delegates Chief Justice of the Supreme Court. John Rutledge of South Carolina, who had served for two years earlier as an Associate Justice before going off to become chief justice of his own state, was chosen in 1795 to replace the first Chief Justice, John Jay, who left to become Governor of New York. When

Rutledge, who served only for a single term, was not confirmed by the Senate, Washington named Oliver Ellsworth of Connecticut, who was. Later, Ellsworth and another former delegate, William R. Davie of North Carolina, would be sent by John Adams as commissioners to France to negotiate an agreement with Napoleon in 1800.

Of the four former delegates who would serve as Associate Justices of the Supreme Court, three, including John Rutledge, were appointed by Washington to the first Court. John Blair of Virginia and James Wilson of Pennsylvania were the others. Wilson, whose unwise investments had brought him close to bankruptcy at the time of the Convention, was still juggling his heavy debts when he joined the Court. When he plunged even deeper into land speculation, disaster overtook him.

Jailed for debt by a Northern creditor in 1797, Wilson managed to extricate himself from a cell in Burlington, New Jersey, and fled south. Discovered in Edenton, North Carolina, by a Southern creditor, his erstwhile Convention colleague Pierce Butler of South Carolina, he was jailed again. Butler finally relented, and Mr. Justice Wilson, broken in mind and body, holed up in a room in an Edenton tavern, still convinced he could somehow save himself from financial ruin. Two months after his release from jail, he was felled by a stroke. He died in Edenton in August 1798. Butler, to whom Wilson reportedly owed nearly $200,000, was then between two separate terms as a United States Senator. Later, he would serve as a director of the Bank of the United States.

The fourth former delegate to serve on the Supreme Court was William Paterson, the diminutive lawyer who had presented the New Jersey Plan to the Convention. Elected first to the Senate in 1789 and to the governorship of New Jersey in 1790, he was appointed by Washington to the Court in 1793 and served until his death in 1806.

Two former delegates were unsuccessful presidential candidates: Charles Cotesworth Pinckney, in 1804 and 1808, after failing as a vice presidential candidate in 1800; and Rufus

King, in 1816, after similar failures to capture the vice presidency in 1804 and 1808. Like King, Pinckney would also serve as Minister to a foreign country, in his case, France.

By the end of Washington's second term as President, ten of the fifty-five former delegates had died. William Churchill Houston of New Jersey, who had left the Convention early because of illness, was the first to go, in 1788. William Pierce of Georgia, who had spent part of his time at the Convention writing sketches of the others, died the following year. The next year, 1790, saw the deaths of four more: David Brearley and William Livingston of New Jersey, Daniel of St. Thomas Jenifer of Maryland, and the man who was senior to them all, eighty-six-year-old Benjamin Franklin of Pennsylvania. Franklin's last public act was to sign a memorial to Congress on behalf of the Pennsylvania Society for Promoting the Abolition of Slavery, of which he was president. The memorial, which asked for an end to slavery, was referred to a committee which reported, as Franklin must have known it would, that Congress had no authority to interfere in the internal affairs of the states.

In 1792, Virginia's George Mason, who had refused to sign the Constitution, died at his home, Gunston Hall, at the age of sixty-seven. Next to go was Connecticut's Roger Sherman, the pious, practical Yankee, who had served in the first House of Representatives and died a United States Senator at seventy-two in 1793. In 1796, Daniel Carroll of Maryland died, having just completed a four-year stint as commissioner laying out the boundaries of the District of Columbia. Nathaniel Gorham of Massachusetts, who had chaired the Convention's Committee of the Whole, died the same year. Like his Convention colleague James Wilson, whom he preceded to the grave by two years, he died of the same cause—a stroke—and in the same condition—financially ruined by land speculation.

Wilson and George Read of Delaware, who both died in 1798, were the eleventh and twelfth to go. Like Wilson, Read died in office, in his case, as chief justice of Delaware. Unlike Wilson, Read died both solvent and at peace, most likely still cherishing his part in assuring that Delaware was the first state to ratify the Constitution.

The man who had presided over the Convention and then for eight years over the more perfect Union it created, the venerated George Washington, lived on just two years after leaving the presidency. Retiring from office in 1797, he planned once more to spend the rest of his days at Mount Vernon. But just as the Philadelphia Convention and the presidency had brought him out of retirement, so now did worsening relations and the possibility of war with France. Appointed lieutenant general and commander in chief by his successor, John Adams, in 1798, Washington set about planning the new army. When the crisis faded, planning ended. And in December 1799, just two months short of his sixty-seventh birthday, Washington died at Mount Vernon. He might well have lived longer but for the then-current practice of bleeding patients with sore throats.

John Rutledge, who had served on five Convention committees and had chaired the important Committee of Detail, died in 1800, five years after the Senate rejection of his appointment as Chief Justice of the Supreme Court.

Three other former delegates died that year, one of them, John Blair of Virginia, four years after retiring from the Supreme Court. The second, Thomas Mifflin, who had served three terms as Governor of Pennsylvania, lived lavishly and died broke. The third was William Blount of North Carolina. Blount, who had become Governor of the Tennessee Territory in 1790, was elected to the United States Senate when the territory became a state in 1796. Like so many of his countrymen, he lost heavily in land speculations. His involvement in a scheme to transfer control of Spanish Florida and Louisiana to Great Britain brought his expulsion from the Senate in 1797. His impeachment by the House of Representatives was later dismissed, but he had meanwhile been elected to the state senate in Tennessee and died while serving as its speaker.

New York's Robert Yates, who with John Lansing, Jr., had left the Convention early and had opposed the ratification of the Constitution in his home state, died in Schenectady in 1801, three years after resigning as chief justice of New York. The next three to go all died at the hands of others: Richard Dobbs Spaight of North Carolina, in 1802, and Alexander Hamilton of New York, in 1804, as a result of wounds sustained in duels. The third, Chancellor George Wythe of Virginia, who died in 1806, succumbed to arsenic poisoning at the hand of a great-nephew displeased with a provision in his granduncle's will.

Spaight had served as Governor of North Carolina and later in the House of Representatives. Wythe, who resigned as judge of Virginia's high court of chancery in 1801, was one of the few former delegates who did not serve in the new federal government. Hamilton, on the other hand, served with such vigor and success as Washington's Secretary of the Treasury that he almost single-handedly put the new government on a firm financial foundation while at the same time creating endless antagonism and bitterness among those who, like Jefferson, saw his bold aggressiveness in exercising the powers of the Constitution as a menace to the government itself.

William Paterson of New Jersey died in 1806, still serving on the Supreme Court thirteen years after his original appointment. Robert Morris, the erstwhile "richest man in America" and Washington's host during the Philadelphia Convention, died the same year. Ruined by land speculation, he had spent three and a half years in debtors' prison before his release in 1801 to eke out his miserable last five years of life in a small house owned by his wife and paid for by his former business protégé, Gouverneur Morris. The man who had helped to finance the American Revolution died reportedly owing an assortment of creditors more than three million dollars.

In 1807, Oliver Ellsworth joined the growing list. He had retired as Chief Justice after five years in 1801. Alexander Martin
of North Carolina, four times elected Governor of his state and
once its United States Senator, died the same year. Abraham
Baldwin died in Washington, D.C., in 1807 after ten years as a
member of the House and eight as a Senator.

With the death of John Dickinson of Delaware in 1808 at
the age of seventy-five and that of his colleague, Jacob Broom,
two years later, the toll of former Convention delegates had
reached its midpoint. In 1811, it was the turn of Thomas Fitzsimons of Pennsylvania, who had served in the House of Representatives for its first six years. He was followed the next
year by Delaware's Gunning Bedford, Jr. Bedford, who had
provided the Convention with its high-water mark of vitriol
with his "I do not, gentlemen, trust you" speech, served the
twenty-three years from 1789 until his death as a federal judge
in his home state of Delaware.

George Clymer of Pennsylvania was the next to go, and that
same year, 1813, also saw the death of Edmund Randolph, the
second of the three who had refused to sign the Constitution.
Randolph, after resigning as Washington's Secretary of State
in 1795, had returned to Virginia to practice law in Richmond.
There, in 1807, he had acted as senior counsel in the successful
defense of Aaron Burr against the charge of treason.

Nicholas Gilman of New Hampshire served eight years in
the House of Representatives and the last nine years of his life
as a United States Senator. He died in 1814, the same year as
Elbridge Gerry of Massachusetts, the third nonsigner. Gerry,
who had accepted the Constitution after its ratification, served
two terms in the first House of Representatives, and in 1797
was sent by President John Adams to France (along with former Convention delegate Charles Cotesworth Pinckney and
John Marshall) to attempt to patch up the faltering American
alliance. When Talleyrand, the French Foreign Minister, solic-
ited a bribe through go-betweens known only as X, Y, and Z
as the price of negotiations, Pinckney and Marshall wisely

went home, while Gerry, convinced that the French would declare war if he, too, left, stayed on and allowed Talleyrand to negotiate secretly with him until he was ordered home.

Returning to Massachusetts, Gerry was beaten four times in the annual race for Governor by his erstwhile Convention colleague Caleb Strong before he finally won in 1810. In an attempt to hold power by redrawing election districts, Gerry's Massachusetts Republicans bequeathed to American politics the misshapen "gerrymander" and enabled Caleb Strong to defeat Gerry once again. Elected Vice President as James Madison's running mate in 1812, Gerry died after two years in office.

Richard Bassett of Delaware died in 1815. Bassett, who had somehow managed to sit through the entire Philadelphia Convention without uttering a word, stirred himself sufficiently afterward to serve four years in the United States Senate and two years as Governor of Delaware. Maryland's James McHenry, who had called the meetings of his Maryland colleagues after hearing the report of the Committee of Detail, died in 1816, having served as Secretary of War under both Washington and Adams.

That same year, Gouverneur Morris, who had played one of the major roles at the Convention, died after a full and happy life. The man who had attempted to limit the vote to freeholders became, shortly after the Convention, a freeholder with few peers when he purchased the family manor in the Bronx he had been denied as an inheritance and moved from Philadelphia back to New York to live. Soon he was off to France as a business agent for Robert Morris, arriving in Paris in February 1789 in time for a ringside seat at the French Revolution.

Morris remained in Europe for nearly ten years, served as Washington's Minister to France from 1792 to 1794, and weathered the Terror in spite of his known sympathy for the French monarchy and key role in a plot to rescue Louis XVI from the Tuileries. Returning to the United States in 1798, he was elected to the United States Senate in 1800. His last years were spent in building a new mansion at Morrisania in the Bronx, marrying, finally, a Randolph of Virginia, and chairing the commission that began development of the Erie Canal.

John Langdon of New Hampshire, who had paid his own and Nicholas Gilman's expenses to get to the Philadelphia Convention, died in 1819 after serving twelve years as a United States Senator and six years as Governor of New Hampshire. Three other former Convention delegates died that year: Caleb Strong, after one term in the Senate and eleven years as Governor of Massachusetts; William Samuel Johnson, who had retired as President of Columbia in 1800, having served Connecticut simultaneously in the Senate from 1789–91; and Hugh Williamson, who left North Carolina in 1793 to spend the rest of his life in New York.

The following year brought the death of Williamson's North Carolina colleague William R. Davie, who had moved to South Carolina in 1805 for life as a plantation owner. In 1821, John Francis Mercer of Maryland, who had arrived at the Convention late and left early, leaving behind little more than his unsolicited statement that he disliked the whole plan of the Constitution, died after three years in the House of Representatives and two more as Governor of Maryland.

Pierce Butler of South Carolina joined the long procession to the grave in 1822 after two separate periods of service in the Senate. Jared Ingersoll of Pennsylvania, who had spoken only once, and that on the last day of the Convention, died the same year. He had served as Attorney General of Pennsylvania for fifteen years. He was followed in 1823 by John McClurg, the Richmond physician appointed to the place in the Virginia delegation left empty by Patrick Henry's refusal to serve.

Jonathan Dayton of New Jersey was the next to go. He died in 1824 after serving eight years in the House and six in the Senate and then destroying his political career by his involvement in Aaron Burr's separatist schemes. His indictment for treason was eventually dropped. That same year, Charles

Pinckney, the younger of the two South Carolina cousins, died after a life largely devoted to politics. Three times Governor of South Carolina, once a Senator, and for four years Thomas Jefferson's Minister to Spain, he served in the House of Representatives between 1819 and 1821.

The elder Pinckney, Charles Cotesworth, followed his cousin to the grave in 1825. Between 1791 and 1795, he had turned down offers from Washington to command the army, to sit on the Supreme Court, to be Secretary of War, and finally, to be Secretary of State. When he accepted the post of Minister to France in 1796, the French Directory refused to recognize him. Appointed by Adams to the three-man special mission to France in 1797, he was confronted by Talleyrand's XYZ maneuver. For a brief period during the crisis with France that followed, Pinckney returned to the army as a major general. Finally, the man who had rejected so many offices sought, unsuccessfully, the vice presidency (under Adams) in 1800, and the presidency (against Jefferson) in 1804 and (against Madison) in 1808.

In 1826, Luther Martin of Maryland, whose volubility at the Convention had so infuriated Oliver Ellsworth, died in New York, ruined by extravagance and drink. Twice the Attorney General of his state (1778–1805 and 1818–22), Martin had successfully defended Supreme Court Justice Samuel Chase, a fellow Marylander, in impeachment proceedings in 1804–05 and unsuccessfully represented Maryland in the landmark *McCulloch versus Maryland* case in 1819. In between, he had served under Edmund Randolph in the defense of Aaron Burr in his treason trial of 1807, and it was in the grateful Burr's New York City house that Martin, a destitute, half-paralyzed alcoholic, passed his final days.

The next year, 1827, it was the turn of Rufus King, formerly of Massachusetts but since the Convention, by ardent choice, a New Yorker. A Senator from 1789 to 1796, he had then put in seven fruitful years as United States Minister to Great Britain. Unfazed by his two defeats as a candidate for Vice President in 1804 and 1808, he served again in the Senate from 1813 to 1825, with time out in 1816 to run unsuccessfully for President against James Monroe. When President John Quincy Adams urged him to serve once more as Minister to Great Britain, the indefatigable King acceded, but it was not to be. Shortly after his arrival in England in 1825, he became ill. By the time he reached home, he had less than a year to live.

William Few of Georgia, who had said nothing but had served on one committee at the Convention, died in 1828 after four years as a Senator and three as a federal judge in Georgia and then moving to New York in 1799. The next year, John Lansing, Jr., of New York disappeared from the scene—literally. Having served his state as justice, chief justice, and finally chancellor, he had retired in 1814 to the private practice of law in Albany. In New York City on business in December 1829, Lansing went out to mail a letter and was never seen again.

When William Houstoun of Georgia died in 1833, there remained but a single survivor of the Philadelphia Convention. James Madison, then eighty-two and living in retirement with Dolley at Montpelier in Orange County, Virginia, had just recovered from a long bout of rheumatism and fever. That September, he was again well enough to leave the house to "ride out every day, three or four miles."

Near the end of his life, Madison drafted a preface to his notes of the debates in the Philadelphia Convention. Of his colleagues of 1787, now all departed, he said "that there never was an assembly of men, charged with a great and arduous trust, who were more pure in their motives, or more exclusively or anxiously devoted to the object committed to them, than were the members of the Federal Convention of 1787, to the object of devising and proposing a constitutional system which should best supply the defects of that which it was to replace, and best secure the permanent liberty and happiness of their country."

On June 28, 1836, James Madison died quietly at breakfast in his bed. He was eighty-five years old. The Constitution was not quite forty-nine.

Author's Note

For fifty-three years after the Constitution was signed on September 17, 1787, only two men had in their possession a firsthand, daily account of virtually everything that had taken place at the Convention. One was James Madison, who, as we have seen, had painstakingly taken voluminous notes of the debates as they occurred. The other was his close friend Thomas Jefferson, to whom Madison later entrusted his original notes so that a copy might be made for safekeeping.

It was widely known that Madison had performed this task, and he was often urged to publish his notes, not least for the help they might provide in interpreting various constitutional provisions. On that point, Madison never wavered. ". . . whatever veneration might be entertained for the body of men who formed our Constitution," he said in the House of Representatives in 1796, "the sense of that body could never be regarded as the oracular guide in expounding the Constitution. As the instrument came from them it was nothing more than the draft of a plan, nothing but a dead letter, until life and validity were breathed into it by the voice of the people, speaking through the several State Conventions. If we were to look, therefore, for the meaning of the instrument beyond the face of the instrument, we must look for it, not in the General Convention, which proposed, but in the State Conventions, which accepted and ratified the Constitution."

Still, the hope of somehow discovering the "intent of the framers" in the debates of the Convention—by judges, lawyers, legislators, politicans, and scholars—has never ceased.

And in the light of the Supreme Court's frequent recourse to the Convention's proceedings after Madison's notes of the debates were finally published in 1840, it is an ironic fact that the Court somehow managed to interpret the Constitution for its first fifty-one years without them. All of the major decisions of Chief Justice John Marshall on constitutional law were rendered before Madison's notes were made public. Marshall himself never saw them, having died five years before they were published.

But Madison had another reason for withholding publication for so long. "In general," he wrote in explanation in 1821, "it had appeared to me that it might be best to let the work be a posthumous one; or at least that its publication should be delayed till the Constitution should be well settled by practice, & till a knowledge of the controversial part of the proceedings of its framers could be turned to no improper account." And this, too, was a decision he stuck to.

Since their publication, Madison's notes of the debates have been of major interest to scholars in history, law, political science, and American government. Together with the previously published *Journal* of the Convention, which contained none of the debates, and the incomplete and largely fragmentary notes of other Convention delegates published earlier, they gave the world its first detailed account of what historian Clinton Rossiter has called "an event about whose nature, meaning, origins, purposes, staging, techniques, cast of characters, and consequences men have been speculating in print ever since."

A key word here may well be "speculating," for in the outpouring of books about the Convention and the fifty-five men who attended it, only a handful of authors has chosen simply to tell the straightforward, dramatic story of what happened in Philadelphia that summer for an audience of ordinary readers. One who did, Carl Van Doren, remarks in the preface of his book *The Great Rehearsal*, that "even historical novelists, who hunt everywhere for memorable events to celebrate, have hardly touched the event without which there would have been a United States very different from the one that now exists; or might have been no United States at all." His explanation for this strange oversight is convincing: "The Constitution has so long been rooted so deeply in American life—or American life so deeply rooted in it—that the drama of its origins is often overlooked." And he is surely correct when he characterizes those origins as "the most momentous chapter in American history."

Clinton Rossiter, whose *1787: The Grand Convention* leans more toward interpretation than narrative, agreed about the importance of the event: "1787 was, beyond all but the faintest shadow of a doubt, the most fateful year in the history of the United States." The framers of the Constitution, Rossiter believed, "made a gamble with the destiny of the American people so hazardous and yet so calculated, so contingent and yet so prudent, that they command the highest homage granted to the makers of history: an endless retelling of the manner of their ascent to glory."

What first struck me when I began reading about the Philadelphia Convention of 1787 was its vitality simply as a story. Later, as I became more familiar with it, I could see its inherent dramatic structure. With the gathering of the delegates in mid-May and their departure in mid-September as opening and closing curtains, the Convention itself became the stage on which was played out the crucial struggle for the survival of the nation. Infused with all the tension and conflict of a great trial (which in a way it was), driven by its own internal suspense, with dramatic and sometimes passionate speeches by many of the leading characters of the time and place, it seemed almost extravagant that it should also be true.

It was a story, though, that for the most part I had to piece together myself from the available materials. Dramatic scenes often appeared between long pages of explanation, hints of brilliant speeches in the midst of detailed analysis. The forming and re-forming of blocs and coalitions of delegates lurked, sometimes only dimly visible, behind paragraphs of documentation or argument. But through it all, there were striking glimpses of earnest men, torn between their roles of local politician and national statesman, impatient at being kept so long from home, family, and occupation, yet unwilling to abandon the effort of constructing a new government while their country seemed on the verge of collapse.

There was a promise of story, of engrossing narrative, in almost everything I read, but it was constantly surfacing and then submerging in a sea of interpretation and explication. While I welcomed—and needed—both, I found myself increasingly impatient with digressions that took me far from the scene of action. What I craved was an understanding that emerged from the story itself, an interpretation implicit in the presentation of characters and events. In a country addicted to rousing tales of its improbably adventurous past, it seemed almost absurd that this one had not been written again and again, to be endlessly transformed into novels, plays, movies, and television documentaries and dramatic series. That was the book I wanted to read. It is the book I have attempted to write.

It was written, however, not only to attempt to fill a void and remedy an oversight but also to assure that the generation of Americans that celebrates the bicentennial of its Constitution in 1987 can, if it wishes, find the exciting narrative of how it was made in a single book. Ultimately, of course, it was written because, having found the story I was looking for, I was compelled to set it down.

I have mentioned Carl Van Doren's *The Great Rehearsal* and Clinton Rossiter's *1787: The Grand Convention*. They were published a generation apart: Van Doren's book in 1948, Rossiter's in 1966. A generation before Van Doren, in 1928, a third historian, Charles Warren, infused his account of the Convention—*The Making of the Constitution*—with pertinent letters and newspaper stories of the time.

For their details of the Convention debates, all three of these important books depended heavily on the encyclopedic resources of Max Farrand's *The Records of the Federal Convention of 1787*, originally published in 1911 and revised in 1937. Here, in four volumes, is to be found the most comprehensive collection of materials about the Convention in existence. Two volumes contain day-by-day entries of the official *Journal*, Madison's notes, and the more scattered notes of delegates Robert Yates, Rufus King, James McHenry, William Pierce, William Paterson, Alexander Hamilton, Charles Pinckney, and George Mason. A third volume contains a wealth of peripheral material in the form of letters, diary entries, and official documents. The final volume provides, in addition to a general index and a helpful index by clauses of the Constitution, corrections and additions to the other volumes.

Among the many sources I consulted for this book, these four have been the most consistently helpful. Of the four, Farrand's *Records* has been indispensable.

I have sought to tell the story of the 1787 Convention chronologically, as a narrative of the men who attended it, as they themselves experienced it. I have, in a word, sought to take the reader to Philadelphia, to experience what happened as it happened. To accomplish this, I have, where appropriate, transposed the third-person, past-tense renderings of Convention speeches by Madison and others back into the first-person, present-tense in which they were originally spoken. Abbreviations have been largely eliminated, and punctuation, spelling, and capitalization mostly modernized. Where notes were made in incomplete sentences, I have restored what I felt must have been the original sentence structure. In a very few instances, where old usages tended to obscure meaning, I have substituted a more familiar one. Thus, "They want information" has become "They lack information." Beyond this, I have not ventured. It was not necessary. The story was there, waiting to be told, Even the emphases I have included (expressed in italics) in quotations from speeches and letters are reproduced as they were in my sources.

I am indebted to a number of people for both help and encouragement in the research underlying this book as well as for trying to make sure I avoided the more obvious pitfalls. Gordon S. Wood, Professor of History at Brown University, has supported my efforts from the outset. He knows this chapter of American history far better than I will ever know it; yet he has been unfailingly enthusiastic and helpful in my attempt to retell it in my own way.

Paul A. Freund, Carl Loeb Professor Emeritus of Harvard Law School, has also been of great assistance, both in pointing out gaps and in helping me to fill them. His belief in what I set out to do helped enormously to make it seem possible.

Stanley M. Katz, Professor of Law, Liberty, and Public Affairs of the Woodrow Wilson School of Public and International Affairs at Princeton University; Jack P. Greene, Professor of History at Johns Hopkins University; and Robert Allen Rutland, Editor of the James Madison Papers at the University of Virginia, have all been more than generous with their time, comments, criticism, and corrections. What errors may remain are, of course, my own.

William Peters
Branford, Connecticut

Sources

The vast majority of material in this book has been mined from a single source, Max Farrand's *The Records of the Federal Convention of 1787* (Yale, 1911, 1937; rev. ed., 4 vols., 1966). Since the Convention speeches excerpted from this source have for the most part been given their appropriate dates in the text itself, the originals will be easily found in the first two volumes of that work. Letters, diary entries, and other documents cited in the text will most often be found in the third volume, which is also arranged chronologically.

Among the many sources I have consulted, the following have proved most useful:

Billias, George Athan. *Elbridge Gerry: Founding Father and Republican Statesman.* New York: McGraw-Hill, 1976.

Bowen, Catherine Drinker. *Miracle at Philadelphia: The Story of the Constitutional Convention, May to September, 1787.* Boston: Little, Brown, 1966.

Brant, Irving. *The Fourth President: A Life of James Madison.* Indianapolis: Bobbs-Merrill, 1970.

————. *James Madison: A Biography.* (6 vols.) New York: Macmillan, 1941–1961.

Corwin, Edward S. *The Constitution and What It Means Today.* 14th ed. Princeton: Princeton University, 1978.

Cunliffe, Marcus. *George Washington: Man and Monument.* New York: New American Library, 1958.

Elliot, Jonathan, ed. *The Debates in the Several State Conventions as Recommended by the General Convention at Philadelphia in 1787, Together with the Journal of the Federal Convention.* (5 vols.) New York: Burt Franklin, 1974.

Farrand, Max. *The Framing of the Constitution of the United States.* New Haven: Yale, 1913.

————, ed. *The Records of the Federal Convention of 1787.* New Haven: Yale, 1911, 1937, rev. ed. (4 vols.) 1966.

Flexner, James Thomas. *George Washington.* (3 vols.) Boston: Little, Brown, 1969, 1970.

————. *Washington: The Indispensable Man.* Boston: Little, Brown, 1974.

Freeman, Douglas Southall. *George Washington: A Biography.* (7 vols.) New York: Scribner's, 1948–1957.

Garrity, John A., ed. *Quarrels That Have Shaped the Constitution.* New York: Harper & Row, 1964.

Ketcham, Ralph. *James Madison: A Biography.* New York: Macmillan, 1971.

Mason, Alpheus Thomas. *The States Rights Debate: Antifederalism and the Constitution.* Englewood Cliffs, N.J.: Prentice-Hall, 1964.

Padover, Saul K. *The Living U.S. Constitution.* New York: New American Library, 1968.

Peterson, Merrill D., ed. *James Madison: A Biography in His Own Words.* New York: Newsweek, 1974.

Rossiter, Clinton. *1787: The Grand Convention.* New York: Macmillan, 1966.

Rutland, Robert Allen. *The Birth of the Bill of Rights, 1766–1791.* Chapel Hill: University of North Carolina, 1955.

———— et al., eds. *The Papers of James Madison.* Vol. 11, Charlottesville: University of Virginia, 1977.

Smith, Charles Page. *James Wilson: Founding Father, 1742–1798.* Chapel Hill: University of North Carolina, 1956.

Smith, Edward Conrad, ed. *The Constitution of the United States with Case Summaries.* New York: Barnes & Noble, 1979.

Storing, Herbert J. *What the Anti-Federalists Were For.* Chicago: University of Chicago, 1981.

Van Doren, Carl. *Benjamin Franklin.* New York: Viking, 1938.

————. *The Great Rehearsal: The Story of the Making and Ratifying of the Constitution of the United States.* New York: Viking, 1948. Reprint. New York: Penguin Books, 1986.

Warren, Charles. *The Making of the Constitution.* New York: Barnes & Noble, 1967.

Wood, Gordon S. *The Creation of the American Republic, 1776-1787.* New York: Norton, 1969.

Appendix

CONSTITUTION
OF THE UNITED STATES

Proposed by Convention September 17, 1787
Effective March 4, 1789

WE the people of the United States, in order to form a more perfect union, establish justice, insure domestic tranquillity, provide for the common defense, promote the general welfare, and secure the blessings of liberty to ourselves and our posterity, do ordain and establish this Constitution for the United States of America.

ARTICLE I

SECTION 1.   All legislative powers herein granted shall be vested in a Congress of the United States, which shall consist of a Senate and House of Representatives.

SECTION 2.   1.   The House of Representatives shall be composed of members chosen every second year by the people of the several States, and the electors in each State shall have the qualifications requisite for electors of the most numerous branch of the State legislature.

2.   No person shall be a representative who shall not have attained to the age of twenty-five years, and been seven years a citizen of the United States, and who shall not, when elected, be an inhabitant of that State in which he shall be chosen.

3.   Representatives [and direct taxes]* shall be apportioned among the several States which may be included within this Union, according to their respective numbers, [which shall be determined by adding to the whole number of free persons, including those bound to service for a term of years, and excluding Indians not taxed, three fifths of all other persons.]† The actual enumeration shall be made within three

* See the 16th Amendment.
† See the 14th Amendment.

259

years after the first meeting of the Congress of the United States, and within every subsequent term of ten years, in such manner as they shall by law direct. The number of representatives shall not exceed one for every thirty thousand, but each State shall have at least one representative; and until such enumeration shall be made, the State of New Hampshire shall be entitled to choose three, Massachusetts eight, Rhode Island and Providence Plantations one, Connecticut five, New York six, New Jersey four, Pennsylvania eight, Delaware one, Maryland six, Virginia ten, North Carolina five, South Carolina five, and Georgia three.

4.   When vacancies happen in the representation from any State, the executive authority thereof shall issue writs of election to fill such vacancies.

5.   The House of Representatives shall choose their speaker and other officers; and shall have the sole power of impeachment.

SECTION 3.   1.   The Senate of the United States shall be composed of two senators from each State, [chosen by the legislature thereof,]* for six years; and each senator shall have one vote.

2.   Immediately after they shall be assembled in consequence of the first election, they shall be divided as equally as may be into three classes. The seats of the senators of the first class shall be vacated at the expiration of the second year, of the second class at the expiration of the fourth year, and of the third class at the expiration of the sixth year, so that one third may be chosen every second year; and if vacancies happen by resignation, or otherwise, during the recess of the legislature of any State, the executive thereof may make temporary appointments until the next meeting of the legislature, which shall then fill such vacancies.*

3.   No person shall be a senator who shall not have attained to the age of thirty years, and been nine years a citizen of the United States, and who shall not, when elected, be an inhabitant of that State for which he shall be chosen.

4.   The Vice President of the United States shall be President of the Senate, but shall have no vote, unless they be equally divided.

5.   The Senate shall choose their other officers, and also a president *pro tempore,* in the absence of the Vice President, or when he shall exercise the office of the President of the United States.

6.   The Senate shall have the sole power to try all impeachments. When sitting for that purpose, they shall be on oath or affirmation.

* See the 17th Amendment.

When the President of the United States is tried, the chief justice shall preside: and no person shall be convicted without the concurrence of two thirds of the members present.

7.   Judgment in cases of impeachment shall not extend further than to removal from office, and disqualifications to hold and enjoy any office of honor, trust or profit under the United States: but the party convicted shall nevertheless be liable and subject to indictment, trial, judgment and punishment, according to law.

SECTION 4.   1.   The times, places, and manner of holding elections for senators and representatives, shall be prescribed in each State by the legislature thereof; but the Congress may at any time by law make or alter such regulations, except as to the places of choosing senators.

2.   The Congress shall assemble at least once in every year, and such meeting shall be on the first Monday in December,* unless they shall by law appoint a different day.

SECTION 5.   1.   Each House shall be the judge of the elections, returns and qualifications of its own members, and a majority of each shall constitute a quorum to do business; but a smaller number may adjourn from day to day, and may be authorized to compel the attendance of absent members, in such manner, and under such penalties as each House may provide.

2.   Each House may determine the rules of its proceedings, punish its members for disorderly behavior, and, with the concurrence of two thirds, expel a member.

3.   Each House shall keep a journal of its proceedings, and from time to time publish the same, excepting such parts as may in their judgment require secrecy; and the yeas and nays of the members of either House on any question shall, at the desire of one fifth of those present, be entered on the journal.

4.   Neither House, during the session of Congress, shall, without the consent of the other, adjourn for more than three days, nor to any other place than that in which the two Houses shall be sitting.

SECTION 6.   1.   The senators and representatives shall receive a compensation for their services, to be ascertained by law, and paid out of the Treasury of the United States. They shall in all cases, except treason, felony, and breach of the peace, be privileged from arrest during their attendance at the session of their respective Houses, and in going to and returning from the same; and for any speech or debate in either House, they shall not be questioned in any other place.

* Modified by the 20th Amendment.

2. No senator or representative shall, during the time for which he was elected, be appointed to any civil office under the authority of the United States, which shall have been created, or the emoluments whereof shall have been increased during such time; and no person holding any office under the United States shall be a member of either House during his continuance in office.

SECTION 7. 1. All bills for raising revenue shall originate in the House of Representatives; but the Senate may propose or concur with amendments as on other bills.

2. Every bill which shall have passed the House of Representatives and the Senate, shall, before it becomes a law, be presented to the President of the United States; if he approves he shall sign it, but if not he shall return it, with his objections to that House in which it shall have originated, who shall enter the objections at large on their journal, and proceed to reconsider it. If after such reconsideration two thirds of that House shall agree to pass the bill, it shall be sent, together with the objections, to the other House, by which it shall likewise be reconsidered, and if approved by two thirds of that House, it shall become a law. But in all such cases the votes of both Houses shall be determined by yeas and nays, and the names of the persons voting for and against the bill shall be entered on the journal of each House respectively. If any bill shall not be returned by the President within ten days (Sundays excepted) after it shall have been presented to him, the same shall be a law, in like manner as if he had signed it, unless the Congress by their adjournment prevent its return, in which case it shall not be a law.

3. Every order, resolution, or vote to which the concurrence of the Senate and the House of Representatives may be necessary (except on a question of adjournment) shall be presented to the President of the United States; and before the same shall take effect, shall be approved by him, or being disapproved by him, shall be repassed by two thirds of the Senate and House of Representatives, according to the rules and limitations prescribed in the case of a bill.

SECTION 8.   The Congress shall have the power

1. To lay and collect taxes, duties, imposts, and excises, to pay the debts and provide for the common defense and general welfare of the United States; but all duties, imposts, and excises shall be uniform throughout the United States;

2. To borrow money on the credit of the United States;

3.   To regulate commerce with foreign nations, and among the several States, and with the Indian tribes;

4.   To establish a uniform rule of naturalization, and uniform laws on the subject of bankruptcies throughout the United States;

5.   To coin money, regulate the value thereof, and of foreign coin, and fix the standard of weights and measures;

6.   To provide for the punishment of counterfeiting the securities and current coin of the United States;

7.   To establish post offices and post roads;

8.   To promote the progress of science and useful arts, by securing for limited times to authors and inventors the exclusive right to their respective writings and discoveries;

9.   To constitute tribunals inferior to the Supreme Court;

10.   To define and punish piracies and felonies committed on the high seas, and offenses against the law of nations;

11.   To declare war, grant letters of marque and reprisal, and make rules concerning captures on land and water;

12.   To raise and support armies, but no appropriation of money to that use shall be for a longer term than two years;

13.   To provide and maintain a navy;

14.   To make rules for the government and regulation of the land and naval forces;

15.   To provide for calling forth the militia to execute the laws of the Union, suppress insurrections and repel invasions;

16.   To provide for organizing, arming, and disciplining the militia, and for governing such part of them as may be employed in the service of the United States, reserving to the States respectively, the appointment of the officers, and the authority of training the militia according to the discipline prescribed by Congress;

17.   To exercise exclusive legislation in all cases whatsoever, over such district (not exceeding ten miles square) as may, by cession of particular States, and the acceptance of Congress, become the seat of the government of the United States, and to exercise like authority over all places purchased by the consent of the legislature of the State in which the same shall be, for the erection of forts, magazines, arsenals, dockyards, and other needful buildings; and

18.   To make all laws which shall be necessary and proper for carrying into execution the foregoing powers, and all other powers vested by this Constitution in the government of the United States, or in any department or officer thereof.

SECTION 9.   1.   The migration or importation of such persons as any of the States now existing shall think proper to admit, shall not be prohibited by the Congress prior to the year one thousand eight hundred and eight, but a tax or duty may be imposed on such importation, not exceeding ten dollars for each person.

2.   The privilege of the writ of *habeas corpus* shall not be suspended, unless when in cases of rebellion or invasion the public safety may require it.

3.   No bill of attainder or *ex post facto* law shall be passed.

4.   No capitation, or other direct, tax shall be laid unless in proportion to the census or enumeration hereinbefore directed to be taken.*

5.   No tax or duty shall be laid on articles exported from any State.

6.   No preference shall be given by any regulation of commerce or revenue to the ports of one State over those of another: nor shall vessels bound to, or from, one State be obliged to enter, clear, or pay duties in another.

7.   No money shall be drawn from the treasury, but in consequence of appropriations made by law; and a regular statement and account of the receipts and expenditures of all public money shall be published from time to time.

8.   No title of nobility shall be granted by the United States: and no person holding any office of profit or trust under them, shall, without the consent of the Congress, accept of any present, emolument, office, or title, of any kind whatever, from any king, prince, or foreign State.

SECTION 10.   1.   No State shall enter into any treaty, alliance, or confederation; grant letters of marque and reprisal; coin money; emit bills of credit; make anything but gold and silver coin a tender in payment of debts; pass any bill of attainder, *ex post facto* law, or law impairing the obligation of contracts, or grant any title of nobility.

2.   No State shall, without the consent of the Congress, lay any imposts or duties on imports or exports, except what may be absolutely necessary for executing its inspection laws; and the net produce of all duties and imposts laid by any State on imports or exports, shall be for the use of the treasury of the United States; and all such laws shall be subject to the revision and control of the Congress.

3.   No State shall, without the consent of the Congress, lay any duty of tonnage, keep troops, or ships of war in time of peace, enter into any agreement or compact with another State, or with a foreign

* See the 16th Amendment.

power, or engage in war, unless actually invaded, or in such imminent danger as will not admit of delay.

ARTICLE II

SECTION 1. 1. The executive power shall be vested in a President of the United States of America. He shall hold his office during the term of four years, and, together with the Vice President, chosen for the same term, be elected as follows:

2. Each State* shall appoint, in such manner as the legislature thereof may direct, a number of electors, equal to the whole number of senators and representatives to which the State may be entitled in the Congress: but no senator or representative, or person holding an office of trust or profit under the United States, shall be appointed an elector.

The electors shall meet in their respective States, and vote by ballot for two persons, of whom one at least shall not be an inhabitant of the same State with themselves. And they shall make a list of all the persons voted for, and of the number of votes for each; which list they shall sign and certify, and transmit sealed to the seat of the government of the United States, directed to the president of the Senate. The president of the Senate shall, in the presence of the Senate and House of Representatives, open all the certificates, and the votes shall then be counted. The person having the greatest number of votes shall be the President, if such number be a majority of the whole number of electors appointed; and if there be more than one who have such majority, and have an equal number of votes, then the House of Representatives shall immediately choose by ballot one of them for President; and if no person have a majority, then from the five highest on the list the said House shall in like manner choose the President. But in choosing the President, the votes shall be taken by States, the representation from each State having one vote; a quorum for this purpose shall consist of a member or members from two thirds of the States, and a majority of all the States shall be necessary to a choice. In every case, after the choice of the President, the person having the greatest number of votes of the electors shall be the Vice President. But if there should remain two or more who have equal votes, the Senate shall choose from them by ballot the Vice President.†

* See 23rd Amendment.
† This paragraph was superseded by the 12th Amendment.

3. The Congress may determine the time of choosing the electors, and the day on which they shall give their votes; which day shall be the same throughout the United States.

4. No person except a natural born citizen, or a citizen of the United States, at the time of the adoption of this Constitution, shall be eligible to the office of President; neither shall any person be eligible to that office who shall not have attained to the age of thirty-five years, and been fourteen years a resident within the United States.

5. In case of the removal of the President from office, or of his death, resignation, or inability to discharge the powers and duties of the said office, the same shall devolve on the Vice President, and the Congress may by law provide for the case of removal, death, resignation, or inability, both of the President and Vice President, declaring what officer shall then act as President, and such officer shall act accordingly, until the disability be removed, or a President shall be elected.*

6. The President shall, at stated times, receive for his services a compensation, which shall neither be increased nor diminished during the period for which he shall have been elected, and he shall not receive within that period any other emolument from the United States, or any of them.

7. Before he enter on the execution of his office, he shall take the following oath or affirmation:—"I do solemnly swear (or affirm) that I will faithfully execute the office of President of the United States, and will to the best of my ability, preserve, protect and defend the Constitution of the United States."

SECTION 2. 1. The President shall be commander in chief of the army and navy of the United States, and of the militia of the several States, when called into the actual service of the United States; he may require the opinion, in writing, of the principal officer in each of the executive departments, upon any subject relating to the duties of their respective offices, and he shall have power to grant reprieves and pardons for offenses against the United States, except in cases of impeachment.

2. He shall have power, by and with the advice and consent of the Senate, to make treaties, provided two thirds of the senators present concur; and he shall nominate, and by and with the advice and consent of the Senate, shall appoint ambassadors, other public ministers and consuls, judges of the Supreme Court, and all other officers of the United States, whose appointments are not herein otherwise provided

* See the 25th Amendment.

for, and which shall be established by law: but the Congress may by law vest the appointment of such inferior officers, as they think proper, in the President alone, in the courts of law, or in the heads of departments.

3. The President shall have power to fill up all vacancies that may happen during the recess of the Senate, by granting commissions which shall expire at the end of their next session.

SECTION 3. He shall from time to time give to the Congress information of the state of the Union, and recommend to their consideration such measures as he shall judge necessary and expedient; he may, on extraordinary occasions, convene both Houses, or either of them, and in case of disagreement between them with respect to the time of adjournment, he may adjourn them to such time as he shall think proper; he shall receive ambassadors and other public ministers; he shall take care that the laws be faithfully executed, and shall commission all the officers of the United States.

SECTION 4. The President, Vice President, and all civil officers of the United States, shall be removed from office on impeachment for and conviction of, treason, bribery, or other high crimes and misdemeanors.

ARTICLE III

SECTION 1. The judicial power of the United States shall be vested in one Supreme Court, and in such inferior courts as the Congress may from time to time ordain and establish. The judges, both of the Supreme and inferior courts, shall hold their offices during good behavior, and shall, at stated times, receive for their services, a compensation, which shall not be diminished during their continuance in office.

SECTION 2. 1. The judicial power shall extend to all cases, in law and equity, arising under this Constitution, the laws of the United States, and treaties made, or which shall be made, under their authority; —to all cases affecting ambassadors, other public ministers and consuls; —to all cases of admiralty and maritime jurisdiction;—to controversies to which the United States shall be a party;—to controversies between two or more States;—between a State and citizens of another State;*— between citizens of different States;—between citizens of the same State claiming lands under grants of different States, and between a State, or the citizens thereof, and foreign States, citizens or subjects.

* See the 11th Amendment.

2. In all cases affecting ambassadors, other public ministers and consuls, and those in which a State shall be party, the Supreme Court shall have original jurisdiction. In all the other cases before mentioned, the Supreme Court shall have appellate jurisdiction, both as to law and to fact, with such exceptions, and under such regulations as the Congress shall make.

3. The trial of all crimes, except in cases of impeachment, shall be by jury; and such trial shall be held in the State where the said crimes shall have been committed; but when not committed within any State, the trial shall be at such place or places as the Congress may by law have directed.

SECTION 3. 1. Treason against the United States shall consist only in levying war against them, or in adhering to their enemies, giving them aid and comfort. No person shall be convicted of treason unless on the testimony of two witnesses to the same overt act, or on confession in open court.

2. The Congress shall have power to declare the punishment of treason, but no attainder of treason shall work corruption of blood, or forfeiture except during the life of the person attained.

ARTICLE IV

SECTION 1. Full faith and credit shall be given in each State to the public acts, records, and judicial proceedings of every other State. And the Congress may by general laws prescribe the manner in which such acts, records and proceedings shall be proved, and the effect thereof.

SECTION 2. 1. The citizens of each State shall be entitled to all privileges and immunities of citizens in the several States.*

2. A person charged in any State with treason, felony, or other crime, who shall flee from justice, and be found in another State, shall on demand of the executive authority of the State from which he fled, be delivered up to be removed to the State having jurisdiction of the crime.

3. No person held to service or labor in one State under the laws thereof, escaping into another, shall, in consequence of any law or regulation therein, be discharged from such service or labor, but shall

* See the 14th Amendment, Sec. 1.

be delivered up on claim of the party to whom such service or labor may be due.*

SECTION 3. 1. New States may be admitted by the Congress into this Union; but no new State shall be formed or erected within the jurisdiction of any other State; nor any State be formed by the junction of two or more States, or parts of States, without the consent of the legislatures of the States concerned as well as of the Congress.

2. The Congress shall have power to dispose of and make all needful rules and regulations respecting the territory or other property belonging to the United States; and nothing in this Constitution shall be so construed as to prejudice any claims of the United States, or of any particular State.

SECTION 4. The United States shall guarantee to every State in this Union a republican form of government, and shall protect each of them against invasion; and on application of the legislature, or of the executive (when the legislature cannot be convened) against domestic violence.

ARTICLE V

The Congress, whenever two thirds of both Houses shall deem it necessary, shall propose amendments to this Constitution, or, on the application of the legislatures of two thirds of the several States, shall call a convention for proposing amendments, which in either case, shall be valid to all intents and purposes, as part of this Constitution when ratified by the legislatures of three fourths of the several States, or by conventions in three fourths thereof, as the one or the other mode of ratification may be proposed by the Congress; Provided that no amendment which may be made prior to the year one thousand eight hundred and eight shall in any manner affect the first and fourth clauses in the ninth section of the first article; and that no State, without its consent, shall be deprived of its equal suffrage in the Senate.

ARTICLE VI

1. All debts contracted and engagements entered into, before the adoption of this Constitution, shall be as valid against the United States under this Constitution, as under the Confederation.

2. This Constitution, and the laws of the United States which shall

* See the 13th Amendment.

be made in pursuance thereof; and all treaties made, or which shall be made, under the authority of the United States, shall be the supreme law of the land; and the Judges in every State shall be bound thereby, anything in the Constitution or laws of any State to the contrary notwithstanding.

3. The senators and representatives before mentioned, and the members of the several State legislatures, and all executive and judicial officers, both of the United States and of the several States, shall be bound by oath or affirmation to support this Constitution; but no religious test shall ever be required as a qualification to any office or public trust under the United States.

ARTICLE VII

The ratification of the conventions of nine States shall be sufficient for the establishment of this Constitution between the States so ratifying the same.

Done in Convention by the unanimous consent of the States present the seventeenth day of September in the year of our Lord one thousand seven hundred and eighty-seven, and of the independence of the United States of America the twelfth. In witness whereof we have hereunto subscribed our names.

George Washington—President and deputy from Virginia
Attest WILLIAM JACKSON *Secretary*

New Hampshire	{ JOHN LANGDON NICHOLAS GILMAN
Massachusetts	{ NATHANIEL GORHAM RUFUS KING
Connecticut	{ WM: SAML. JOHNSON ROGER SHERMAN
New York	ALEXANDER HAMILTON
New Jersey	{ WIL: LIVINGSTON DAVID BREARLEY WM. PATERSON JONA: DAYTON

Pennsylvania	B. FRANKLIN THOMAS MIFFLIN ROBT. MORRIS GEO. CLYMER THOS. FITZ SIMONS JARED INGERSOLL JAMES WILSON GOUV MORRIS
Delaware	GEO: READ GUNNING BEDFORD jun JOHN DICKINSON RICHARD BASSETT JACO: BROOM
Maryland	JAMES MCHENRY DAN OF ST THOS. JENIFER DANL CARROLL
Virginia	JOHN BLAIR JAMES MADISON JR.
North Carolina	WM: BLOUNT RICHD. DOBBS SPAIGHT HU WILLIAMSON
South Carolina	J. RUTLEDGE CHARLES COTESWORTH PINCKNEY CHARLES PINCKNEY PIERCE BUTLER
Georgia	WILLIAM FEW ABR BALDWIN

Articles in addition to, and amendment of, the Constitution of the United States of America, proposed by Congress, and ratified by the legislatures of the several States pursuant to the fifth article of the original Constitution.

AMENDMENTS

First Ten Amendments passed by Congress Sept. 25, 1789.
Ratified by three-fourths of the States December 15, 1791.

ARTICLE I

Congress shall make no law respecting an establishment of religion, or prohibiting the free exercise thereof; or abridging the freedom of speech, or of the press; or the right of the people peaceably to assemble, and to petition the government for a redress of grievances.

ARTICLE II

A well regulated militia, being necessary to the security of a free State, the right of the people to keep and bear arms, shall not be infringed.

ARTICLE III

No soldier shall, in time of peace be quartered in any house, without the consent of the owner, nor in time of war, but in a manner to be prescribed by law.

ARTICLE IV

The right of the people to be secure in their persons, houses, papers, and effects, against unreasonable searches and seizures, shall not be violated, and no warrants shall issue, but upon probable cause, supported by oath or affirmation, and particularly describing the place to be searched, and the persons or things to be seized.

ARTICLE V

No person shall be held to answer for a capital, or otherwise infamous crime, unless on a presentment or indictment of a grand jury, except in cases arising in the land or naval forces, or in the militia, when in actual service in time of war or public danger; nor shall any person be subject for the same offense to be twice put in jeopardy of life or limb; nor shall be compelled in any criminal case to be a witness against himself, nor be deprived of life, liberty, or property, without due process of law; nor shall private property be taken for public use without just compensation.

ARTICLE VI

In all criminal prosecutions, the accused shall enjoy the right to a speedy and public trial, by an impartial jury of the State and district wherein the crime shall have been committed, which district shall have been previously ascertained by law, and to be informed of the nature and cause of the accusation; to be confronted with the witnesses against him; to have compulsory process for obtaining witnesses in his favor, and to have the assistance of counsel for his defense.

ARTICLE VII

In suits at common law, where the value in controversy shall exceed twenty dollars, the right of trial by jury shall be preserved, and no fact tried by a jury shall be otherwise reëxamined in any court of the United States, than according to the rules of the common law.

ARTICLE VIII

Excessive bail shall not be required, nor excessive fines imposed, nor cruel and unusual punishments inflicted.

ARTICLE IX

The enumeration in the Constitution of certain rights shall not be construed to deny or disparage others retained by the people.

ARTICLE X

The powers not delegated to the United States by the Constitution, nor prohibited by it to the States, are reserved to the States respectively, or to the people.

ARTICLE XI

Passed by Congress March 4, 1794. Ratified February 7, 1795.

The judicial power of the United States shall not be construed to extend to any suit in law or equity, commenced or prosecuted against one of the United States by citizens of another State, or by citizens or subjects of any foreign State.

ARTICLE XII

Passed by Congress December 9, 1803. Ratified July 27, 1804.

The electors shall meet in their respective States, and vote by ballot for President and Vice President, one of whom, at least, shall not be an inhabitant of the same State with themselves; they shall name in their ballots the person voted for as President, and in distinct ballots, the person voted for as Vice President, and they shall make distinct lists of all persons voted for as President and of all persons voted for as Vice President, and of the number of votes for each, which lists they shall sign and certify, and transmit sealed to the seat of the government of the United States, directed to the President of the Senate;—The President of the Senate shall, in the presence of the Senate and House of Representatives, open all the certificates and the votes shall then be counted;—The person having the greatest number of votes for President, shall be the President, if such number be a majority of the whole number of electors appointed; and if no person have such majority, then from the persons having the highest numbers not exceeding three on the list of those voted for as President, the House of Representatives shall choose immediately, by ballot, the President. But in choosing the President, the votes shall be taken by States, the representation from each State having one vote; a quorum for this purpose shall consist of a member or members from two thirds of the States, and a majority of all the States shall be necessary to a choice. And if the House of Representatives shall not choose a President whenever the right of choice shall devolve upon them, before the fourth day of March* next following, then the Vice President shall act as President, as in the case of the death or other constitutional disability of the President. The person having the greatest number of votes as Vice President shall be the Vice President, if such number be a majority of the whole number of electors appointed, and if no person have a majority, then from the two highest numbers on the list, the Senate shall choose the Vice President; a quorum for the purpose shall consist of two thirds of the whole number of Senators, and a majority of the whole number shall be necessary to a choice. But no person constitutionally ineligible to the office of President shall be eligible to that of Vice President of the United States.

ARTICLE XIII

Passed by Congress January 31, 1865. Ratified December 6, 1865.

SECTION 1. Neither slavery nor involuntary servitude, except as punishment for crime whereof the party shall have been duly convicted,

* See 20th Amendment.

shall exist within the United States, or any place subject to their jurisdiction.

SECTION 2. Congress shall have power to enforce this article by appropriate legislation.

ARTICLE XIV

Passed by Congress June 13, 1866. Ratified July 9, 1868.

SECTION 1. All persons born or naturalized in the United States, and subject to the jurisdiction thereof, are citizens of the United States and of the State wherein they reside. No State shall make or enforce any law which shall abridge the privileges or immunities of citizens of the United States; nor shall any State deprive any person of life, liberty, or property, without due process of law; nor deny to any person within its jurisdiction the equal protection of the laws.

SECTION 2. Representatives shall be apportioned among the several States according to their respective numbers, counting the whole number of persons in each State, excluding Indians not taxed. But when the right to vote at any election for the choice of electors for President and Vice President of the United States, representatives in Congress, the executive and judicial officers of a State, or the members of the legislature thereof, is denied to any of the male inhabitants of such State, being twenty-one years of age, and citizens of the United States, or in any way abridged, except for participation in rebellion, or other crime, the basis of representation therein shall be reduced in the proportion which the number of such male citizens shall bear to the whole number of male citizens twenty-one years of age in such State.

SECTION 3. No person shall be a senator or representative in Congress, or elector of President and Vice President, or hold any office, civil or military, under the United States, or under any State, who having previously taken an oath, as a member of Congress, or as an officer of the United States, or as a member of any State legislature, or as an executive or judicial officer of any State, to support the Constitution of the United States, shall have engaged in insurrection or rebellion against the same, or given aid or comfort to the enemies thereof. But Congress may by a vote of two thirds of each House, remove such disability.

SECTION 4. The validity of the public debt of the United States, authorized by law, including debts incurred for payment of pensions and bounties for services in suppressing insurrection or rebellion, shall not be questioned. But neither the United States nor any State shall assume or pay any debt or obligation incurred in aid of insurrection or rebellion against the United States, or any claim for the loss or emancipation of any slave; but all such debts, obligations, and claims shall be held illegal and void.

SECTION 5.   The Congress shall have power to enforce, by appropriate legislation, the provisions of this article.

ARTICLE XV

Passed by Congress February 26, 1869. Ratified February 3, 1870.

SECTION 1.   The right of citizens of the United States to vote shall not be denied or abridged by the United States or by any State on account of race, color, or previous condition of servitude.

SECTION 2.   The Congress shall have power to enforce this article by appropriate legislation.

ARTICLE XVI

Passed by Congress July 2, 1909. Ratified February 3, 1913.

The Congress shall have power to lay and collect taxes on incomes, from whatever source derived, without apportionment among the several States, and without regard to any census or enumeration.

ARTICLE XVII

Passed by Congress May 13, 1912. Ratified April 8, 1913.

The Senate of the United States shall be composed of two senators from each state, elected by the people thereof, for six years; and each senator shall have one vote. The electors in each State shall have the qualifications requisite for electors of the most numerous branch of the State legislature.

When vacancies happen in the representation of any State in the Senate, the executive authority of such State shall issue writs of election to fill such vacancies: *Provided,* That the legislature of any State may empower the executive thereof to make temporary appointments until the people fill the vacancies by election as the legislature may direct.

This amendment shall not be so construed as to affect the election or term of any senator chosen before it becomes valid as part of the Constitution.

ARTICLE XVIII*

Passed by Congress December 18, 1917. Ratified January 16, 1919.

After one year from the ratification of this article, the manufacture, sale, or transportation of intoxicating liquors within, the importation thereof into, or the exportation thereof from the United States and all territory subject to the jurisdiction thereof for beverage purposes is hereby prohibited.

The Congress and the several States shall have concurrent power to enforce this article by appropriate legislation.

This article shall be inoperative unless it shall have been ratified as an amendment to the Constitution by the legislatures of the several States, as provided in the Constitution, within seven years from the date of the submission hereof to the states by Congress.

ARTICLE XIX

Passed by Congress June 4, 1919. Ratified August 18, 1920.

The right of citizens of the United States to vote shall not be denied or abridged by the United States or by any State on account of sex.

The Congress shall have power by appropriate legislation to enforce the provisions of this article.

ARTICLE XX

Passed by Congress March 2, 1932. Ratified January 23, 1933.

SECTION 1. The terms of the President and Vice President shall end at noon on the 20th day of January, and the terms of Senators and Representatives at noon on the 3d day of January, of the years in which such terms would have ended if this article had not been ratified; and the terms of their successors shall then begin.

* Repealed by the 21st Amendment.

SECTION 2.   The Congress shall assemble at least once in every year, and such meeting shall begin at noon on the 3d day of January, unless they shall by law appoint a different day.

SECTION 3.   If, at the time fixed for the beginning of the term of the President, the President-elect shall have died, the Vice President-elect shall become President. If a President shall not have been chosen before the time fixed for the beginning of his term, or if the President-elect shall have failed to qualify, then the Vice President-elect shall act as President until a President shall have qualified; and the Congress may by law provide for the case wherein neither a President-elect nor a Vice President-elect shall have qualified, declaring who shall then act as President, or the manner in which one who is to act shall be selected, and such person shall act accordingly until a President or Vice President shall have qualified.

SECTION 4.   The Congress may by law provide for the case of the death of any of the persons from whom the House of Representatives may choose a President whenever the right of choice shall have devolved upon them, and for the case of the death of any of the persons from whom the Senate may choose a Vice President whenever the right of choice shall have devolved upon them.

SECTION 5.   Sections 1 and 2 shall take effect on the 15th day of October following the ratification of this article.

SECTION 6.   This article shall be inoperative unless it shall have been ratified as an amendment to the Constitution by the legislatures of three-fourths of the several States within seven years from the date of its submission.

ARTICLE XXI

Passed by Congress February 20, 1933. Ratified December 5, 1933.

SECTION 1.   The Eighteenth Article of amendment to the Constitution of the United States is hereby repealed.

SECTION 2.   The transportation or importation into any State, Territory, or possession of the United States for delivery or use therein of intoxicating liquors in violation of the laws thereof, is hereby prohibited.

SECTION 3.   This article shall be inoperative unless it shall have been ratified as an amendment to the Constitution by conventions in the several States, as provided in the Constitution, within seven years from the date of the submission thereof to the States by the Congress.

ARTICLE XXII

Passed by Congress March 21, 1947. Ratified February 27, 1951.

No person shall be elected to the office of the President more than twice, and no person who has held the office of President, or acted as President, for more than two years of a term to which some other person was elected President shall be elected to the office of the President more than once.

But this article shall not apply to any person holding the office of President when this article was proposed by the Congress, and shall not prevent any person who may be holding the office of President, or acting as President, during the term within which this article becomes operative from holding the office of President or acting as President during the remainder of such term.

This article shall be inoperative unless it shall have been ratified as an amendment to the Constitution by the legislatures of three-fourths of the several states within seven years from the date of its submission to the states by the Congress.

ARTICLE XXIII

Passed by Congress June 16, 1960. Ratified March 29, 1961.

SECTION 1.   The District constituting the seat of Government of the United States shall appoint in such manner as the Congress may direct:

A number of electors of President and Vice President equal to the whole number of Senators and Representatives in Congress to which the District would be entitled if it were a State, but in no event more than the least populous state; they shall be in addition to those appointed by the states, but shall be considered, for the purpose of the election of President and Vice President, to be electors appointed by a state; and they shall meet in the District and perform such duties as provided by the twelfth article of amendment.

SECTION 2.   The Congress shall have power to enforce this article by appropriate legislation.

ARTICLE   XXIV

Passed by Congress August 27, 1962. Ratified January 23, 1964.

SECTION 1.   The right of citizens of the United States to vote in any primary or other election for President or Vice President, for electors for President or Vice President, or for Senator or Repesentative in Congress, shall not be denied or abridged by the United States or any State by reason of failure to pay any poll tax or other tax.

SECTION 2.   The Congress shall have the power to enforce this article by appropriate legislation.

ARTICLE XXV

Passed by Congress July 6, 1965. Ratified February 10, 1967.

SECTION 1.   In case of the removal of the President from office or his death or resignation, the Vice President shall become President.

SECTION 2.   Whenever there is a vacancy in the office of the Vice President, the President shall nominate a Vice President who shall take the office upon confirmation by a majority vote of both houses of Congress.

SECTION 3.   Whenever the President transmits to the President pro tempore of the Senate and the Speaker of the House of Representatives his written declaration that he is unable to discharge the powers and duties of his office, and until he transmits to them a written declaration to the contrary, such powers and duties shall be discharged by the Vice President as Acting President.

SECTION 4.   Whenever the Vice President and a majority of either the principal officers of the executive departments, or of such other body as Congress may by law provide, transmit to the President pro tempore of the Senate and the Speaker of the House of Representatives their written declaration that the President is unable to discharge the powers and duties of his office, the Vice President shall immediately assume the powers and duties of the office of Acting President.

Thereafter, when the President transmits to the President pro tempore of the Senate and the Speaker of the House of Representatives his written declaration that no inability exists, he shall resume the powers and duties of his office unless the Vice President and a majority of either the principal officers of the executive department, or of such other body as Congress may by law provide, transmit within four days to the President pro tempore of the Senate and the Speaker of the House of Representatives their written declaration that the President is unable to discharge the powers and duties of his office. Thereupon Congress shall decide the issue, assembling within 48 hours for that purpose if not in session. If the Congress, within 21 days after receipt of the latter written declaration, or, if Congress is not in session, within 21 days after Congress is required to assemble, determines by two-thirds vote of both houses that the President is unable to discharge the powers and duties of his office, the Vice President shall continue to discharge the same as Acting President; otherwise, the President shall resume the powers and duties of his office.

ARTICLE XXVI

Passed by Congress March 23, 1971. Ratified June 30, 1971.

SECTION 1.   The right of citizens of the United States, who are eighteen years of age or older, to vote shall not be denied or abridged by the United States or any state on account of age.

SECTION 2.   The Congress shall have the power to enforce this article by appropriate legislation.

Index